JEWISH
FEMINISM
AND
INTERSECTIONALITY

SUNY series in Feminist Criticism and Theory

Michelle A. Massé, editor

JEWISH FEMINISM AND INTERSECTIONALITY

MARLA BRETTSCHNEIDER

Published by State University of New York Press, Albany

© 2016 State University of New York

All rights reserved

Printed in the United States of America

No part of this book may be used or reproduced in any manner whatsoever without written permission. No part of this book may be stored in a retrieval system or transmitted in any form or by any means including electronic, electrostatic, magnetic tape, mechanical, photocopying, recording, or otherwise without the prior permission in writing of the publisher.

For information, contact State University of New York Press, Albany, NY
www.sunypress.edu

Production, Ryan Morris
Marketing, Fran Keneston

Library of Congress Cataloging-in-Publication Data

Names: Brettschneider, Marla, author.
Title: Jewish feminism and intersectionality / Marla Brettschneider.
Description: Albany : State University of New York Press, [2016] | ©2016 |
  Series: SUNY series in feminist criticism and theory | Includes
  bibliographical references and index.
Identifiers: LCCN 2015018364 | ISBN 9781438460338 (hardcover : alk. paper) |
  ISBN 9781438460345 (paperback : alk. paper) | ISBN 9781438460352 (e-book)
Subjects: LCSH: Feminism—Religious aspects—Judaism. | Gender
  identity—Religious aspects—Judaism. | Race—Religious aspects—Judaism.
  | Social conflict—Religious aspects—Judaism. | Queer theory—Religious
  aspects—Judaism. | Feminism. | Gender identity. | Race. | Social
  conflict. | Queer theory.
Classification: LCC BM729.W6 B7466 2016 | DDC 296.3/8—dc23
LC record available at http://lccn.loc.gov/2015018364

10 9 8 7 6 5 4 3 2 1

This book is dedicated to Paris and to Toni,

And in loving memory of my mother, Phyllis Brettschneider

Contents

Acknowledgments		ix
Introduction		1
1.	To Race, to Class, to Queer: Jewish Feminist Contributions to Intersectionality Studies	17
2.	Jewish Feminists and New Diaspora Theorizing: The Life and Work of Jamaica Kincaid	41
3.	Race, Gender, Class, Sexuality, and the Jewish *Goldbergs* in the Suburbs	61
4.	Ritual Encounters of the Queer Kind: A Political Analysis of Jewish Queer Ritual Innovation	75
5.	Jewish Feminism, Race, and a Sexual Justice Agenda	99
6.	Reproductive Justice: Costs of Increased Adoption Access	113
Conclusion: Jewish Race Segregation and Jewish Feminism		127
Notes		147
Works Cited		169
Index		187

Acknowledgments

Every project, certainly one as large as a book, is a communal endeavor. In addition to the many specific appreciations offered in the coming pages, this book would not have been possible without the support of Burt Feintuch and the University of New Hampshire Center for the Humanities, the College of Liberal Arts Dean's Office, the Department of Political Science, and the Women's Studies Program. Marcie Anderson, Michael Cole, and Dee-Ann Dumas have provided invaluable assistance; Faina Bukher has been an outstanding colleague. Also at UNH I would like specifically to thank Jessica Compton, Jessica Rosenthal, Richard Barney, Chelsea Moyer, Tobi Afolayan, Cassie Travers, Rachel Draper, Alden Reed, and the Women's Studies Program assistants team: Emily Sorey-Backus, Emerson Dorion, Stephanie Kuhn, and Cecilia Martins as well as Abigail Carpenter-Winch from Hampshire College.

    I am grateful for the access to the Jewish Museum's National Jewish Archive of Broadcasting, New York City, and the opportunity to work with Andy Ingall and Joanne Jacobson. Even during a rough time in the midst of a recession, the Hadassah–Brandeis Institute was able to fund a portion of my time during sabbatical for this work. B'not Esh continues to sustain me in many ways, as well as the Jewish Multiracial Network, Jews for Racial and Economic Justice (JFREJ), Nehirim, the National Havurah Institute, as well as the Jewish Queer Think Tank for the seven years that we worked together. I also acknowledge the International Society for the Study of African Jewry, with which I connected during the process of working on this book and which has greatly contributed to developments in my work. The participants in the Newton, MA Jewish feminist text study group that Ronnie Levin so graciously initiated and keeps afloat have been a great source of connection. Daughters of Abraham and Kids4Peace have been wonderful communities in New England for supporting my work on diversity. Jen Chau, and all of Swirl's work with, and on behalf of, mixed-race individuals and families have been important for me and this work.

Much gratitude goes to Rebecca Alpert, Lori Marso, Patricia Moynagh, Sarra Lev, Randi Dubnick, and the many anonymous reviewers who have given generously of their time and expertise to help make this work as strong as it can be. It is incredible Jewish feminists such as Martha Ackelsberg and Melanie Kaye/Kantrowitz who have cut paths in so many ways for activist scholars like me to do our work.

I could not have made it through without the sensitivity and brilliance of Suzy Lowinger (may her memory be a blessing) and Lanie Resnick. As always, I thank my sisters, Beth and Nina, and my father, Solomon, as well as Dawn Rose. I write in loving memory of my mother Phyllis Brettschneider. I still cannot say how parents manage to research and write while raising kids, but I am eternally blessed by Paris's and Toni's presence in my life. (I showed this line to Paris as I was working in our kitchen. In response she upped the volume on her pop music while emptying the dishwasher. I think she got the irony.)

Of course, any errors are my own alone.

The following are adapted and reprinted with permission:

Portions of chapter 1: 2006. "To Race, to Class, to Queer: Jewish Contributions to Feminist Theory." In Bat-Ami Bar On and Lisa Tessman, eds. *Jewish Locations: Traversing Racialized Landscapes.* Rowman & Littlefield/Altimira Press.

Portions of chapter 3: 2003. "Ritual Encounters of the Queer Kind: A Political Analysis of Jewish Lesbian Ritual Innovation." *The Journal of Lesbian Studies: Special Issue on Lesbians and Ritual* 7, no. 2. Taylor and Francis Ltd, http://www.taylorandfrancis.com.

Portions of chapter 4: 2008: "Jewish Feminism, Sexuality, and a Sexual Justice Agenda." *Jewish Feminism.* Ed. Elyse Goldstein. Woodstock, VT: Jewish Lights.

V.
Lowell, MA
2015

Introduction

Jewish Feminism and Intersectionality is intended to offer readers exposure to how one might include Jews and Jewish matters of interest into the field of intersectionality studies. This book is equally designed to demonstrate a range of ways that Jewish feminist work can operate with the best of what intersectionality studies has to offer. With the completion of the main portion of the manuscript in the summer of 2014, this work felt more relevant than ever.

There are always horrible things happening around the world, but the summer of 2014 seemed more formidable than many. In late spring, I was planning a research trip to Nigeria for another work on the Jewish phenomenon in Sub-Saharan Africa, when hundreds of girls, mostly ranging from sixteen to eighteen years old, were abducted from their school in Chibok Nigeria by Boko Haram. Boko Haram (meaning "Western education is forbidden") is an Islamic fundamentalist group considered to have sold the teens into "forced marriages" or other forms of sexual slavery. Hoping to travel with my own teen girls, I was in the elite position of being able to change our travel plans—a distinct privilege of agency regarding trying to keep my own children safe, to which too few people across the globe have access.

In midsummer, Israel and Gaza began bombing each other. Following the kidnapping and killing of three Israeli teen boys, a revenge killing of a Palestinian teen, and a major crackdown in the Occupied Territories, the events turned catastrophic. Israelis were for the most part successfully protected from the bombs coming from Gaza with the "Iron Dome" technology that prevented most of the bombs from actually falling within Israel. Psychologically, however, terrors ran high as citizens from all walks of life were running to bomb shelters with a frequency this generation had not yet experienced, and the military was activated at high levels. The humanitarian fiasco in Gaza grew to previously unimaginable proportions. Facing Israel's military attack from air and on land, over two thousand people were killed, including mostly civilians and over five hundred children, and many were sent into exile, creating yet a new refugee emergency. Over fifteen thousand homes in Gaza were destroyed, leaving approximately one-third of the population homeless.

In response to this situation in Israel and Gaza, Jews and Jewish businesses and organizations were being targeted around the world at a level not seen since the Nazi-perpetrated Holocaust. High-security threats were issued for Jewish tourists across the globe. At the start of the US portion of my route to Casablanca in July 2014, a rabbi in that city was beaten up as retaliation for Israel's early bombing. By the time I arrived there the following calendar day, others had been victims of retaliatory violence as well. In a day of meetings with Jewish communal representatives in Casablanca, the official line was "Wait and see." I was told many times, "We as Jews can be Moroccan citizens now. That is good. But when there are tensions, there are still tensions." It seemed to me a bundle of contradictions about how to understand the community's place and situation.

The violence against Jews, not just Israelis—not that random violence against Israelis is justifiable either—continued to worsen. I had moved on to Western and Central Africa, visiting with Jewish and Jewishly related communities in different countries for the other book project. By the time I was preparing to leave the continent, the ebola virus breakout had grown to epidemic proportions, the worst outbreak in history. Thousands of victims resulted in what is clearly not simply a biological issue, but one of race, class, and international equity. As of this writing, there are reported to be ten thousand deaths, and we had seen the first cases in the US.

The Islamic State organization, operating under different names since the 1990s, invaded Mosul early in June. Their tactics and successful advance strategy spread fear through the regions in which they are active and around the world. National leaders seemed just as inept at dealing with what they considered the threat of this group as they had been with the last spate of top "terror" groups, and the US seems engaged in perpetual war.

Then there was Ferguson. I live on the US East Coast. But Ferguson, Missouri felt like it was around the corner. On August 9, 2014, a Missouri teenager named Michael Brown was shot dead after he had raised his hands and pleaded, "Don't shoot." In the town of Ferguson in St. Louis county, this African-American youth was killed by a white police officer, setting off riots, solidarity demonstrations, soul searching, and activism around the country for the rest of the year.

In addition to the general examinations, my inbox was bursting with notes about how Jews of all races were responding, what they had been doing, what they could do. Notices from Jews of color were circulating to "white" Jewish allies. US Jewish organizations were busy working, preparing analyses, offering support, standing up and speaking truth to power. Jewish organizations such as the Shalom Center and the US T'ruah: The Rabbinic Call for Human Rights were very visible. I had received many e-mail forwards with a letter by Susan Talve,[1] the rabbi of Central Reform Congregation of central St. Louis, with concrete information from a Jewish, local, multiracial perspective.

In Talve's list of actions to take, the fifth item reads: "Please tell every community across America to wake up. This is not just about Ferguson. 'Find your Ferguson.'" Find your Ferguson—when a little girl who acts like a tomboy is raped to "make her more feminine." As I argue in chapter 4 on the political power of ritual for sexual and gender justice aspirations, we must each hold our communities accountable. As Talve coined the phrase, "Find your Ferguson" when Jews around my parents' age organized "eat-ins" in Middle Eastern and South Asian groceries and restaurants after September 11, 2001, when such businesses were being vandalized and proprietors were being beaten up in broad daylight (like Jews were in 2014–15 across the globe). Many were of an age that they were not able to walk in the peace marches, but they could demonstrate concrete support and show haters that violence is unacceptable by being public and present in their urban communities. Then Iranian, Iraqi, and others Jews were rounded up along with the other Middle Eastern men forced to register with local authorities in cities across the US. This roundup was occurring even as many European-heritage Jews, who are the majority of the Jews in the United States today, did not even know that many Middle Eastern and North African Jews live here and were directly impacted by the registration requirement.

Find your Ferguson . . . when a local politician puts back on the legislative agenda a requirement of birth control for young women of color to be eligible for bail, and in another case, the state terminates a mother's parental rights because her being late again (the city bus was delayed) was the last straw in assessing her "fitness" as a parent. As we will see in chapter 5, Jews were a primary target of eugenic campaigns in the US earlier in the nineteenth century. Hitler was quite clear in *Mein Kampf* about learning from US experiences. Jewish women and the US Jewish community have always been at the forefront of what emerged as the reproductive rights movement. Now we must listen and shift these efforts toward what is being called by today's primary targets reproductive justice.

In chapter 3 I will be discussing popular culture from a Jewish feminist multitiered intersectional perspective. There I analyze the movement of many European heritage Jews from the cities to the suburbs at mid-twentieth century and the costs of the racial re-assignment (from nonwhite to honorary whites) that went along with segments of the Jewish community's upgrade into the middle class. I argue that Gertrude Berg's successful radio and television show *The Goldbergs* crashed after one season of the fictive family's move from the Bronx to the suburbs. US Americans hadn't yet figured out, and I would argue still haven't figured out, how to end discrimination against others if those others were not able to assimilate into "American Dream" versions of "America." The end of *The Goldbergs* was in the 1950s. But in 2014 Talve's action-item number five continues: "And Ferguson is not in the city. It is a nice suburb that many people moved to get away from the problems of the city. But no one was paying attention as the majority grew to be the Black middle class and the government and the police force stayed white. This population is especially vulnerable because many are one crisis away from being in the poverty cycle again." The summer 2014 riots in Ferguson, and ally actions across the country, were about race, and they were about class, and gender, and police brutality. And in later August, my older daughter Paris entered high school. One high school in this small diverse city with around four thousand kids. Paris was immediately taken aback by the police presence and the ways the guards yelled at all those brown-skinned kids.

Talve's action-item number four states: "Explode the myth that Jews are white people living in the suburbs. We have many black members with black sons scared for their lives. One of my bar mitzvah and confirmation students is a very tall 16 year old who is black and lives in Ferguson. No school for another week. He is scared to leave his apartment. This is personal. It is about us." Before two other members of B'not Esh, a Jewish feminist group with which I have been involved for over twenty years and in which Talve has also been a member, sent additional forwards of Talve's letter, Yavilah McCoy sent B'not Esh members a copy of a piece she wrote some years ago about being targeted by white police when her family had moved to the heavily white and Jewish Newton, MA. McCoy is Jewish African-American and sought to remind her white Jewish colleagues how white people can stand, and take risks as allies, with all Black people. In Ferguson, MO, and wherever we are. Jews for Racial and Economic Justice in New York City, the Progressive Jewish Alliance in Los Angeles, the Council on Urban Affairs in Chicago, the national Jewish Multiracial

Network, and countless Jewish organizations and activists across the US had an extra-busy, Ferguson summer (fall, and winter) in 2014.

The conclusion of this book opens with a story of my younger daughter when she was in grade school in this small New England City—trying to get through a day as an African-American Jewish kid in an underfunded public school with rampant racism, sexism, homophobia, classism, ableism, and the gamut from total cluelessness about Jews to outright anti-Semitism. As I edit this introduction in spring 2015, Toni is turning fourteen and about to become a bat mitzvah. As part of her *tzedakah* (justice) project for this life cycle event, she recently prepared a speech and delivered it at a local #blacklivesmatter rally, also commemorating the fiftieth anniversary of the assassination of Malcom X. Toni stood up in our city as a Black Jew and told the crowd gathered just exactly why she thought white police officers killing black men more often than they do white men is ridiculous. And that black women and girls face racism. We got connected to the local #blacklivesmatter activists through a Jewish friend I know from years ago, who recently moved to a nearby town. Jews, African Americans, African-American Jews, and many others continue to "work on this problem," as Toni said at the rally.

I argue in the conclusion of this book that intersectionality scholars' and activists' avoidance of Jewish issues, critiques of Christian privilege and Christian hegemony, and anti-Semitism is disastrous. The left's inability to integrate Jewishly identified experiences and critique directly serves multilevel status quo and right-wing agendas. This inability explicitly bolsters the work of those in the Christian right. We cannot address the issues of mass incarceration and state-sanctioned murder of African Americans, all too common in the US today, as well as many other deadly and apparently intractable issues before us, without a deeper and broader capacity to undertake multifaceted critiques, including Jewish critical race contributions.

In the book's conclusion, I also argue that an antiracist agenda is crucial for Jewish feminism. I offer a number of reasons for these claims. Jewish feminists are at the forefront of antiracist and other social justice work. However, among the reasons for Jewish feminists needing to get more serious about antiracism *within* Jewish feminist work are that racism is deadly, and if Jewish feminism cannot help us understand and cope, as well as resist this multipronged force, then Jewish feminism is not helping us with a central facet of our lives and experience in the US today. I would be happy to have to argue harder as a political theorist and not have the litany of experiences such as Ferguson as empirical evidence. But that is not our lot. The treatment of Rodney King, Trayvon Martin, Michael Brown, Eric Garner, and so many others are travesties. As much as they are travesties, each one, these men are also the more well-known faces of an aspect of a constant lethal racism in the US today. The classism, racism, homophobia, transphobia, anti-Semitism, sexism, ableism, and other brutal facets of the contemporary US landscape are all too alive and well. The more that we can understand how these facets are cocreated and work to reinforce each other, the better our abilities to resist and find alternatives will be. The better our capacities to be allies will be. The more that we will be able to face "our" issues and have built the relationships wherein others "have our backs." The more daring will be our art, our loving, our laughter, our activism, our scholarship. Jews need support in being part of this historical moment that requires everyday bravery and big acts of kindness. And movements that can include Jews will be that much richer for our deep and diverse experience.

Jewish Feminism and Intersectionality is a scholarly book in which I explore a range of opportunities to apply and build intersectionality studies from within the life and work of Jewish feminism in the US today. It is a celebration of the vibrancy and array of Jewish feminist subjects contributing to the field. And it is an intervention, as there is almost no mention, let alone serious analysis, of this dynamic Jewish feminist and queer subfield in intersectionality studies to date.

Intersectionality studies has taken the academic and activist worlds by storm. One cannot attend an academic conference in almost any discipline without seeing on the program many papers on intersectionality. Some disciplines have independent sections on intersectionality studies. Works in this new field have increasingly been making their way into print, as books, articles, and new academic journals emerge whose missions are devoted specifically to furthering and advancing intersectionality studies (e.g., *Politics, Groups, and Identities*). On the ground, one can hear activists and ordinary people in all manner of organizational planning, classrooms, and board meetings intoning the concept of intersectionality.

This is a welcome development in many ways. Particularly, second-wave and more recent feminists of color have argued that we cannot separate the major vectors of power that structure our societies and life circumstances, such as race, class, sexuality, and gender. Critical legal scholar Kimberlé Crenshaw is noted as having coined the term *intersectionality* in a 1989 article, "Demarginalizing the Intersection of Race and Sex: A Black Feminist

Critique of Antidiscrimination Doctrine, Feminist Theory and Antiracist Politics."[2] Before and since Sojourner Truth's famous "Ain't I a Woman?" speech delivered at the 1851 Women's Convention in Ohio, black and other feminists have been inspired over time to challenge sexism and the ways in which race, class, gender, and other relevant markers work together in contouring oppression. Cutting-edge Black feminists introduced the concept of double jeopardy,[3] and for a while feminist scholars and activists discussed the concept of multiple oppressions.[4] Some scholars and activists are able to include sexuality and gender identity in the context of the emerging field of trans studies, and nationality and language.[5] At least since the reclamation of the Combahee River Women's Collective statement[6]—demanding that we not leave parts of ourselves at the door—many scholars have taken up the charge arguing in differing terms that reality is comprised of the intersections of multiple politically salient identity factors, and scholarly and activist work must operate with that knowledge as a baseline.[7] White-identified feminists (many of whom are Jewish) have taken up the charge as well.[8]

As Ange-Marie Hancock (2007) notes, the roots of intersectionality studies run deep, and have done so long before Combahee. Feminist scholars are actively pondering the strengths and weaknesses of the intersectionality paradigm and its methodology.[9] Some critics argue that intersectionality is too vague to be of serious scholarly use. One view proposed is that intersectionality's open-endedness, sometimes noted as a weakness, is also its strength.[10] Many scholars and activists are able to undertake quite complex and nuanced work on multiple levels for multiples groups, offering helpful critiques of intersectionality as they also develop distinct contributions.[11] Certainly one flaw for many is that some people do take intersectionality to connote discrete identity signifiers that "intersect"/cross or overlap at distinct moments; and it is those moments that scholars and activists are examining within the framework of intersectionality studies. Instead of devoting specific attention to more critique of intersectionality (and the ways it falls short of some of its own goals), this book project seeks to build on the best of what has been done in the field, offering what I hope will be read as constructive internal critique along the way. Additionally, I seek then to continue the critique through examples of alternative ways to do this important work.

Additionally, this work as a whole serves as a friendly critique of (and pushing on) the "overlap" or "intersect" paradigms sometimes used in what is referred to as intersectionality. The more sophisticated among intersectionality theorists acknowledge that they are not so much positing an approach based on an idea of independent and previously formed identities that then come into contact with each other, such as at a stop light. Instead they discuss the ways that different politically salient (with such salience contextual itself) identity signifiers cocreate and mutually constitute each other. Further, from a Jewish perspective, I find myself, comrades, and colleagues often work on multiple planes, and not usually within only two vectors of identities. I will develop these arguments regarding mutual constitution theory with multiple vectors more fully in the following chapter. I will also clarify that I am working from a nonidentitarian (sameness) paradigm when examining identity communities. As a whole, this book works from within the premise of mutually constructing multiple aspects of fluid and porous identities and demonstrates how this operates in different ways and in application to a variety of subjects to concretize that argument.

Significantly, this book offers another productive form of "doing the work," instead of focusing on additional criticism of existing intersectionality literature. As with multiculturalism—the dominant concept of the 1980s that set the stage for the intersectionality studies of today—Jewishly identified people and issues are largely absent in the emerging field. Among the litany of "isms" scholars and activists challenge, anti-Semitism remains problematically absent from the lists. As with multiculturalism, this is noteworthy as the amount of work contributed to the field by Jewish—and particularly Jewish feminist and queer scholars and activists—is significant. It was what appeared to be the odd eclipse of Jews in multiculturalism that led me, in the late 1980s, to begin to prepare the award-winning volume, *The Narrow Bridge: Jewish Views on Multiculturalism*, with a forward by Cornel West. In that work, I situated Jewish experience and history within multiculturalism and asked some of the best minds of the day to apply a Jewish multicultural framework in a variety of fields. That work brought together Jewish and multicultural studies in a book-length project for the first time. It assisted those interested in multiculturalism in recognizing the strength of including Jewish matters of import in the field, as it helped Jewish scholars more systematically use the insights of multiculturalism. These decades later, it is time for a similar Jewish intervention in intersectionality studies.

I personally have good experiences offering Jewish lenses on multiple and co-constructed identity theory, but these individual experiences would not characterize the reception or inclusion of Jewish work in the field of intersectionality more broadly. For example, my own Jewishly related paper proposals have had 100 percent acceptance at academic conferences, I am asked to conduct manuscript reviews with a frequency I cannot manage, and interactions with scholars who are not in Jewish studies are always productive. At the same time, Jews, Jewish issues, and Jewish orientations more generally continue to be lacking in the growing field of intersectionality studies. Early on in this development, we had activist scholars such as Barbara Smith declaring in 1984 (257–258): "I have often wished I could spread the word that a movement committed to fighting sexual, racial, economic and heterosexist oppression, not to mention one which opposes imperialism, anti-Semitism, the oppressions visited upon the physically disabled, the old and the young, at the same time that it challenges militarism and imminent nuclear destruction is the very opposite of narrow."[12] Joint projects such as the 1984 Elly Bulkin, Minnie Bruce Prat, and Barbara Smith volume *Yours In Struggle: Three Feminist Perspectives on Anti-Semitism and Racism* became rarer as intersectionality studies developed as a field. Beyond such an occasional mention of Jewish feminists or of anti-Semitism among a matrix of oppressions, Jews and Jewish issues are basically absent in this intellectual and activist turn.[13] This book is meant to bridge that gap. It is theoretical and broad in scope, while focused on issues significant in feminist—and otherwise Jewish—intersectionality studies.

Similarly, it is only to our peril that we ignore Jewish interventions in perpetuating injustice, and Jewish contributions to multitiered intersectionality study. A problematic marginalization of Jews is argument enough for challenging the seemingly Jew-free space of intersectionality studies. Though there is more to say on the matter. US progressives, religious and secular, are troubled by the explosion of Christian right popularity and reactionary Christian success in mainstream US thinking and politics (and certainly internationally). Intersectionality scholars, along with all those seeking social justice, will do well to more consciously link the erasure of Jewish contributions, the devaluing of an insistent anti-Semitism, and the persistence of Christian privilege and Christian hegemony with the rising popularity of right-wing Christian appeal. While it is not only Jewish contributions and critique that will interrupt these ultraconservative Christian developments (upsetting to many Christians as well as others), Jewish insights and activism can help clarify the work before us that needs to operate on many fronts at once (including supporting both self-defined and those not self-identified as Christians in the social justice movement). We cannot avoid the rising tide of anti-Muslim propaganda and action, at both the community and state levels. We cannot continue to avoid the Christian hegemonic aspects of such targeting directly threatening us all. Jews are key partners and allies in the work to expose and disrupt such anti-Muslim rage and systemic policy development. While Jewish specificity is of course different, Jewish historical experience and communal organization contributes much to such work. Similarly, the weight of assimilationist expectations bear down on so many minorities and new immigrant groups. Various Jewish modes of coping with the implicit and explicit genocidal aspects of what are dangled before us in the United States as freedom and equality have much to offer intersectional resistance to US liberal forms of ending discrimination by ending difference itself. Overall, intersectionality studies that ignore Jewish critical insight will remain hindered.

Thus, *Jewish Feminism and Intersectionality* undertakes a variegated intersectional analysis of matters of import in queer, critical race, class-based, feminist studies within a Jewish context. Instead of lamenting the absence of Jewish content in most intersectional feminist theory, this work provides such analysis. Readers will see distinctive Jewish themes and approaches, as they will also note how Jewish feminists are a core part of feminist intersectionality work in the academy and on the ground.

Relevant Literature of Note

The intersectionality literature has been growing in scope, able to include scholars and input from a variety of communities. Much to its detriment, however, the swiftly increasing and exciting multidisciplinary and interdisciplinary literature in intersectionality studies virtually excludes examination of Jewish experience and perspectives. There is, however, a long and ongoing history of outstanding Jewish feminist academic literature and activism on the ground addressing class, race, ability, gender, nationality, and sexuality that ought to be considered foundational for any study of intersectionality and as we all seek to work beyond the limits of this field as it stands currently.

In the early 1970s, we began to see numerous works by Jewish feminists hitting the larger feminist movement who would become known as pathbreakers for Jewish feminists (e.g., Paley 1974, Rich 1976, Piercy 1976, and as Starhawk's work came to be in the 1980s). In 1976 Koltun's and Baum, Hyman, and Michel, and then Falk's 1977 works were groundbreaking for their time. In 1979 Judith Plaskow's engagement with Carol Christ on *Women's Spirit Rising: A Feminist Reader in Religion* was revolutionary for putting Jewish feminist liturgical imaginaries in print along with feminist works across communities. Evelyn Torton Beck's 1982 *Nice Jewish Girls: A Jewish Lesbian Anthology* was innovative for its naming and sharing the visions of lesbians in a still very much budding, though lesbian-free, Jewish feminist context. Susannah Heschel's 1983 *On Being a Jewish Feminist* was pivotal. Melanie Kaye/Kantrowitz and Irena Klepfisz's 1986 *The Tribe of Dina: A Jewish Women's Anthology* set the stage for contemporary Jewish feminist examination and action in the context of diversity studies, including issues of sexuality, race, ability, class, anti-Semitism, and ethnicity.

Among later Jewishly related single author books, feminist writings such as Klepfisz's 1990 *Dreams of an Insomniac*, Alpert's 1997 *Like Bread on a Seder Plate*, Brodkin's 1998 *How Jews Became White Folks*, Adler's 1998 *Engendering Judaism*, and Schultz's 2001 *Going South: Jewish Women in the Civil Rights Movement* are all important contributions. Each individually takes on issues of race, class, gender, and sexuality; however, each could use these modes of inquiry in more fully imbricating ways. From this period, mainly the work of Melanie Kaye/Kantrowitz (*The Issue Is Power* and *The Color of Jews*) can be said to do the work of intersectionality, although like many of her generation, she does not actually use the word *intersectionality*. Pinsky's 2010 *Jewish Feminists: Complex Identities, and Activist Lives* does try to work in the context of intersectionality theory; while this work is interesting, it does not offer a critical race lens.

Among Jewishly related edited volumes, Balka and Rose's 1989 *Twice Blessed: On Being Lesbian or Gay and Jewish*; Elwell, Idelson, and Alpert's 2001 *Lesbian Rabbis: The First Generation*; and Aviv and Shneer's 2002 *Queer Jews* are among the works that address GLBTQ topics directly. The individual contributions in *Queer Theory and the Jewish Question* 2003 (Boyarin, Itzkovitz, and Pellegrini), *Insider/Outsider: American Jews and Multiculturalism* (1998 Biale, Galchinsky, and Heschel) and *Jewish Locations: Traversing Racialized Landscapes* 2001 (Tessman and Bar On) are very good. In addition, Belzer and Pelc's 2003 *Joining the Sisterhood: Young Jewish Women Write Their Lives*, Ruttenberg's 2001 *Yentl's Revenge: The Next Wave of Jewish Feminists*, Goldstein's 2008 *New Jewish Feminism: Probing the Past, Forging the Future* and Rose, and Green, Kaiser, and Klein's 2007 *Righteous Indignation: A Jewish Call for Justice* all strive to reach multigenerational audiences and were fresh contributions.[14]

In terms of publications that have specifically challenged the normative Ashkenazi/Euro-centeredness of (US) American Jewish thinking since Kaye/Kantrowitz and Klepfisz, Khazzoom's 2013 edited work *The Flying Camel: Essays on Identity by Women of North African and Middle Eastern Jewish Heritage*, Azoulay's 1997 *Black, Jewish, and Interracial: It's Not the Color of Your Skin but the Race of Your Kin and Other Myths of Identity*, and Daniels and Johnson's 1995 *Ruby of Cochin* deserve attention.[15] Rebecca Walker's 2001 *Black, White, and Jewish* was an important addition.[16]

There are many more important Jewish feminist contributions beyond the space of this introduction in the disciplines of history, queer studies, theology, sociology, psychology, politics, literature, immigration studies, diaspora studies, colonialism, and global feminisms, across disciplines and of course in Jewish and Middle East Studies. In sum, there are many publications addressing aspects of the material covered in *Jewish Feminism and Intersectionality*. As an interdisciplinary text, the book has many excellent affiliates. These cross-cutting discourses are in a dynamic moment. *Jewish Feminism and Intersectionality* brings a critical Jewish eye to these discussions, demonstrates how mutual constitution theory can bypass its current limits, and cuts a new—Jewish feminist—path in intersectionality studies.

Chapter Breakdown

This book contains six content chapters and a conclusion. In each chapter I bring together and develop principally feminist, queer, class-based, critical race and diaspora theories by informing the discourse with Jewishly grounded theorizing as it brings these critical theories to bear on an analysis of aspects of Jewish history and thought. Overall, the book serves to enact the political and methodological commitment of intersectionality studies to push through the supposed binary of the normative and the empirical, as well as the presumed divide of theory and action.

Chapter 1 situates this Jewish project in the field of intersectionality in a more scholarly way than does this introduction. I use Elizabeth Spelman's primary contribution to what is now called intersectionality to note some differences between Jewish possibilities and those in feminist theory more broadly. By juxtaposing the ontological frame in my reading of a brief Talmudic text to Spelman's, I offer a more complex form of mutual construction-type intersectionality theory. This chapter offers a Jewish "countertext" to demonstrate how analysis can be enriched with Jewish perspectives, specifically arguing that many leaders in the field, such as Spelman, remain more tied to an Aristotelian frame than her critique suggests.

Chapter 2 also offers a theoretical argument, but more specified, in the field of diaspora thinking. Important for Jews and a range of communities, particularly in the current age of so much population displacement, diaspora theorizing has moved beyond being a primarily Jewish field. However, Jewish works and those of others remain cut off from each other, barely in conversation. Demonstrating both the theory and method of mutual construction intersectionality, this chapter uses the life and work of Jewish Afro-Caribbean writer Jamaica Kincaid, herself a product of three diasporas (Jewish, African, and Caribbean) to bring together multiple conversations in new diaspora theorizing. Chapter 2 makes a unique contribution in feminist terms for the need for more nuanced and subtle understandings of diaspora beyond its historic binary formulation of home/away.

Moving the theoretical work along, chapter 3 begins to work more solidly in application in the context of popular culture. In the fall of 2013, ABC began airing a new sitcom called *The Goldbergs*. In this show, the Goldbergs are a Jewish, white-coded family living in the suburbs of Philadelphia in the 1980s. They are loud and act badly (as is common in this genre of sitcoms) with occasional Jewishly coded references. Interestingly, sixty years ago, the first Jewish-themed television sitcom to air was also called *The Goldbergs*, produced by Gertrude Berg. In comparison, the original *Goldbergs* began as a radio show, and then a Bronx apartment-based television show. For its time, its Jewish content was also considered relatively slight, though it would be considered far more Jewishly inflected today. This chapter analyzes creator Gertrude Berg's work in the wildly successful radio and television show *The Goldbergs*. Using mutual construction intersectionality theory—bringing together Jewish, feminist, queer, race, and class analyses—the chapter offers an examination of the moment when the producers moved the locale of the show from the minority ethnically infused Bronx to the suburbs, and why this moved ended the long career of *The Goldbergs*. As part of media history, at the start of television as a popular medium, Gertrude Berg was centrally located in a historical moment in the United States that was open to some ethnic diversity. Gertrude Berg and her work, unusually placed as a successful woman comedian, were later eclipsed by the *Lucille Ball Show*. Intersectionality theory helps us understand this significant shift in popular culture that ended the possibility of *The Goldbergs* at that historical moment, so that in 2013 a new television sitcom with the same name began to air, which considered the suburban placement quite ordinary.

The next three chapters of the book work more explicitly in application in related fields of primary import to feminist studies. The three separate cases explored in these chapters bring the empirical into the analysis in ways broadly useful in intersectionality studies. Chapter 4 addresses an aspect of sexual and gender justice. It provides a consciously mutually constitutive intersectionality analysis of ritual innovation for GLBTQ life cycle needs. Ritual innovation has been a prime area of Jewish feminist work since the 1970s, and, similarly, has been among numerous ethnic and faith communities. But the development of ritual has also been part of the work of explicitly secular communities to reclaim traditions and recover multiple forms and sources of power in the face of hegemonic modes of "power over." From pride parades, drag shows, and the AIDS quilt to life cycle celebrations—for coming out, for transitioning, for relationships, retirement, and for child-rearing queers—these have drawn on feminist efforts to retrieve rituals lost in history and to create new and innovative rituals meaningful to our lives today. However, as in most areas, when such efforts do not pay explicit attention to the co-construction of multiple identities, they can turn into essentialist spectacles. This chapter addresses diversity issues of sexual and gender justice work in the context of intersectional queer ritual innovation.

Chapter 5 names key issues in the area of reproductive justice in a Jewish context. This is an excellent way to place these final two content chapters of the text, because European heritage Jews are a majority among Jews in the United States, but a minority among global Jewry, and European heritage Jewish women have been at the center of the struggle for sexual and reproductive rights. While earlier in the twentieth century, Jewish women (primarily of European heritage) were a main target of eugenic movements, which overlapped with feminist reproductive rights activism, Jewish feminist work in this field has suffered from its own gaps in taking into account the racial diversity within the Jewish community, even in the United States, as well as moving into a parallel leadership role in the critical race transformation of sexual and reproductive rights to reproductive justice.

The final content chapter of *Jewish Feminism and Intersectionality* operates in the most applied sense of the book chapters. Chapter 6 takes up the significant subject of reproductive justice work. While feminists have done important work, a tendency to focus on more elite women has brought the reproductive rights movement to focus, usually, on issues of stopping pregnancy and childbirth. However, as (even Euro-heritage) Jewish feminists should have seen long ago, a main issue for more marginalized communities is the "right" to have children and to parent the children that they birth. For its particular focus, chapter 6 takes up the sticky political issues of transracial adoption from an intersectional Jewish perspective. Here I argue that moves touted as progressive accomplishments—frequently by women and GLBTQ folk, including Jewish feminists and queers—often come at the expense of women and families of color. Opening up to transracial placements has occurred with a concurrent move to make it more difficult for women and families of color to protect their parental rights. This chapter emerges out of the work on my book: *The Family Flamboyant: Race Politics, Queer Families, Jewish Lives*. I do not argue against transracial adoption per se. Instead, I argue for the need for Jews, feminists, queers, and antiracist activists (and those who are any combination of these) and their allies who may understand themselves as directly implicated in and impacted by the reproductive justice assault on primarily women of color to get active. I also see the chapter as a call to take more responsibility for these applauded developments increasing transracial adoptions in the US context.

Conclusion

Whereas not all works cover every aspect of import in intersectionality studies, Jewish feminist activism and scholarship has been excellent on many layers of class, sexuality, ability, and transgender matters. Though much work is being done on race, an area currently most in need of attention for Jewish feminist intersectionality is multiple areas of critical race theory. Intersectionality work has as a key methodological and political aspiration that scholars and activists from a variety of communities come into contact, and inherently hold each other in view when addressing societal challenges. In a similar vein, the book's conclusion presents an argument specifically that antiracism is inherently bound to Jewish feminism and Jewish feminists must more actively include an antiracism agenda within the purview of Jewish feminism as a social justice project. Like the introduction to the book, this chapter uses a more accessible style compared to the academic tone in the content chapters. It rounds out the examinations to be found in *Jewish Feminism and Intersectionality* to assist intersectionality scholars and activists to make use of Jewish feminist contributions and horizons and similarly to support Jewish feminists to more consciously integrate developments of intersectionality studies into their work.

Chapter 1

To Race, to Class, to Queer

Jewish Feminist Contributions to Intersectionality Studies*

Introduction

This chapter continues the introductory analysis with a more detailed discussion of doing intersectionality in a Jewish feminist context. It is intended to set the terms for the later chapters, which will increasingly apply the methodology explored here of racing queer studies and queering race studies, for example, from a Jewish feminist critical race perspective. This chapter is specifically historically situated in some of the most helpful literature from what is sometimes called the feminism's second wave (though treating developments as linear and progressive has been named as unhelpful in intersectionality studies) and critical responses, mainly to white feminists' work of that period. It is intended to (re-)introduce readers to some of the core texts of feminist intersectionality studies, with the Jewish frame made explicit. This will enable us in future chapters to examine various aspects where we can find generative Jewish work and experiences for those also interested in broadening the current trends in intersectionality studies.

The project of racing queer studies and queering race studies in a class-conscious Jewish context must be seen as a part of a larger, and changing, historical context of feminist activism and thought.[1] Feminist theorizing of identity has changed since the beginning of the second wave of the feminist movement. The origins of what we may call contemporary identity politics, since Karl Marx's focus on a liberatory politics based explicitly on class grounds, lay in identifying individual characteristics such as gender, culture,

---

*Revised and updated from the original publication in Bar On and Tessman (2001).

race/ethnicity, ability, or sexual orientation that are singled out for analysis. This form of identity politics was also identitarian, assuming a sameness, or cohesion of a well-bounded identity community. The one identity aspect was often universalized and set at the center of visions for ending oppression. For Jewish feminists active in this period, universalizing one discrete and identitarian aspect of identity proved limiting.[2] Activists and scholars eventually were able to articulate that the choice of being either a woman or a Jew for communal and political purposes was indeed a false choice.[3] Oppression works through multiple mechanisms, identities are porous and morphing and cannot be seen in isolation from one another.

Discourse about multiple identities and oppressions gave way to self-criticism, including the recognition that identities were not simply many, but interconnected in an indefinite variety of ways. We cannot just add critical race theory to feminist analysis, for example, because the way one's life is gendered does not stand on its own as clearly distinguishable and then get added to the way one's life is raced. Causes for celebration and resistance for Jewish women as feminists, for example, do not come in neat ahistorical packages for them as women, and then other times in other neat essentialist packages for them as Jews. Many feminists, then, began to talk about the connection between identities or even the ways that oppressions "intersect."[4]

While extremely popular still today, for others, however, intersectionality was not enough. Feminists theorized the ways in which identity signifiers are actually mutually constitutive (a premise that, when they are queried, most intersectionality scholars say they are working from). What they mean is that, for example, gender itself is a raced/classed/sexed/cultured category, as race is a gendered/classed/sexed/cultured category. Gender can be seen as mutually constitutive of the construction of sexual orientation so that being male or female only makes sense in the context of compulsory heterosexuality. The personal and social constructions of one's life as a Jewish lesbian feminist is a historically situated Jewishly and gendered sexing, a sexed and gendered Jewing, and simultaneously a sexed and Jewed gendering.

In large part, it has been the work of African-American, Latina, and other lesbians and feminists of color that most clearly articulated this point of analysis. In earlier works such as *Ain't I a Woman*, the anthologies *Home Girls*; *This Bridge Called My Back*; *Making Face, Making Soul*, and the most appropriately titled *All the Women Are White, All the Blacks Are Men, but Some of Us Are Brave*,[5] many women of color worked at describing and investigating the ways that race, class, culture, and sexuality all nuance and shift gender construction. There were certainly formally trained philosophers writing in these books. In hindsight, however, we can now see that there were both strengths and weaknesses involved in the appropriation of insights from these volumes into the works of formally trained feminist philosophers outside these marginalized communities. Further, despite the widespread activities of Jewish feminists, less attention has been paid to Jewish experiences and insights within these discussions of identities and multiple modes of power and oppression. From multiculturalism to intersectionality, Jewish people, experience, and analysis is largely missing in these literatures.

It is my intention in this chapter to constructively address these strengths and weaknesses and to situate Jewish feminist queer thinking within the philosophical discussion of intersectionality and mutual construction. To do so, the next session takes up an early important text in the development of intersectionality studies and mutual constitution theory, that by Elizabeth V. Spelman, as a helpful, yet limited, example of philosophical writing on the mutual constitution of identities. I then offer a critical reading of a specific Talmudic text as an alternative to Spelman's reliance on a hegemonic Western philosophical tradition. In the final section, through an analysis of early works by Rebecca Alpert and Melanie Kaye/Kantrowitz, I discuss the ways that insights from both Western feminist and Talmudic traditions may be found at work in Jewish feminist queer discussions of what is termed today *intersectionality politics*.

Mutual Constitution Theory in Feminist Philosophy

It is probably all too obvious that those doing higher-level feminist philosophy have tended to be white women, or women not identifying in their written work with a nonwhite/Christian minority.[6] The second point of import here, addressed more specifically to conceptual content, is that although some have managed to include numerous aspects of identities into their analyses, in fact, some of the most insightful academic philosophical demonstrations of this view of multiple identity signifiers as mutually constitutive have used a two-tiered model.[7] Early pivotal work by Spelman, for example, demonstrated that gender and race mutually constitute each other.[8] As helpful as this scholarship is, however, it also has significant limitations. Such work has tended to slip from focusing on two identity signifiers into privileging one or two at the cost of others. In Spelman's case, despite the significant contribution of her critique of such practices in the development of intersectionality studies, she tends to privilege race as an identity category and this seems to follow from her reliance on standard canons of hegemonic Western civilization.

Spelman's Argument

In *Inessential Woman*, Spelman presents the following analysis of race and gender categories. According to Spelman, we often find ourselves and our political commentators asking about, for example, the status of women and Blacks in the military.[9] She reminds us that such a statement actually makes no sense, since some women in the military are Black and some of the Blacks are also women. Not only is this faulty use of language, but given the racist biases in gender analysis and the sexist biases in race-based analysis, the category "women" is taken then to mean non-Black women, and the category "Black" is taken to mean Blacks who are not women. This structure leaves out an important group of human beings: Black women.

Spelman seeks to introduce the Black woman into (traditionally white) scholarly discourse and ultimately (back) into the modes of political production. In order to make her point, she demonstrates that the additive method for understanding identity (adding one discrete identity signifier such as gender to another discrete identity signifier such as race, and so on) is insufficient for including Black women. The only way to end the exclusion of Black women is to understand identities such as race and gender, not just as connected or as one added to the other, but to understand that the very category of gender is raced and the category of race is gendered.

Spelman's Method

Spelman begins her argument with a critique of race and gender in Plato, and hones the discussion further in a second chapter on Aristotle. There were certain distinctions that Aristotle made between human beings that set them into particular categories with respect to power. Not all people were considered citizens. In fact, children, women, slaves, and foreigners were expressly considered to exist by nature outside the bounds of possible citizenship. It is, however, the specific designations of women and slaves that mostly concern Spelman. Again, motivated by who is left out of theoretical treatises on the subject of "women and slaves in ancient Greece," including feminist ones,[10] Spelman reminds us that some females were slaves, as much as some slaves were female. Among nonslave Athenians, Aristotle distinguished between the men and the women. When referring to slaves, the distinction of gender is not made.[11] Spelman skillfully demonstrates, therefore, that when Aristotle referred to women (presumably the gendered category of females),[12] he was referring specifically and exclusively to nonslave females. Thus, for Aristotle, the very category of women exists only within a certain elite segment of the population.

It is at this point that Spelman's use of the hegemonic Greek text takes a problematic turn. She notes that the ancient Greek category of "slave" resembles a cross between our contemporary categories of race and class. She suggests that, for expository ease, this race/class category will have to be simplified. Driven by her own motivations within the context of contemporary political concerns, Spelman chooses to translate the ancient Greek notion of slave into the modern idiom of race.[13] The potential for a class-based analysis effectively drops out at this point.[14] We are left with a dual axis discussion of identity, based on gender and race.[15] Due to this particular interpretation, although Spelman eloquently shows that gender is raced, her argument that race is gendered functions slightly differently and brings her use of the Greek text into further difficulties.

As mentioned earlier, Spelman points out that Aristotle does not address gender distinctions among slaves. Allowing Aristotle's work here to function as a hegemonic text, Spelman, therefore, also does not make such a distinction.[16] Although for critical purposes she writes about this issue in Aristotle's writing, she also does not distinguish between the maleness and femaleness of slaves.[17] Therefore, although she will ultimately argue that gender is raced and race is gendered, her explanations of the two understandably are not parallel. Gender, on this account, is raced because one needed to be of a certain race to have a gender at all. Race is gendered, in this story, because the distinction of races is marked by those who have genders and those who do not. In short: free Athenians have genders; slaves do not.

The issue of concern for intersectionality studies is the way that Spelman's construction of the race of gender and the gender of race does not sufficiently reflect the relations of power and identity in many of our lives, and therefore is limited in the ways it might be helpful in the work to overcome oppressions as they operate in our lived lives (not only in our philosophical heritage). By setting up race and gender in the way that she does with the help of Aristotle, Spelman assumes that Athenian women stand above all slaves, whether male or female, in the social hierarchy. Spelman writes: "Since there are no natural rulers among slaves, a man who is a slave is not the natural ruler of a woman who is a slave (and surely not of a free woman)," and "whatever biological superiority male slaves have to female slaves, they are inferior to the wives of male citizens."[18] I could not say whether such a depiction is accurate. What is important is that Spelman then projects this set of relationships onto those she conceives of as among similar groups of our day. Thus, Spelman presumes that white women, in the contemporary political context, always stand above all African Americans.[19]

Critique

From within Spelman's theory, one loses the ability to continue a critical gender analysis within a critical discussion about race. When Spelman relates Aristotle's view of slaves to the reality of African Americans, she also transfers what she understands as Aristotle's homogenizing characterization of slaves. As a result, in her argument, race trumps gender. If in Spelman's reading of Aristotle, slaves had no genders, then modern oppressed races have no genders. If modern oppressed races have no genders, then gender-based analysis cannot be applied. But, when critical gender analysis is not applied, maleness is the assumed norm and patriarchy goes uncontested. In effect, Spelman has thus erased the existence of African-American women and their concerns. Ironically, this is precisely the problem that inspired Spelman's inquiry to begin with.

There are, though, two additional problems. First, despite the obvious pervasiveness of racism in the contemporary context, all white women simply do not always have distinct power over all Black men. This was the case long before, and will be long after, Barak Obama beat Hilary Clinton for the Democratic Party presidential nomination. Second, Spelman tends to essentialize the groups of Black men and white women in her characterization; thus, the structure of her argument causes her at times to lose sight of diversity among white women, and also among Black men and women. Bringing these two points together, we can say that within classes, for example, Black men often enjoy male privilege over all women in their own or lower classes, often enough including white women and trans people and also queer, non-Christian, non-citizen, and disabled women and other genders of various races. Spelman's unfortunate refusal to work within the reality of such renders this aspect of her argument absurd. Moreover, real life has us often moving in and out of differing positions of power and this dynamic ought to be core to any intersectionality study, but Spelman does not adequately prepare us for the work.

Although Spelman's account of Aristotle focuses on his two-tiered model of free/slave-male/female, at the moment Spelman chooses to translate the ancient Greek slavery from what she herself notes as a more complicated convergence of contemporary class and race, she limits the power of her own insights as well. However, it is my argument that Spelman's thesis on the mutual constitution of multiple identities is not inherently limited. My suggestion is that one reason she falls short of her own goals involves her particular methodological reliance on Aristotle, a preeminent Western canonical figure, in her critique of the dominant framework. Perhaps we will be better able to do the work Spelman sets out for us if we look for alternative ways of conceptualizing the issues from sources and traditions outside the Western canon. In light of this suggestion, I turn now to a discussion of countertexts.

There are certainly any number of texts that could be employed in order to help Spelman's analysis stay critical, multifaceted, and more flexible (which I imagine she intended) by applying a critique of a hegemonic text. What one ought to look for is a text capable of conceiving multiple categories as mutually constitutive that relies on an alternative epistemological framework to that relied on by hegemonic texts. We may look for answers to these questions in traditional, ancient Jewish texts.

Having said this, I realize that some people who are familiar with feminist and queer studies might find this statement implausible. Due to the sexism practiced and institutionalized in so many Jewish communities, feminists often presume there is nothing left of worth in traditional Jewish thinking and texts. Similarly, due to religious—and explicitly biblical—invocations used to justify extreme homophobia, queers of all kinds may assume that the Torah is inherently tainted with a heterosexist norm. What we also find, however, is that the epistemological framework manifest in certain ancient Jewish texts offers alternatives to current attempts at theorizing our multiple identities as mutually constitutive.

Jewish Texts as Countertexts

In this section, I develop a close reading of a Talmudic text.[20] Posing difficult dilemmas, the Babylonian rabbis puzzled through what Jewish tradition would prescribe in myriad specific circumstances. I engage a particular analysis of this text as an example of a countertext that can help perform the interrogatory function that Spelman's theory needs to stay critical. Before presenting the textual analysis, however, a few words are in order on the use of these texts as countertexts.

Political and Philosophical Potential of Countertexts for Intersectionality Studies

As feminist and queer scholars have argued, it is often helpful to turn to countertexts in order to see through myths of dominant cultural norms.[21]

If we look at a nonhegemonic text (or even a text that is hegemonic but in a subaltern context), we might be better able to explore the multiple layers of the ways identity categories are mutually constituted. Using Spelman's concern about lists of identities, and about how the additive approach blinds us to the reality of whole groups of people, we can look at a particular ancient Jewish text that resembles the Aristotelian model of listing "slaves and women," but with significant differences. I want to suggest that with the help of Spelman, an analysis of the countertext I will present holds more promise for those in intersectionality studies interested in theorizing the mutual constitution of multiple identities and the ways in which they are complicated, than that of Spelman's use of the canonical Greeks only. Further, we can find this methodology used in many Jewish feminist lesbian and queer theorizings, however unself-consciously.

Methodologically, it seems we would want to be able to say more about a text that qualifies in specific contexts as a countertext than that it is simply outside the canon.[22] A comparative analysis of the differences between Talmudic texts in the context of their use in Jewish history and Western political theory would take volumes. What I find most interesting in this set of countertexts for the subject of this chapter, however, is how they help us circumscribe the problems of modernist standpoint theory that could (and at times do) plague Jewish feminist queer, critical race, and class work.

The main distinction that is important at this point, between the method of thinking in the Aristotelian-based tradition and that found in rabbinic texts, relates to how Aristotle's universalism relies on sameness to define identity concepts.[23] This is the foundational assumption in the problematic nature of essentialism. Jewish tradition has not worked this way, for the most part. It is not a universalist tradition, but rather it is usually particularist. As will be demonstrated, differences comprise the world of rabbinic and other Jewish understandings of identity.[24] This suggests that what I present as "additional" categories to the two-tiered approach of Spelman are not merely multiplying, or adding, categories as is often found in the additive move, and critiqued by those wary of standpoint theory.[25] The Talmudic categories are not "added" to some essential and unchanging identity, as somehow external to one's "core" identity as a Jew.[26] The categories are internally constitutive of Jewishness itself; they explicitly make one the kind of Jew one is.

What I find interesting in the Talmudic text (later replicated in much Jewish feminist work) is the alternative system of complex hierarchies.[27] In the structure erected in this text, there is no single standpoint from which to gain perspective. These texts are therefore both extremely problematic for their content vis-à-vis the history of Jewish communities and also extremely promising for complex contemporary theorizing. Further, in using a countertext, I do not wish to suggest that we can get outside of oppressive discourses simply by looking outside *dominant* oppressive discourses. What I am offering is the idea that other noncanonical modes of thinking—even if oppressive in their own contexts—might highlight aspects of the dominant mode in need of critique. They can provide a set of instances that disrupt the first set of oppressive categorizations.[28]

The following analysis of a countertext will also demonstrate the reciprocal benefit of using a more multicultural analysis. Relying on canonical texts can often reinforce problematic modes of thinking. Looking to marginalized works may provide us with more alternative conceptualizations. But this is not all. Bringing together analytic discussions of concern in the dominant framework with those in marginalized communities can provide transformative insight into the problems faced by those within the marginalized framework as well.[29] This layer of countertextual analysis is imperative, because not making the reciprocal move to hold the subaltern text to critical scrutiny runs the risk of cultural essentialism by not acknowledging the interpretive struggles and historical power dynamics in the minority community. Without the reciprocal move in countertextual analysis, the critique potentially sets up the historically dominant powers within the minority culture as an unproblematized and representative norm. For Jewish feminist queers, this will simply not do. Finally, failing to engage in the reciprocal countertextual critique implicitly prioritizes justice work for those in the dominant community over those in the marginalized minority community.[30] As such, the following pages will point to the potential of both using Jewish texts to revive Spelman's thesis, as well as using Spelman to challenge the power relationships in the Jewish text.

Talmudic Hierarchical Classifications for Saving a Life

Contemporary scholars and practitioners working in a Jewish framework often turn to historically significant Jewish texts to understand the ancient logic of the rabbis in order to help solve contemporary problems. For example, we might imagine a dilemma for contemporary medical ethicists where in urgent cases, such as those of modern emergency rooms, the question of how to prioritize patients for triage is life-threateningly pressing. In examining the particular case of what a physician should do when faced with two patients of equal ill health at the same time, Jewish ethicists may turn to Talmudic sources for answers. In their search they are likely to come upon a text from the Babylonian Talmud Horayot 13b–14a, which addresses "matters concerning the saving of a life."

In this case the rabbis reasoned through a maze of categories and came up with a specific answer. The rather shocking and very practical answer to this question of enormous gravity is that the male patient is treated before a female patient, for it says in the Mishnah, "A man takes precedence over a woman in matters concerning the saving of life." Interestingly enough, the reasoning does not stop here in order to make sure that the writing can answer the problem completely. Gender categories are not the only significant categories in traditional Jewish culture, nor is this binary notation cohesive as the Talmud also discusses various additional gender categories (Lev 2004, 2007, 2010; Fonrobert 2007). The text thus goes on to rank numerous groups of people in the order in which they should receive attention.

The next ranking runs according to the ancient Jewish caste system: One must treat a Cohen before a Levite, and a Levite before an Israelite. The Gemara also includes ten ranked subcategories of Cohens and some challenges to its chosen order. This system of categorization, which I have called caste-based, actually works according to religious rights and responsibilities in ancient Israel. It is still in use today under certain circumstances and explains common Jewish surnames in the United States: Cohen, Cohn, Cahan, Kahane, Kane; Levi, Levy, Levitan, Levinson, Lewinsky; and Israel, Israeli, and so on. These names, or other familial identifications, tell where those individuals fall in the three-thousand-year-old Jewish caste system. As a concrete example, I am of the Israelite caste.

This is not all. The next set of categorizations are what might best be understood today as national (i.e., who belongs to the nation). The Mishnah states that Cohens, Levites, and Israelites are all to be treated before bastards, "a bastard over a nathin,[31] a *nathin* over a proselyte, and a proselyte over an emancipated slave." The text does not mention slaves as a group at all. What is also interesting about this category of national membership is that there are three subcategories of membership in the nation: biological, cultural, and geographic. Although these categories are presented in a simple hierarchy at this stage, the text in full through the Gemara interpretation keeps the relations between these three subcategories challenged within the text and thus may be seen as potentially fluid and shifting. Let us look at an example of this complex and hierarchy.

What is presented in terms of textual order, as the last category, scholars, actually turns out to override all the previous categories. This is the subversive category of the Talmud.[32] The Mishnah states clearly: "This order of precedence applies only when all these were in other respects equal. If the bastard, however, was a scholar and the High Priest an ignoramus, the learned bastard takes precedence over the ignorant High Priest." (The high priest refers to the Cohen caste, within which the Gemara makes sure to delineate many subcategories as well.) Mixing in political categories of hierarchical ordering, the Gemara also explains, "A scholar takes precedence over a king of Israel, for if a scholar dies there is none to replace him," and "A king takes precedence over a High Priest." There is a final category that crosses the political and religious—prophets—who are ranked below the political category of king. None of these classifications refer to those that affect women as a group as women, such as marital status.

Co-Constructionist Intersectionality, Spelman, and the Confusion of the Talmudic Hierarchies

Given the multiplicity of categories and their nature, the Talmudic text can be quite interesting to contemporary political theorists working on intersectionality, and more promising than the twofold framework of Spelman's translated Aristotle. Due to the complexity of the Talmudic rankings, I will first attempt to clarify the conceptual incoherences and the nuances of the hierarchical orderings that often turn in on themselves. To do so I will use Spelman's methodology. First, a gender classification is in some ways distinct from the collection of castes among Cohens, Levites, and Israelites. These are, in turn, in certain aspects distinct from the national collection of bastards, *nathins*, converts, and emancipated slaves, which are to some degree distinct from the scholarly, political, and political/religious classifications. In this case, the fact that slaves are not even mentioned is a silence waiting to be theorized.

The use of the term *Israelite* in this listing is particularly confusing for those who yearn for discrete and separable identity groupings, because it sometimes refers only to the priestly order (as when it is used in the list of religious caste order), and at other times it means all the rest of the people of Israel (as in the reference to a king of Israel), which would include those named under the gender, national, scholarly, political, and political-religious listings as well as Cohens, Levites, and kings.[33] Also, historically there were instances when individuals moved in or out of the Levite cast, making that designation far more fluid than such placement in the list suggests. Further, in common understandings of Jewish law, once a person has become a Jew, there is to be no distinction, let alone discrimination, made between one who converted to become a Jew and one who is Jewish by virtue of being born to a Jewish mother. Here, on the matter of literal life and death, we find a substantial distinction. Otherwise, Israelites may have been converts, bastards, or *nathins* and could be among the group designated as emancipated slaves. Finally, aside from Cohens, Levites, and kings, all the other categories mentioned might be composed of both men, women, and (and what we might consider today) queerly gendered.

Using Spelman to destabilize the Jewish text proves to be quite interesting. It forces a contemporary scholar to look at the multiplicity of categories and question their internal logic in ways not traditionally questioned. To explicate this for those less familiar with the mechanisms of this particular historical tradition, Jewish law is steeped in distinctions based on gender—though not necessarily only in a binary frame. In this case, the two top religious caste categories do not even include women. Laws for women apply to women only sometimes in the Israelite designation and usually in all the other categories designated; laws for men sometimes apply to all men and at other times apply to men according to their membership in these other classes. The scholarly and religious-political references would usually refer to men, but on occasion women scholars and prophetesses have been named. No woman was ever king. Although one might conclude that gender trumps all other distinctions, due to its appearance at the top of the original list, Spelman's analysis helps us to see that such a conclusion is nonsensical. In ancient Israelite society, women could be converts, nathins, bastards, and current or freed slaves. À la Spelman, saying "women and Israelites," or "women and converts" makes no sense and excludes those who fall into both categories. It also does not help us understand women and the caste system or myriad decisions regarding (in contemporary terms) gender queers.

The Talmud and the Problem of a Two-Tiered Intersectionality Method

Due to the particularist tendency of Talmudic thinking, that there are many categories previously named does not mean that the categories of identity of interest to Spelman are simply multiplied. Instead, we find a complex system of overlapping, shifting, and internally challenged hierarchies. This makes the use of the additive method basically impossible. The following is intended to help clarify this point.

Regarding the Jewish text, one must do the following (not necessarily lexically):

1. Put all these sets of relationships together.

2. Figure out if including women and those beyond a gender binary into categories where they fit means that bastard males take precedence over bastard females.

3. Rerank categories that include men and women and all genders.

4. Open the possibility that women could stand above men in the case where a woman is a scholar.

5. Include the groups not mentioned in even this long list but crucial to its implementation, such as those beyond a modern gender binary, slaves and divorced women, wives of Cohens, Levites, Israelites, and kings.

6. Rerank according to how the unnamed groups change the hierarchy of the named.

7. Figure out what to do in frame 5 where a Cohen and a Levite are both above Israelites and are Israelites themselves.

8. Notice that it is impossible to perform steps 1 through 7.

The above set of steps demonstrates conceptually the classifications, group names, and power relationships in the two examples, Spelman's Aristotle and this particular Talmudic text. The difference between Spelman's Aristotle and the Talmudic text is not simply that more classifications and groups are named in the Talmud, but that the internal logic of the Talmudic text challenges its own named categories as discrete and separable entities and makes it impossible to develop a linear presentation of power relationships at all, let alone one that is stable or fixed.

Using this countertext to help destabilize Spelman's Aristotelian categorizations, we can see that if this had been the model that Spelman had relied on, she might not have translated the complicated racial/classed category of slave into the single contemporary signifier of race. It would not have helped her to do so. She would, therefore, also probably not have theorized race as a gendered category in the way that she does. Some particulars from this Jewish example are that certain castes have women and other genders, others do not; women and other genders in the families of the Cohen or Levite men led different lives in the social context than those in other castes; and divorced women and other genders, yet another category, were generally exempted from the possibility of marrying males in the Cohen caste. Like life, the situation is more complicated than the easy slave/not-slave bifurcation, and importantly, the line of gender is not drawn on a dualistic model. In looking at the rabbinic text, we are forced to deal with multiple categories and myriad relationships that are often counterindicative and can change, given different contexts. We would have to examine the whole complex of gender, caste, class, politics, learnedness, marital status, foreign origin, and so on, as it works in its own unique way through each constellation, as well as what similarities might run throughout, even as the categories and their relations themselves are questioned and shift. This model is probably more productive for contemporary intersectionality thinkers seeking to theorize identities and power dynamics in the vast complex multiplicity of our lives.

The Talmudic Example and Jewish Lesbian Feminist Analyses

We must ask, therefore, how we can make use of this alternative mode, as found in traditional Jewish texts, for contemporary work in critical queer, class, and race studies. In some ways, many Jewish feminists and queer (or queer-conscious) activists and thinkers have long been working out the answer to this question. Although the majority of queer and feminist Jewish intellectuals and organizers are not likely to be familiar with Talmudic or other ancient texts,[34] we can find an interesting correlation between their epistemological assumptions. In addition, although many Jewish queers would not necessarily see themselves as consciously engaged in a contemporary application of ancient Jewish wisdoms, *we* might see them as such nevertheless.

There are two reasons for this that I think are important to highlight in the context of this chapter. First, there is a relationship between contemporary intersectionality perspectives that look for, embrace, and honor particularities and the epistemological framework found in some rabbinic reasoning mentioned earlier. Second, the basic life experiences of feminist Jewish queers demands attention to their multiple identities—and concomitant power relations—beyond a dual grid. Even white, European-heritage and Ashkenazi Jewish lesbians who have not yet begun to problematize their racial/cultural/class location in a US context do, at least, engage in the tripartite complex hierarchies of sexuality, gender, and Jewishness. In many Jewish feminist and queer activist organizations and writings, we find sensitivity to the complexity of power dynamics operating on multiple layers that not only shade one another, but often change shape and turn in on each other as well, depending on the context. Since this may be difficult to understand abstractly, I would like to present an analysis of early exemplary works by two Jewish lesbian feminist activists and scholars. The first, Rebecca Alpert, is also a rabbi and therefore familiar with Talmudic texts (although I do not mean to imply that her book is a conscious application). The second, Melanie Kaye/Kantrowitz, is a secular Jew with less exposure to such texts. In looking at a central early work by each woman, we can see more specifically how we may use Spelman's insights recast with a Talmudic legacy of multiple identities in theorizing Jewish issues in the complex nexus of race/nationality, gender, sexuality, and class.

The Lesbian Legacy of "Bread on the Seder Plate"

Alpert is a Jewish lesbian feminist activist rabbi, and also a scholar in the secular academy. The goal of her 1997 book, *Like Bread on the Seder Plate*, is to "determine strategies" for Jewish lesbians to "participate [more] fully, as lesbians, in Jewish life."[35] Alpert does not seek inclusion of lesbians into Jewish communal life in an assimilationist mode (as in the universalist reliance on sameness). Instead, she seeks an inclusion of this previously ignored—and other times marginalized—group through means no less radical than the fundamental transformation of Judaism itself. Similar to the way that the Talmud both establishes authority even as it challenges it, at the outset of Alpert's vision we find that Jewish tradition is itself open and changing rather than essentially static. In order to make possible this deep change in Jewish history, Alpert primarily takes on the traditional Jewish task of reinterpreting texts. There is, however, nothing essentially traditional in the aims of her methodology. Alpert offers lesbian-critical insights from readings of ancient religious texts, introduces new texts for consideration as part of a transformed canon, and develops suggestions for the creation of new sacred texts out of the lives of Jewish lesbians from the history of today and the future.

As the Talmudic example works with multiple, overlapping, and shifting categories to establish its newly authoritative perspective, Alpert deftly works a tripartite analysis of identities and their mutual constitution. She takes on gender, sexual orientation, and Jewish affiliation in a fluid weave. Within her tripartite analysis, Alpert is able to acknowledge and incorporate multiple aspects of difference though she privileges three categories. She is able to do so often enough without always treating the multiple aspects as discrete and separative. For example, Jewish diversity is not limited to factors of sexual orientation and gender (her two other privileged categories). Jews are one group in the privileged triplet, even as Jews are diverse according to historical context, race, geography, religious expression, nationality, and so on. Similarly, analysis of the category of lesbian crosses Jewish and non-Jewish examinations as it is also related to gay male, bisexual, transgender, and queer categories. Her treatment of gender also draws on both Jewish and non-Jewish sources and complicates the very idea of gender through discussion of lesbian and other gender nonconformist interstices.

Alpert's project faces a number of challenges, however, when viewed through the lens of an attempt to race queer studies and queer race studies in a Jewish context. Most obviously, despite brief acknowledgment of other politically salient issues of identity such as race and class, Alpert's mode of exploration in this particular text is not sufficiently open to race- and class-critical analyses. Having said this, there is actually another consideration that I would like to focus on more specifically: the delicate difficulty of privileging the conceptual category of lesbian over queer without incorporating the baggage of second-wave feminism's history of essentialism.

Although the reclamation of "queer" became a hallmark of 1990s politics in the United States, it did not become—or remain—so without contestation. The concept of queer is in need of such contestation. I do not use the term *queer* here to suggest that it simply surpasses all essentialisms. It does not. As one example, many can collapse queer, often taken to suggest multiplicity and fluidity, into its own binary essentialism over and against heteronormativity. Many communities, often depending on age, race, class, and cultural diversity, do not use the term *queer* in self-identification. Significantly also for the purposes of this chapter, many lesbians in particular have resisted self- and movement-labeling as queer because of the legacy of sexism within gay men's activist movements and within society at large. Sexist tendencies to eclipse the experiences, concerns, and contributions of women in their diversity have found their place in coalitions among sexual minorities and in queer studies and activism. Lesbians, in particular, but not only those deeply situated in the second-wave feminist movement, have often continued to demand distinct lesbian spaces, organizations, and modes of analysis. This, of course, has become increasingly challenging as transfolk speak up and speak back in supposedly feminist women's spheres. Albert's project focused on lesbians, although it was clearly situated within a broader spectrum of sexual minorities, gender variance, and queer ideology in particular. In many ways the book itself demonstrates the need for such a prioritization.

However, as Spelman's work is designed to demonstrate, some aspects of second-wave feminism relied on various modes of essentialist thinking. Women were taken to be the subject of feminist political movement, and too often even the feminist employment of the category of women reflected hegemonic patriarchal characterizations of who these "women" are. As has been much discussed, despite long-term activism among women from an array of minority communities, the closer one was to a white, middle-class, heterosexual, Christian, and able norm, the more likely one's voice was to be heard within feminist movement and in the US media. Internalizing a narrow and/or static view of women, even as they often radicalized it, many second-wave feminists represented lesbians at an apex of the "feminist woman." While not specifically the trajectory of Alpert's work, the lesbian identity that often emerged out of radical second-wave feminism was, as a political act, defined more through a feminist lens of the person being "woman identified" than through a lens of sexuality and/or status as a sexual or gender outlaw.[36]

The consequence of this trend among feminists was that lesbians of this milieu more frequently aligned themselves with "women" than with gay men, bisexuals, and transgender people. In fact, the nature of certain strains of feminist critique explicitly distanced lesbian identity and community from cultural forms developing in both gay men's communities (such as drag and male-to-female cross-dressing) and other forms of queer women's culture (such as role-playing, cross-dressing, female-to-male transitioning, or sadomasochism). This set of political alignments also often set lesbian feminists against lesbians whose identity was forged prior to the advent or outside the centers of second-wave feminism. This meant, for example, that lesbian identities in rural areas and small cities without a college campus (specifically an elite or radical college campus) were frequently marginalized as politically incorrect, not only as feminists, but also as women and as lesbians. The same may be said for racial and class dichotomies: The radical feminist assertion of "feminism as the theory, lesbianism as the practice" emerged largely outside of working-class and poor lesbian worlds, as well as outside most lesbian communities of color.

Feminist movements presuming the priority of women *as* women left no room for women *as* anything else. Put more specifically, the notion of women as women assumed an essential identity of womanness that could be abstracted from other identity constructions and stand universally on its own. In fact, this essentialized universal womanness was of course a raced, classed, sexed, and cultured conception. Without attending to this fact, however, women from communities not assumed in the class/race/culture/gender/sexuality norm were seen as less purely *women*—including often Jewish women in their diversity. Identifications imbricated with a cross section of other communities were seen as tainted. This problem of essentialism is directly related to Spelman's excellent work on race and class in the text analyzed in this chapter. For all the critical work her contribution accomplishes, it also can make it difficult to do gender-based critique in the context of the vast array of power dynamics, even among the group she refers to as women.

We cannot overlook at this point that these imbricating identities are ones that women would share with men as well as with other women and those gender identified beyond the binary. Just as Jews invested in Jewish patriarchy found identifying as feminists an act of mutiny, as it was assumed impossible to identify with women *and* Jews, some feminists found continued identification with class struggle and racial and ethnic/religious communities an act of treason. In class, racial, and ethnic/religious communities, women could not be women *as* women exclusively; they shared these politics with groups of men, trans, and all gender queer people. This bind within feminism was at times replicated within lesbian politics. Moreover, to the degree that lesbians were seen as hyperwomen (in a radical feminist sense), the elite pressure to define identities and align politically with women made coalition and joint identity construction with males and gender/sexual outlaws culturally and politically criminal. This has led to the more recent reemergence of some self-identifying as "radical feminists" as virulently antitrans. This usurpation of the identifier radical is problematic. Jewishly it tends to make less sense. Jewish feminism has always needed feminism to be more open and variegated in its radicalness, or anti-Semitism remained intact in ways similarly found in hegemonic patriarchal and racist societal norms.

I want to be clear here: I am not saying that these elements of exclusionary thinking are directly present in *Like Bread on the Seder Plate*. Alpert provides a helpful framework for those seeking to work in critical lesbian theory, which avoids the worst of these movement problematics. For example, Alpert explicitly concludes the book with her "visions for the future." In this chapter Alpert points out that many of her concerns for a lesbian feminist Jewish agenda are shared with numerous other Jews: heterosexual feminists, gay men, heterosexual intermarried couples, bisexuals, transgendered people, single heterosexuals, those not traditionally observant, liberal Jews in general, progressive educators, "scholars of women's history, mysticism, and Mizrachi Jewish communities." This single mention of nonwhite/

non-Ashkenazi Jews suggests, however, that they may be absent from the writer's and readers' conceptualizations about the other groups and may not even be interpreted to mean Mizrachi (Eastern) Jewish communities at all, but "scholars of." No mention was made at that historical juncture of Jews of color of whatever Jewish ethnic tradition, though Alpert's work has changed since the publication of this particular text. Further, Jewish lesbian feminists have made clear that tensions between lesbians and other sexual outlaws in the Jewish community, especially those involving "men" of various sorts, will not be adequately addressed until bisexual women take responsibility for certain aspects of relative privilege, and until men, including trans men, make antisexist work central to their agendas. However, this does not exempt lesbians from taking responsibility as well. The history of essentialist thought at work not only in feminism, Spelman's focus, but also in lesbian feminism has affected some aspects of Jewish lesbian feminism. Gathering together in specific communities is necessary as we do the work of social justice. However, attending to some of the problematic aspects that gathering has relied on historically is also a necessary part of justice work. In this, lesbian feminists must also take seriously the potentially essentialist bases informing some of our choices historically to identify as lesbians.

The Issue Is Power

At this juncture I would like to undertake a brief review of one other earlier work by a Jewish lesbian feminist that was also interestingly able to avoid the trap of essentialism. At the time Melanie Kaye/Kantrowitz was writing the essays for her book, *The Issue Is Power: Essays on Women, Jews, Violence and Resistance*, she was not using the term *queer*; her radical feminist identification as lesbian and dyke does not, however, exactly recall the historical problems of essentialism in feminist thought in the same way that Alpert's work can and Spelman's work did. Clearly advancing a lesbian-critical agenda, Kaye/Kantrowitz shows us that we need constantly to see the relationship between anti-Semitism, racism, classism, sexism, and homophobia if we are to build an inclusive, multicultural, and effective left in this "toxic wasteland" of our lives.[37] However, we must build these bridges with "our frail/sturdy human hearts outraged by injustice and committed to generosity."[38]

The Issue Is Power contains speeches from political events and essays of various lengths developed over a fifteen-year period. Kaye/Kantrowitz's message is delivered always in the cadence of a poet, with the urgency of an activist, and the sensitivity, kindness, and self-criticism of a Brooklyn-born

Jew re-created in the civil rights, women's, and lesbian liberation movements. From pieces on art and culture to politics, identity, and sexuality, Kaye/Kantrowitz shows over and over that the issue most certainly is power and that we had better wise up, allow ourselves to feel it, talk to each other about it, and take action.

The book opens with a long essay on violence.[39] She opens the introduction: "First I learned about rape. I mean, I always knew, cannot remember learning. First I learned about the Holocaust. I mean, I always knew, cannot remember learning."[40] Kaye/Kantrowitz, who is antimilitaristic, takes the issue of violence seriously and has decided that it is "a contradiction to be a Jew and a pacifist," that "pacifism is a luxury" because "victims resist every way they can . . . victims must fight back."[41]

But this is no diatribe through which Kaye/Kantrowitz might seduce you into any form of action and resistance if you are not careful. Her work on violence is far from a glorification, or a love affair such as Hollywood, the news media, or the nation-state have. Kaye/Kantrowitz, speaking with the insight of the oppressed, immediately asks: "What does it mean to be a *victim*? How does one/can one use violence to free oneself? And then how does one stop? When is one strong enough to stop?"[42] In this essay, Kaye/Kantrowitz is able to focus on violence against women and articulate what she has learned from resistance to such violence. But like any of the mutually constitutive categories of the Talmudic text, women do not stand alone in this piece as a separative category. What she knows about violence against women is made possible by what she has mutually come to know about anti-Semitic, class-based, racial violence, and militarism as well.

Many of the other essays treat topics of Jewish identity and politics more directly. Similar to what we saw in Alpert and in contrast to an essentialist view, Kaye/Kantrowitz benefits from a traditional legacy that values historical continuity as it presumes major disruptions and new developments within that historical trajectory. In these pieces, she keeps in motion the movement to redevelop US Jewish identity. This emerging identity is Jewish and is placed in history; in her words, "to be a Jew is to tangle with history."[43] It is also well rooted in and relevant to our contemporary (US) American experience, in the spirit of those with an unflinching commitment to morality and pride, both personal and collective. Kaye/Kantrowitz takes for her base a quote from Muriel Rukeyser, "To be a Jew in the twentieth century is to be offered a gift,"[44] and adds that "To be a Radical Jew in the Late 20th Century" is . . . is . . . well, maybe we don't know yet exactly what it is." But in the face of the pain and loss particularly associated with assimilation, to be a radical Jew in the late twentieth century and still today begins with "the need to know the self, the people, the culture," to "figure out how to undo assimilation without being nostalgic or xenophobic," as we, as radical Jews, "tangle with Jewish identity and its relationship to Jewish culture, tradition and politics."[45]

In these essays, then, Kaye/Kantrowitz shares with us the delight and pain involved in her gradual process of "coming out as a Jew" and coming more wholly into her Jewishness. In the fashion of the Talmudic example discussed above, Kaye/Kantrowitz can celebrate a particular aspect of identity even as it is imbricated with other facets of human identity and therefore situated within complex and shifting sets of power dynamics. She writes that she (like how many Jews on the left?) "did not know what it meant to be a Jew, only what it meant to be a *mentsh*. [She] did not know that *mentsh* was a Jewish word in a Jewish language."[46] But having moved "along a mostly unconscious, gradual, zig-zag, and retrospectively inevitable path,"[47] she can now suggest that we must "reach out and in at the same time," in order to live our lives and do our work as radical Jews. Such work requires exploration and experience within "Jewish space," as well as coalition work based on solidarity, rather than guilt.

On the issue of class and Jewish power, Kaye/Kantrowitz correctly points out, "The problem is not relative Jewish success. The problem is a severe class system that distributes success so unequally."[48] The author asks us to confront relative Jewish success as a community in the United States in this historical period. She writes, "Used well, education, choice, even comfort can strengthen people, individually and collectively. . . . The question is what do we do with our education, our choice, privilege, skills, experience, passion for justice: our power." In holding the community responsible for its access and resources, Kaye/Kantrowitz does not mistake this communal situation for an assumption of wealth or access among particular Jews. Too often, work on Jewish communal comparative success eclipses the reality of poor and working-class Jews, of the gendered, transphobic, and heterosexist aspects of Jewish wealth, and of the severe class injustice operative within the Jewish community, which will be addressed in later chapters.[49] As in the anti-universalist tendency of the Talmudic tradition, Kaye/Kantrowitz is able to name communal responsibilities while simultaneously identifying particular intracommunal differentials. I wonder what would happen if, as Kaye/Kantrowitz suggests, we all (poor and privileged Jews) could be "proud of our collective strength, confident that we can use it right." I wonder what would happen if we as a community could make our *collective* strength more accessible for those within and without the Jewish community who need it most?[50] Yes, whether individually we are working class or middle class, or of the top 1 percent, as Jews we will likely be reminded that "someone will always call us pushy," but "Isn't it time to really push?"[51]

Relevant for the serious lack of attention to Jewish matters in contemporary intersectionality studies, Kaye/Kantrowitz also brings the issue of class into a discussion of race, stating that "anti-Semitism—Jew hating—is not taken seriously because it hasn't kept Jews poor,"[52] but she writes unequivocally that "anti-Semitism protects christian wealth."[53] The author clarifies for us that, given the confluence of race and class, "Race relations in the U.S. are usually presented as a Black-white paradigm which disguises both the complexity of color and the brutality of class."[54] Her insights on this point make good use of the Talmudic example of the capacity to work with mutually constitutive categories in a way that clarifies power dynamics rather than masking them. She adds that by framing the Jewish role in this situation in terms of "the Black-Jewish Question" we obscure both Christian hatred and white privilege embodied within the class system. Additionally, we obscure the realities of Black Jews (and other Jews of color), in the same way Spelman points out that Black women are obscured in the formation of Blacks and women. Kaye/Kantrowitz brings many years of antiracism work—since her days as a seventeen-year-old in the civil rights movement to her position as the first executive director of the New York City–based Jews for Racial and Economic Justice—to these essays. She redefines race issues in the United States along a white/colored/Black continuum and discusses how some Jews in this country chose and then learned how to be white, and the cost—the cultural loss—of such a choice.

Intersectionality, Reciprocity, and the Use of Countertexts

Getting inside a differing worldview as experienced by cultures outside the mainstream can help us as scholars and activists to destabilize hegemonic paradigms of the dominant culture. Such cross-cultural study demonstrates the particular nature of dominant constructs that often appear all-encompassing to even critical contemporary theorists and as universal in cultural production. It was not within the purview of Spelman's work to analyze the life and needs of slaves in ancient Greece. However, here I can employ an alternative paradigm to engage in critique of problematic power relations in the dominant mode in the service of justice for those who suffer within the dominant structures. But does this mean that the alternative paradigm is simply more just? Does this mean that although the dominant paradigm is torn asunder and its power dynamics exposed, the alternative mode remains intact? As justice is sought for those in the dominant culture, is not justice also a concern for those whose lives are constructed within subaltern cultures?

The countertext employed in this chapter enables the analysis of the mutual construction of identities necessary in the contemporary period in the West, aiding those such as Spelman (and all of us working with her legacy) in the project we have set up for ourselves. But what a strange countertext I have employed. Few if any contemporary Jewish medical ethicists would be able to use this text at face value given the intensely inegalitarian stance of the reasoning. Thus, the countertext itself is desperately in need of communal reinterpretation and ultimately reconstruction if it is to be helpful for Jews and others today. The project of contemporary Jewish feminist queers is to engage in that reinterpretation so that new insights will be developed.

If the analysis is not self-conscious of the power dynamics in the countertext, the method of countertext itself becomes imperialist. Contemporary movements for social justice often plumb minority cultures for how they help critique the dominant mode, without offering similar critiques of the minority example or working with those seeking justice within the minority groups. The most obvious examples, because of their usurpation in popular US culture, come from native communities. Tidbits of native lifestyles are offered as alternatives and critiques of the individualistic and aggressive mechanisms of the colonizers' liberalism and capitalism. Still, too rarely do those appropriating native imagery, art, or ritual attend to ways in which the materials appropriated have often been the markers of minority/marginalized subjugation within the subaltern community. Scholarship relying on countertexts is seriously lacking if it does not come back to critique the power dynamics within the counterworld, aware of and in the service of the marginalized there.

The complicated and multilayered ranked categories found in the Talmudic texts can help us develop critical insight into the hierarchical categorizations found in hegemonic Western philosophy and keep activist and scholarly revisioning in that sphere more nuanced and liberatory. But the contributions of philosophers such as Spelman, whose work concerns the dominant paradigms, can supply those of us also working to transform power dynamics in the minority Jewish world with critical insight into Jewish texts and paradigms. Spelman's method enables those working with Jewish texts to identify in new ways the absurdity of Talmudic ranked categories. Suddenly one sees that there is an illogic to lists of genders, priestly rankings, birthright, and so on. These lists are sometimes overlapping, and other times mutually exclusive and on the surface do not make sense together. Spelman's insights compel us to look deeper into Jewish traditions and religious texts to understand what the lists are about, how they constitute a complex structural hierarchy, and how we may find newly reconstructed ways to use them. Scholars working within the Jewish framework can see that Spelman's conception of the ways multiple identities are mutually constituted comprises the terrain of hierarchical power within a particular cultural and historical framework. In this case, those seeking justice will better understand this complex Jewish framework and be better able to do the work of *tikkun olam*, social justice, within the Jewish community as well.

In the following chapters, I will extend the more philosophical analysis of this chapter into increasingly applied arenas. Chapter 2 brings this work of intersectionality studies, working in the mode of mutual construction, into an exploration of diaspora theory, important in Jewish contexts and for many communities. We will use the multiply situated life and work of Jewish Afro-Caribbean Jamaica Kincaid to trouble the binaries, the two-tiered presumptions, of both traditional and even some newer diaspora theorizing.

Chapter 2

Jewish Feminists and New Diaspora Theorizing

The Life and Work of Jamaica Kincaid

Introduction

In this chapter, I apply Jewish intersectionality from the more abstract theoretical discussion in chapter 1 to a more focused theory conversation: diaspora theorizing. Jewish feminist contributions to intersectionality studies can take us into important areas of examination for many different communities. If we are to take up the challenges of inequality within the frames of democratic possibility, political thinking needs to employ multilayered intersectionality to parse and reassess the limitations and opportunities of differing experiences of diaspora. A Jewish feminist intersectionality study of the political author Jamaica Kincaid can assist us in working on this project of new diaspora theorizing. Analysis of Kincaid's work requires theorizing the interstices, as well as the gendered nature, of diaspora. This work analyzes Kincaid's contributions to current thinking on the diasporic, specifically by deepening the capacity to appreciate both homes and diasporas, and their varied relationships, without essentializing them.

Given the large numbers of Caribbean immigrants to the United States and England, it is not unusual that Jamaica Kincaid migrated to the United States. It is, however, ironic that Kincaid mostly lived in New England, as her work focuses on diaspora, matters of traditional English colonialism of her Caribbean island home, and the neocolonialism of the United States. As intersectionality analysis will demonstrate, in New England, Kincaid makes a new world without ever really escaping old England or neocolonial forces.[1] While she may have come to New England and remained a resident for any number of reasons, for this Afro-Caribbean Jewish literary figure the fact that she has spent much of her life in New England metaphorically highlights that there is no Archimedean point outside the systems of colonialism and neocolonialism centrally related to diasporic phenomena. Kincaid's multiple diasporas, her literary talent, and her incisive capacity for critique make her and her work an excellent study for an intersectionality project on new diaspora theorizing.[2]

Jewish engagement with the growing interdisciplinary field of diaspora studies is a potentially rich site for nuanced examinations of the politics of peoples' movements in history. I take an intersectional theoretical approach to how we might more fluidly make sense of somewhat balkanized emergent fields (diaspora studies generally, as well as African, Caribbean, and Jewish diaspora studies) in order to place Jewish experiences globally in new ways. The discussion is based on a study of the internationally acclaimed writer Jamaica Kincaid in the context of excavating Jewish feminist political thinking.[3]

Kincaid was raised on the small Caribbean island of Antigua and later moved to the United States. She is also Jewish and active in her Jewish community. There is almost no mention of the basic fact of her Jewishness in the vast literature on Kincaid, nor is there any significant analysis of the meanings of Jewishness in or for her contributions. Placing Kincaid in a Jewish context within intersectionality studies uncovers new meanings in her work which can redirect contemporary Jewish and other diaspora thinking.

Kincaid has come to represent a quintessential Caribbean woman's voice. Her work stands out in any study of Africana, Caribbean, African-American, and African Diaspora literature. Central themes in her work are the devastation of colonialism and imperialism, migration and diaspora, exile and loss, global inequalities, self-exploration, and family relations. Not surprisingly for an intersectionality study, the themes in Kincaid's work are also perennial Jewish themes. Yet we face stumbling blocks in an intersectionality frame when we begin to analyze the import of Kincaid's work to Jewish life and the ways that a Jewish lens deepens the impact of understanding her work in diasporic frames. Analysis of Kincaid's work requires a theorizing the interstices of diasporas as well as the gendered nature of diaspora. While important work is being done in Africana Studies that can bridge significant insights from African, Latin American, and Caribbean diaspora studies for intersectionality analysis, there is little to no coherent articulation of Jewish themes in that field as yet.[4] Similarly, while an intersectional approach to postcolonial studies is crucial to diaspora studies, again Jewish work is not adequately integrated into these overlapping fields.[5] Including new figures and their life experiences into areas where they have previously been absent does more than simply broaden the makeup of existing fields, it transforms them.

From the perspective of intersectionality, what makes this study necessary is also the raced nature of US-based Jewish life and intellectual trends. It is increasingly common to posit Jews in the United States as "postdiasporic." There is much strength in these arguments. However, an unspoken presumption of European heritage reveals the problematically raced frame of much of the discussion. Thus, the current conversation risks irrelevance to, particularly, the millions of African and African-heritage Jews (in the US and globally). For the United States, this is also of particular import for African-heritage Jews from the Caribbean. The proclamation of the "postdiasporic" moment misses opportunities for new Jewish race-critical contributions to diaspora theorizing.[6] A focus on African-heritage Jews in the Americas enables new directions for theorizing intersectional diasporic interstices.

Among contemporary US Jewish thinkers working on matters of diaspora, there is a range of mutually enriching thought. David Biale's work has long challenged dichotomous notions of power and powerlessness, homeland and exile, leaving and returning, continuity and disruption, assimilation and isolation leading to a complex affirmation of Jewish possibilities in diaspora. In an effort to decenter the narrative of Zion, the brothers Daniel and Jonathan Boyarin write to celebrate diasporic living. Multiple trajectories emerge out of this move. One is exemplified in the work of the foremost Jewish feminist intersectionality theorist Melanie Kaye/Kantrowitz, who posits radical diasporism that "embraces diaspora" that is not necessarily exilic in order to "contextualize Jewish experience in a common language" (2007, xi) as part of a social justice project. Another trajectory can be seen in the work of Caryn Aviv and David Shneer, who assess the actual and potential richness of many Jewish diasporic locations, the movement of peoples and the technology to connect them, positing the end of diaspora. Judith Butler's work develops Jewish (and other) diaspora theorizing by noting the relation to non-Jews as inherent in an understanding of Jews. Her work discusses Israel in a political anti-Zionist critique, but not as having valence as a home for some Jews.[7]

Yet, there remains a tendency to revive a static binary of home/exile, as in diaspora theory more broadly, even in negation. In conversation with these pivotal thinkers, in this chapter I thus make three related arguments for current diaspora theorizing in an intersectionality studies framework: (1) there are rich and multilayered opportunities for diverse and thriving cultures in diaspora; (2) given the multiple and contingent moves necessary in imagining radical diasporism, homes/homelands are not necessarily in contradiction with affirming grounded diasporas; and (3) In order to engage in new diasporic theorizing that can both accommodate multiple centers and the vitality of multiply situated communities over time, we must further complicate our models of the diasporic.

This work uses intersectional feminist and critical race Jewish insights in examining the life and thought of Jamaica Kincaid, in order to put forth these three arguments. First, Kincaid offers us portraits of a metropolitan figure, local and global at the same time, each aspect enabling the other in ways new diaspora theorists celebrate. Second, while Kincaid does not return to nor nostalgize any "home," appreciation of her homes and locales of exile is required to understand the power and beauty of her work and vision. Finally, she achieves this apparently contradictory directionality due to the multiplicity of diasporic tropes she uses and creates. Working this multiplicity in an intersectional race critical feminist context assists those of us who seek to continue to re-examine the concept of diaspora for options in postmodern Jewish living.

As the point of this chapter is to complicate the binary of home/diaspora through intersectional feminist analysis of Kincaid's life and work, the following sections layer the exploration of multiple homes and multiple exiles. After briefly introducing Kincaid, I begin looking anew at a source of the framework, the Hebrew Bible. In the section on "Kincaid and Biblical Motifs," I place the ancient Judean exile, source of the trope of the primacy of Zion and much of the binary problem in diaspora theorizing generally, within a more intersectional, multifaceted biblical context and in relation to Kincaid's life and work. Next we explore complications in the theme of home/exile/conquest in the African and (Afro-)Caribbean setting to further interrupt tendencies toward a discourse grounded in binaries commonly found in diaspora thinking that can be more conducive to contemporary intersectionality studies. We then move to an analysis of what meaning we might make from Kincaid's situating herself in New England to note more nuanced complexities and contradictions of exile/home. Finally, I look at Kincaid's navigations in order to use intersectionality to imagine new modes for diaspora theorizing.

Jamaica Kincaid

Jamaica Kincaid was born Elaine Cynthia Potter Richardson in 1949, and raised in St. John's, Antigua. An excellent student who loved literature, she had the ambiguous experience of having the best of an island British colonial education. As a gendered manifestation of her situation as a poor and female colonial subject, she was sent to the US to work as an au pair in 1965—at age sixteen, before earning her high school diploma. She published her first article in 1973. At that time she took the name Jamaica Kincaid, primarily because her family back home disapproved of this writing.

Kincaid developed interesting ties to New England that will become central to this analysis (though she now shares her time between New England and California). Having earned her High School General Equivalency Degree during her time in New York City, she was awarded a full scholarship to the then recently opened and short-lived Franconia College in New Hampshire. She attended school there for about a year in the late 1960s, and never earned a college degree. Since 1985, she lived in Vermont, until recently, and earned honorary degrees from three New England universities (as well as from others).

Kincaid began writing on aspects of gardening in the early 1990s. It is interesting that Kincaid, this nonwhite, non-Christian woman born outside of the United States, later in her life came to "represent" the plant and other life of New England among a small literary set. However, Kincaid made an international name as a young writer for her work on the Caribbean. Since 1977 she has been a finalist for and/or won a stream of prestigious national and international awards for her writings bringing forth Caribbean tableaus and sensibilities.

Given Jamaica Kincaid's "mixed pedigree," an intersectionality focus on her work and life and her theorizing the diasporic will assist in problematizing the presumptions of who Jews are, what they look like, and what their ancestries and backgrounds are. A study of Kincaid is also evocative as she herself is a member of three diasporas (Israel, Africa, Caribbean). Further, while she is known as an Afro-Caribbean, she lived in Vermont longer than any other place.

Kincaid and Biblical Motifs

An intersectional analysis of Kincaid's work helps sharpen a lens on a critical examination of diaspora in a Jewish context, bridging the divide between Jewish, African, and Caribbean diaspora theorizing. The term *diaspora* in its current usage came into being with the Greek translation of the Hebrew Bible. Prior to this biblical translation project, the term *diaspora* in ancient Greek referred to those sent by a conquering empire to live in the acquired lands to govern the new subjects. Introduced in the context of the Israelite's Babylonian exile, the term *diaspora* was used in a new way for the first time in reference to the victims of an imperialist takeover who are then scattered from their homeland. While not all those in diaspora experience themselves in exile, much of diaspora theorizing struggles between binary notions of home/exile, grounded in the Jewish experience of Zion/outside of Israel. However, Jewish exilic thinking does not begin with the Judean exile, and remaining conceptually within this binary does not best describe Jewish life, empirically or normatively. As this chapter seeks (1) to affirm the vitality of diasporic potentiality in a way that (2) does not require negating the importance of homes or a "Zion" to at least some people and Jews in particular, (3) looking at Kincaid's work through an intersectional Jewish feminist lens helps nuance the analysis by challenging a basic binary of home/exile-Zion/diaspora. Thus, this section begins complicating the binary relying on the model of the exile by situating Kincaid in a more disaggregated biblical context.

Kincaid's work is usually discussed in terms of a "prior"-pre-Babylonian-exile. Kincaid was schooled in the British colonial education system.[8] She was taught and often required to memorize long passages (often as punishment) of Milton's *Paradise Lost*.[9] Kincaid's early work (*At the Bottom of the River* and *Annie John*) is often analyzed as recasting a paradise lost, an Edenic rather than Babylonian exile. The relationship of loss and diaspora to power and independence operate on more than one level in both Jewish and Kincaid's literary tropes.

As a small girl, Kincaid was very close with her mother.[10] As she grew to puberty, with the potential for independence and autonomous sexuality, she describes a rejection by the mother.[11] An intersectionality approach helps us to see that this dynamic is a female-gendered parallel, personalized, of a common power dynamic of colonialism. While a colonized population remains perceived as "simple" and easily directed, colonizers can think grandly of themselves as civilizers. When colonized populations begin to clarify a sense of themselves as oppressed, demand redress for grievances, and/or rebel, the dynamics (while certainly always complex) shift. Like the portrayal of Kincaid's mother, the violence of colonialism takes new forms in the face of the potential independence of the colonized population.[12] Similarly, when Kincaid wrote a more directly political tract in her fourth book, *A Small Place*, some commentators felt she lost her "innocence."[13]

The framework often used to analyze Kincaid's early work is an exile from an Edenic original circumstance, the biblical expulsion from the Garden of Eden. This took place "prior" to the dispersion of the Hebrews as a result of Babylonian conquest. However, the story of the expulsion from Eden is told as if humans were given instructions not to eat from "the tree of knowledge of good and evil." As in a colonial or Kincaid's personal story, their doing so challenges the source of the dominant power, god, eliciting an enraged response.

The theme of minority/subject populations' power in a diasporic context is also one in which Exodus is grounded. When a Pharaoh in Egypt arises who "knows not Joseph," he fears the growth and prosperity of this "other" population and forces the Hebrews into slavery. Their growth and self-sufficiency[14] are viewed as threats to the dominant power. Critiques of modern Israel follow similar lines: internationally, some were able to champion Jewish victimhood until Jews built a country (and not some other form of developing a homeland), as a majority population with military power and the bureaucratic infrastructure of a modern sovereign nation state. With this form of independence, Israel must take responsibility for its operations of power in different ways than before statehood, and is constantly called to do so in global contexts.[15] Once successful in terms of creating a state in modern terms, Israel is then understood only as oppressor, as a settler colonialist state. At the same time, Kincaid's work at the nexus of diaspora and postcolonial studies reminds us of the need to be careful of simply associating majority status with power. Kincaid was a member of the majority at home, in Antigua, but was disempowered living as a colonial subject. Diasporic subjects must also wrestle with their nondominant power position but as minority populations. In both cases, as minority and majority, Kincaid's work explores modes of oppression and options for agency for those oppressed in differing contexts helpful to doing intersectionality work.[16]

The exilic theme in Kincaid's work shifts by her third book. In *Lucy*, the young teenage female protagonist is sent off by her parents to the United States to work. Here and in later works, Antigua and the Caribbean, instead of private home and mother, become locations for the metaphor of a paradise lost.[17] Like the biblical Abram and Sarai, Kincaid is sent off to a land she does not know. Kincaid's destination represents a promised land in neocolonial global relations. In this regendered telling, in comparison to the grandiosity of the Abraham and Sarah story, she is a young woman on her own, abandoned by her family in the context of global colonialism. Does she need trust, faith? In what? Hers is a secular telling. She is not guided by a loving god, even perhaps one that humans do not understand. She is sent off alone to a foreign, cold, barren land (in her comparison with the lusciousness of a tropical clime, a theme explored below) in a political context of gendered/raced demands on the impoverished.[18] She is not sent to make a new nation, though we now may celebrate her among the growing ranks of African heritage Jews in the United States. Like Sarah, Kincaid is sent to a new land to make a new life, but for this teenage girl the Promised Land of the United States is also Kincaid's diaspora.[19]

In the biblical telling, the Hebrews have to go—to make a long and arduous journey—to the place that then will be called home. And it is from this place, where Jews were sent to create a new life as an independent nation, that they later become exiled (the origin of the term now used as *diaspora*). However unjust forced exile is, exiles have histories just as much as the creation of homelands. As the modern-day Israel is criticized for being a foreign phenomenon imposed on local inhabitants, those inhabitants scattered or conquered, so too the ancients residing in the land of Canaan. I cannot say whom the Canaanites might have conquered before the biblical telling, but we can presume that there was not simply one cohesively defined people without their own history forged over time through conquest and exchange.

If some contemporary thinkers are compelled to reject diaspora as a Jewish paradigm because they reject the centrality of "Zion," an intersectional feminist analysis demonstrates that such dualistic pairings (of home and away) are unnecessary. Moving beyond an essentialist center-periphery binary frees up diasporic theorizing not only to embrace many possible homes of diaspora but also to choose to stay in relation to communal centers and homes (plural), as well to the degree that such choice expresses one's psychic/political map or that one finds meaning, creativity, and freedom in this multiplicity. In a central contribution to what intersectionality has to offer, Kincaid helps us see that both homes and exiles are not clear-cut phenomena, existing outside of history and politics. For example, Kincaid herself is Afro-Caribbean. Kincaid's notions of home(s)/exile(s) stem from creation of the African diaspora formed through the slave trade, the Caribbean becoming a diaspora. Kincaid then leaves the Caribbean and becomes also part of the Caribbean diaspora. But the Caribs were not the "first" inhabitants of the islands in the region known as home in Kincaid's work. The Carib peoples overtook the Tainos, and—as with the Canaanites—I do not know who the inhabitants before them were. In the creation of the Afro-Caribbean experience, the Caribs are largely genocided. While the near genocide of Carib peoples and cultures is primarily the responsibility of European Christian imperialists, Afro-Caribbean identity still must reckon with its own many instances of genocide, displacement, and the loss of an explicitly Carib people.[20]

For Kincaid, as in Genesis, there are numerous expulsions, devastations of home place, and setting up new homes. For example, the biblical story does not dwell on Noah's experience of the loss of the world as he knows it—but we do know that he turns to drink and that sexual improprieties follow surviving his voyage to a new home. What do the wives of Noah's sons, wrapped up in the story via marriage, experience? Those who moved into a plain in the land of Shinar have their city destroyed (again by God, the supreme ruling force in this ontological frame) and become among those scattered across the face of the earth speaking different languages (the story of the Tower of Babel).[21] Lot does not easily leave Sodom and Gomorra when the most powerful ruling authority he recognizes wipes out these home cities—but he does not technically look back. Alternatively, Kincaid portrays Lot's wife, the woman who will look back.[22] Among many migrations and large-scale loss, the biblical text recounts who is whom and related to whom, reminding us of relationship and community across time and physical wandering. People must bury their dead among strangers (such as Abraham's purchase of the Cave of Machpelah for Sarah) and reconnect to kin across long distances (the search for wives for Isaac and Jacob).[23] These narratives resonate strongly with the phenomena of contemporary diasporic conditions, which I situate here within intersectionality studies. By the exile into Babylon, the story is of a people with much experience of expulsion, chosen and forced wanderings, creation of new homes understood as temporary or hoped to be permanent. Further, during the period of ancient Jewish sovereignty, a majority of Jews voluntarily lived abroad/ in diaspora, as today large numbers of Israeli Jews live outside of Israel. Despite the dualistic trope of home/away found in contemporary diaspora thinking, biblical modes and current realities are far more complex. In an intersectionality context, these stories also seem more fitting to Kincaid's contemporary life and work as well in relating to multiple homes (African, Caribbean, Vermont), multiple conquests (Taino, Carib, European, US), multiple dislocations (out of Israel to other parts of Africa,[24] to the Caribbean, to the US), and multiple efforts to be at home in the world as a diasporic subject. And they are all mutually constitutive of both Kincaid's, and the historic generalized, disaporic experience.

Another instantiation of diaspora brought into relief by an intersectional Jewish feminist examination of Kincaid's work in the biblical context is the way barrenness is linked to diaspora. A common association of diaspora is alienation from a fount of fertile collective culture. Kincaid portrays the evils of colonialism in the barren winter of northern climes.[25] In addition, lamentations are common in diasporic tragedic trajectories, grieving loss. In contemporary diaspora studies, there is also a focus on transforming loss as the central paradigm of diaspora. Many seek to understand the potential gifts of diasporic circumstances, or at least possibilities for the development of new identities and formations of peoplehood.[26] Klagsbrun (1997)[27] reminds us that the first usages for the Hebrew word *akara*—(as opposed to the Greek work *diaspora*)—referring to the "desolate, uprooted nation" (91) of Israel after the exile to Babylon, are in the story of Sarah's barrenness (followed by other stories of barren women). Of exile, Kincaid refers to the "hollow space inside" (*Annie John*, 144). Klagsbrun's reading of the texts makes room for the complex, flawed, strong, conflicted, and beautiful women of Kincaid's life and work as a way to grapple with the concreteness of the dialectic of alienation and renewal in exile.[28] For example, Kincaid presents her love for her mother as intense, and also presents her mother as bitingly imperfect.[29] As Klagsbrun shows that the yearning of the biblical barren women is for sons, Kincaid's expulsion from the paradise of her mother's adoration comes in her lived life with the birth of her younger brothers. This beloved is the same mother who cannot support her daughter emotionally as an emergent independent adult in any way the daughter can appreciate at the time. Still, Kincaid has written that she views her mother as strong, that she writes in her mother's voice.[30]

Africa and the (Afro-)Caribbean

Seeing more complex biblical motifs of home and exile through an intersectional lens is important to understanding Kincaid and new possibilities of diaspora theorizing. There are also more spaces of "home" within which we must situate this intersectional analysis for Kincaid as we work to interrupt the tendency toward binary discursive frames. Kincaid is also of the African diaspora, and Africa plays an important role in Kincaid's works. Yet the actual place of home in Kincaid's writing is not Zion or Africa, but the Caribbean. In this section, I examine aspects of Antigua, the particular location of Kincaid's diasporic political excavations, as we continue to complicate notions of the binary of home/diaspora in Kincaid's work and lived history, forcing us to reconcile multiple homes and many violent ruptures. Thus, this section will briefly address the Caribbean island of Antigua's location in colonial history and the intersectional, inherently related creation of exilic and diasporic historical movements.[31]

While there were earlier European visitors to what became the Americas, 1492 is the oft-mentioned date of European contact and colonialism of the Caribbean, as Kincaid notes: "the vast world that began in 1492" (*See Now Then*, 145).[32] Of the approximately eleven million Africans trafficked during the slave trade, roughly half were traded by the British.[33] According to estimates, four million of these people were brought to the Caribbean.[34] Records indicate that between 1671 and 1763, the British brought 60,820 slaves to Antigua.[35] The British slave trade in the Caribbean ends formally in the early 1800s.[36] Slavery is always hovering in Kincaid's work.[37]

As Kincaid wants us to know, she reminds us in *A Small Place*, for example, the island of Antigua is "a small place . . . a very small place" (56), approximately fourteen miles long by eleven miles wide, with a population just under 70,000.[38] Kincaid often describes the regularity in the environment: the sun rising at 6 a.m. and setting at 6 p.m. In between, the sun is always there and directly overhead.[39] In her writing, this fact takes on meaning for the rhythm and life of the island and its inhabitants in a politically contested context. One aspect of note here is the constancy that location creates culturally. Kincaid notes that Antiguans do not think about the sun always being overhead because it always is. Interestingly for the above discussion of barrenness, while the Caribbean is often portrayed in the global north as wet and lush, geographically this is due to the island's proximity to the equator, its relatively minor fluctuation in temperature year round, and its having one of the lowest rainfall rates in the region. Tourist websites for Antigua tout the fact of the weather's evenness and perpetual sunshine to draw global northerners in ways that resonate perfectly with Kincaid's critique of tourists, the forms of neo-imperialism that draw wealthy others to lay claim to the space, as well as tourists' privileged indifference to the locals' conditions of drought.[40]

By 1684, the British had transformed Antiguan life into one of large-scale sugar production. The transition of majority populations and cultures in the area—earlier tribes to Taino, to Carib, and then to Afro-Caribbean—is bound up with the history of diasporic movement, slavery, and European colonialism.[41] In 1834, Britain formally abolished slavery, putting the new law into use in Antigua. (Other places in the empire took advantage of a possible four-year transition period.) Kincaid's work is situated in the second half of the twentieth century—after slavery has legally been abolished, when the British are the colonial power living off the bloody legacy of slavery and conquest to keep their power over the local population, which was forged through this history.[42] British colonial rule technically ends just when Kincaid herself is exiled to the United States. Her work thus moves between her experience and analysis of being a gendered formal colonial subject and a subject of neocolonialism in the ways it operates in both the Caribbean and her adopted home in the United States.

Jews, Race, and New England

For an intersectional analysis, we cannot neatly separate home and diaspora in Kincaid's thinking or life. At this point then, we move from a focus on home*s* to the diasporic. Kincaid did not immigrate to England, a path that many from the British-controlled Caribbean have taken. Formal British colonial rule has ended, but life in Antigua is controlled in neocolonial global systems in which the United States is a leading power. For many, emigration to the United States represents the possibility of a "better" life. This possibility is due in large part to the advances within the United States, which are enabled by the history of slavery and exploitation of those outside of the country, such as those in the Caribbean.[43] Still, life for many Caribbean immigrants to the United States continues to be extremely difficult, marked by poverty, racism, patriarchy, homophobia, transphobia, and various forms of violence.

Kincaid comes to live in New England, perhaps by the unexpected routes most of our lives take. Her life in New England is not, however, characteristic of Caribbean immigrants to the United States or to New England (one of economic poverty, social stigma, violence, and/or the constancy of the risk of violence). Still, that Kincaid lived most of her life in New England poignantly suggests—both metaphorically and in her own discussions of her life—that even she, who has in many ways freed herself, cannot get outside the reaches of the twin forces of colonialism and neocolonialism.[44]

Neocolonialism and its role in the creation and perpetuation of the injustices of diasporic conditions can be said to be different in kind and degree than colonialism. But neocolonialism is a violent imperial form of relation, nevertheless.[45] Kincaid might not live in England, but she does live in the neocolonial capital of the world. In doing so, Kincaid complicates the notion of New England as a place of white European settlers.[46] She further complicates New England's history as home to freed and nonfreed African-heritage slaves, and of more recent nonwhite immigrants. Kincaid comes to the United States like the many millions of impoverished legal and illegal migrants from the Caribbean, but does not end up in New England as a farmworker, factory employee, or domestic. Gender, heterosexuality, culture, and cultural capital are all factors. She comes to New England because her then husband, from a well-placed New York Jewish intellectual family, got a faculty position at Bennington College. She is among a tiny minority of Black, let alone Afro-Caribbean, immigrants to Vermont and New England. While she writes relentlessly about poverty, migration, and colonialism, she herself arrives in Vermont within the context of significant relative privilege.

Of primary import in this intersectional conversation is that Jamaica Kincaid is also Jewish, served as president of her synagogue, has been active in Jewish affairs, and more recently has been featured a number of times in the English-language Israeli press. The fact that the internationally known diasporic writer and Afro-Caribbean Kincaid is also Jewish deepens our opportunities for complicating the concept of Jews, race, and New England, because of the gaps that Jewish intersectionality studies can assist us in noting for imaging Black New England, Jewish New England, and Black Jewish New England.[47]

Interesting also is the way that New England is often portrayed in US culture as a "quality-of-life" region. Kincaid has an uncanny capacity to do a direct accounting of the contradictions and realities of melancholy, displacement, and sorrow that simultaneously comprise a rich life well lived. Is there a connection between the life afforded Kincaid in a rural New England town and her ability to take on such difficult subjects with such beauty? Within this we see her attention to living life as part of her own challenge to the deadening of exile and both classic and neocolonialism as a Jewish Afro-Caribbean woman.

In her fiction work about her biological father (*Mr. Potter*), Kincaid repeatedly notes that he could not read, thus could not live an examined life, speak for himself, or leave a legacy.[48] This notion is raised similarly in her work about her brother (*My Brother*, 11). She writes that because she learned to read, she can do these things for "others."[49] Further, it is her perch in New England that allows her the capacity to examine these lives she considers unexamined. Meaning, her living in New England enables her to engage in what she associates as an imperial activity: living an examined life. Though she does not eschew this capacity or activity, it is clearly not one possible in her assessment for islanders (given her diasporic location, a category of persons to which she mostly no longer belongs).

New England plays an important role in the images and meaning in Kincaid's work in the context of a diaspora theorizing. Kincaid repeatedly inverts the colonizers' judgments about rich civilizations, cleanliness, and beauty. In her childhood training, in the eyes of her mother in *Annie John*, England and the English are ugly, dirty, and uncouth.[50] Colonialism and the north are often represented in her work by the gray, cold, and alienating climate, and in describing her entry to the northeastern United States in her novel *Lucy*.[51] Yet Kincaid writes some of these works from rural New England, another cold and gray climate that she comes over time to find beautiful.[52] She is privileged to have a garden and "to garden," a possession and an activity that she associates with imperialism. In addition, her garden is one of her answers to alienation; it is bounty countering barrenness (*Among Flowers: A Walk in the Himalayas* and *See Now Then*). We have in the life and work of Jamaica Kincaid New England's cold winter as representative of the ugliness, violence, and loss of dignity that occurs for colonizers. At the same time, New England's iconic winters also serve as a trope for her to consolidate her personal core in the face of uprootedness and the loss inherent in her diasporic existence.

We must also address what it means that Kincaid is mainly an internationally acclaimed writer for her work on Antigua, but has written almost all of her work during the period of her life in Vermont. Questions about privilege, access, and colonialism are key here, with New England holding an interesting place in these questions. For example: in her writing both on Antigua and gardening,[53] Kincaid is clear that Europe and now the United States are dominant and therefore damaged places in the history of (neo) colonialism. She is certain that she could never have become a writer if she had not been trained in the British colonial school system with access to English literature. She is also sure that had she not moved to the United States, she would have never have actually become a writer. That she is able to write, and gain international fame, is inherently related to the access that living inside the foremost neocolonial power is able to afford (not that it affords this to most). She is living in the belly of the violent neocolonial beast. While I assume she faces many challenges, instead of presenting her life in Vermont as a target of common US racial, gendered, and anti-Semitic hatred, Kincaid situates herself in New England, which is how she gains the privilege to survive, by which she means write, and thus thrive.[54] It is interesting then to note that she lives in rural Vermont, not in New York City or in Boston (urban and literary centers and home to more Jews, African, and Caribbean immigrant minorities). The pastoral frame of her lived life, and the presumptions of privilege within a neocolonialist globalizing regime, appear in stark contrast to the content of her writing, her political thinking, and her anticolonial politics.

Living in rural Vermont for a large portion of her life, and attaining and maintaining the status of an internationally acclaimed writer, require attention to power matters on the part of Kincaid. This juxtaposition, rural life and international artist, is made possible through technology in travel, communications, the flow of currencies, and other developments of capitalism that constitute the contemporary context of diasporic living. We see in this facet of Kincaid, representative of New England, made possible through extra-geographical and imperial processes. She has to know people in cities, get to them frequently enough to maintain personal ties, have electronic and other modes of connective communications, and so on to make her rural Vermont town less isolated than a pastoral rendering might suggest. Exemplifying new diaspora thinking—where in the contemporary period technology and travel are said to make the alienation and isolation of the diasporic a phenomenon of the past—the "plugged in" Vermonter can be so because of the ravages of the capitalism Kincaid criticizes, ravages that require the movements of peoples and flux of the contemporary diasporic.[55]

Navigating Complex Tropes: Toward New Diaspora Theorizing

Diaspora has many meanings today. Since the ancient Babylonian conquest of the Jews, the Greek term has come to mean that a more dominant power has caused your people to leave your home and homeland to live in exile. While individuals and groups make new lives in many forms, historically, the experience of exile has been understood as one of alienation, a perpetual death for both the individuals and the people/community—what Kincaid refers to as a breaking of "unbreakable bonds" (*Lucy*, 71). While Biale argues that even in Judaic studies, "the categories of Israel and Diaspora no longer occupy the central place in scholarly agendas they once held" (2003, xxix), these very categories remain central to the organized Jewish community in many ways and continue to drive new diaspora theorizing even in their negation. The Boyarins' 2002 argument repudiates a positive role of Zion and political sovereignty in their affirmation of the diasporic. Thinkers such as Aviv and Shneer (2005) presume that to create vibrant cultural forms, alienation and melancholy become a thing of the past. While this may certainly be possible, it is my argument that in the Jewish context, connection to home—even Zion—and the exilic can function along with the forces opting for new (relatively, as nothing is ever really new), settled life in multiple locales of the diasporic. Butler's 2012 work in diaspora theorizing reclaims non-Zionist thinking in Jewish thought arguing for a binational state in Israel/Palestine. In line with Kaye/Kantrowitz's 2007 more intersectional understanding, in the life and work of Kincaid homes and movement, loss and vitality are not inherently in opposition, but can serve as among many sources out of which the very richness that a radical hereness of new diasporism functions.

Kincaid's work moves within the constant interaction of seeking life and beauty in multiple locations, homes and homelands, exiles, oppressive powers, resistive gestures. Kincaid critiques the dominant powers impacting her and portrays the life of those forced to live among the dominant powers in part through descriptions of climate and flora. Kincaid depicts both the climates of England and the northeastern United States as cold, ugly, and uninviting—contrasted with the ever-bursting warm, wet, and fertile (yet simultaneously drought-ridden) Antigua.[56] This tone and content is developed as a way to also depict the colonial and neocolonial cultures and political implications of life in the different places in the context of power relationships.

Important for this intersectional study of diaspora thinking are the complexities of estrangement and fulfillment, between existential conditions created through power and lived lives constituted in resistance. Interestingly, thus, compared to her writings, when Kincaid herself is in the picture in her lived life, something happens to the lifeless, barrenness of these gray winter neocolonial climes. In her actual life, while living in New England, Kincaid becomes a gardener and is surrounded by beauty and bounty in nature.[57] Concomitantly, while the place of her most recent exile, Antigua, is the primary landscape of her fiction, the Caribbean does not serve as a simplistic primal positively valenced home.[58] Kincaid is able to write in her exile, and so she is able to survive a life of deadness that she understands would have been fated for her had she remained in Antigua. The isolation of the alienation of diaspora is turned on its head in the context of Kincaid's lived life in exile. Here she connects to her people in the Caribbean through the work and product of writing in ways that she says she could never have if she continued to live among those with whom she is so primarily connected. By writing she is able to live, to thrive even though she might not say it that way, and this is only possible for her in exile.

Do we take her to be a traitor to her people for this? Can she be criticized for taking an individualized path to survival while those of her people not forced into exile remain in the cycles of deadening neocolonialism in the Caribbean? It is a complicated question. How might we approach this from an intersectional view? Jewish thinking is steeped in notions of peoplehood. Diaspora presumes a collectivity, and Kincaid seems to distance herself from membership in abstract groups.[59] Kincaid draws the reader into a love of her Caribbean home, both through the beauty of her description and her incisive critique of the forces that have ruined its paradisiacal status.

She also spares Antigua no less than she does England or the United States in her scathing critique.[60] And in this more poked, prodded, and pocked investment in line with more contemporary intersectional feminist theory, Kincaid simultaneously speaks for her peoples, enables connections that sustain communities in exile, and does herself connect in many ways that help her survive her diasporas and exiles.[61]

On the matter of membership in a collective, individualist US ideology says, "Save yourself." The appeal of the US formulation resides within a mythology of freedom understood as "getting away" to create oneself anew. Resonant in postdiaspora thinking, this is a negative form of freedom in the tradition of T. H. Greene and Isaiah Berlin. This reckoning of/with freedom works in the US immigrant context through the presupposition that it is not merely best for you, but actually possible at all, to leave all the heavy "baggage" of home and refashion a lighter, neotech backpack.[62]

The picture for Kincaid, as in an intersectional perspective, however, is never straightforward. She was sent by her parents away from "home," Antigua, without choice. But she stays by "choice" (if rendered as a problematic) in the United States. Does she earn whatever degrees of freedom she has off the backs of those left behind in her Caribbean home?[63] Kincaid understands herself as part of a global capitalist system where the well off and safe are so because of the direct exploitation of others.[64] She has earned her freedom through her writing. In particular, she earned her freedom and fame from writing as a woman on the combination of colonialism/neocolonialism and the diasporic via the Caribbean. Her fame comes through writing difficult though beautiful works about the multilayered realities and the ugliness of exploitation of her peoples, mainly in this context African heritage and Carib. Kincaid cannot be simplistically charged with exploitation because her work and path themselves are replete with an inherent dialectic of accountability regarding those at home and those "away."

Usually the (US) American mythic notion of being able to create oneself anew, to cast off the chains of connection central to the diaspora, comes in a masculine package. George W. Bush succeeded in putting a female gloss on that package, a superficial feminist message, beginning particularly with his media spin on the first invasion of Afghanistan he orchestrated. In this new sense, the United States represents "freedom" for women from the patriarchal backwardness of third world "home" cultures. Kincaid's escape from Antigua and the life she begins in the center of a neocolonial diaspora is one cast in a distinctly female mold. She presents her Caribbean girlhood of *At the Bottom of the River* and *Annie John*, the projected trajectory of her future in the *Autobiography of My Mother*, even the portrayal of the women who love her biological father in *Mr. Potter* and her brother in *My Brother*, as all operating in significantly gender-limited terms. The strength and ingenuity of her female characters located in Antigua are marked, though they are reflective of and simultaneously assisting the development, the co-construction, of this woman outside of Antigua's constraints.[65]

Kincaid's emigration is also a distinctly female emigration. Many parents in third world countries decide that their children cannot finish school due to the pressures of poverty, even when they have excelled as students. Like many, Kincaid is sent to a first world country to relieve the economic burden on the family. While both third world men and women often undertake domestically related labor once in the first world, the path of domestic worker tends to be predominantly gendered female. Kincaid comes to the United States as an au pair, child care being an almost exclusively female immigrant path. But then she gets out of the domestic-worker cycle and not only writes but becomes recognized for her writing. Useful for an intersectional analysis, her story, like that of all women's, does not have a single narrative line: victim/postfeminist. The characters in her work and her own life embody and enable the very idea of the simultaneous realities of patriarchal violence and agency in a world constituted through numerous intersecting and co-constructed modalities of power.

The history of female immigrant domestic labor, of course, crosses many diaspora communities. For the current political movement of Jewish interest, one can look to organizations such as Jews for Racial and Economic Justice in New York City, which have long partnered with groups such as Domestic Workers United, mobilizing reference to a European Jewish immigrant past of a mass of Jewish service workers to bring in the many Jews of New York who may now hire—and often do not know the full rights of—domestic staff. The groups work hard together passing legislation, building coalitions, and hopefully changing some people's lives.[66]

While it may be common today—given the gaps in intersectionality studies of not including Jewish experience—to imagine a middle-class, white US Jewish community, this is a skewed conceptualization that disenables US Jews and all of us to engage in social justice work in a robust fashion. It is significant how segments of the US Jewish community have moved out of their immigrant roots, and/or out of severe economic deprivation.[67] At the same time, there are many portions of the US Jewish community still struggling with their immigrant paths, whose economic positions are precarious and life circumstances compromised.[68] And certainly, there are many Jewish domestic workers in and outside of the United States today. Despite having served as a domestic as a teen, Kincaid might be likely to hire domestics as an adult with the wealth that her work, fame, and intellectually elite heterosexual marriage have afforded her. There remains, however, a fundamental gap between understanding and mobilizing US Jews on such feminist issues as the abuse and rights of domestic workers and connecting to the many people of color and poor people who serve as domestics in our time who are and are not also Jewish. The "Jamaica Kincaids" of the twenty-first century play a key role in imagining a renewed Jewish feminist social justice movement and new paths for antiracist Jewish feminism. Kincaid's experience and writing on the worldviews of immigrant domestic workers is one of many aspects of how Kincaid is an essential figure to study as we reimagine who Jewish feminists are and might be, what a multiracial Jewish feminism is and can be, and what vistas might be open for our lives and futures as Jewish feminists in new and changing diasporic conditions.

Conclusion

Kincaid's work and her life in Vermont—as a relatively cold rural place with very small populations of Jews, African-heritage people as well as Afro-Caribbeans—help us push questions of import for Jews and diaspora significant for intersectionality studies. Regarding community, inherent in the concept of exile is the struggle with alienation, related to separation, isolation from one's people. An aspect of the violence of slavery is the very creation of the African diaspora. Yet we also study how communities re-form in the diaspora.

Kincaid is among those in the Jewish, African, and Caribbean diasporas. An insightful critic of race relations, Kincaid writes as a Jewish brown-skinned woman in a world dominated by those with lighter skin, who are often Christian. The African and Caribbean heritages of the Afro-Caribbean culture about which she writes is explicit in each of her works. In her more recent novel *See Now Then*, she integrates aspects of her Jewish life to the already complex, mutually constitutive portraits she has long painted in her writing. In New England, Kincaid calls into being relationships with others through her writing on the Afro-Caribbean, while doing so from a daily life lived far from her various peoples, broadly defined. Yet she knows that she could not have become a writer, and survived, had she stayed in Antigua. Her separation makes possible her re-creation of relationships connected to Africa, Antigua, the Caribbean, and Israel.

What can we learn from the specificity of Kincaid's circumstances and much of what might seem to be Kincaid's personalized solution? Most people do not become internationally acclaimed writers with the access and privilege this affords Kincaid to create her connections, to cope with her alienation. First, still, we can learn that there are many paths to coping with estrangement created in diaspora experience. Kincaid offers a particular way to do so, lessons from which just might prove more far-reaching than the peculiarities of her personal New England story might at first suggest. Second, at the same time, while Kincaid offers us a vision of a complex affirmation of the potentiality of life and community in diaspora, one cannot understand Kincaid's life or work without Antigua, the import of home, the violence of exile, the devastation of alienation. The co-constructed aspect of these multiple forms are central to intersectionality work. Third, in this, it makes much sense to place Kincaid firmly in a newly configured, intersectional, and more nuanced Jewish feminist and critical race context. The life and work of Kincaid is more resonant with the biblical multilayered legacies of dispersions, re-formations, wanderings, and settlings than contemporary academic bifurcations of Zion and diaspora. With Kincaid in a context of Jewish diaspora theorizing, we can see that outside of a binary model, our lives and histories can and do accommodate many homes and exiles, confront many devastations of places and cultures forced to re-form in new ways in new locales. Without being nostalgic, Kincaid conjures, recalls, and re-creates her home communities in a global context. Clearly a member of oppressed classes also with certain privileges acquired as an adult, she employs tropes of loss, longing, and melancholy to support agency, to survive and to thrive through the creation of beautiful works of art, scathing political analysis, and a life well lived in a nexus of individual and communal relationships.

Chapter 3

Race, Gender, Class, Sexuality, and the Jewish *Goldbergs* in the Suburbs

Introduction

The Jewish television sitcom character Molly Goldberg and her family moved from the Bronx to the suburbs in the 1954–1955 season of the show *The Goldbergs*, its sixth year in syndication.[1] The season starts off hopeful and full of excitement. The first episode for the season has Molly in the Bronx apartment in her infamous pose out the window talking to a neighbor. Well, she's not so much talking as gloating. She is showing off a drawing of her house-to-be in the suburbs, her "saltbox" as she calls it, delighted that there are sixteen on the block, "all the same." "Gracious living." Only once she gets out there, Molly is confronted by an alien world. Or, rather, a world in which hers is suddenly not just one among many nasal Euro-heritage New York Jewish accents, but one in which she is alien, othered, her dignity and morality questionable.

Prior to its television debut, *The Goldbergs* had run successfully as a radio program for two decades. After this long career, one year in the suburbs did the television show in; it was taken off the air. The move from radio, to an urban-site television program, to suburban bliss mirrors the history of technology, ideology, and the changing (US) American imaginary of the period. Much has been written about Gertrude Berg[2] and on the Jewish experience in the development of the US suburbs.[3] With the benefit of previous work, in this chapter I use a co-constructionist intersectional approach and take special note of the phenomenon that the (US) American myth is a story of success, and yet the suburbs killed Molly Goldberg. My central question is: Why? Why was Molly Goldberg not able to survive this latest migration? Looking at multiple vectors of identity and the ways they cocreate each other, what does that say about how Jews and the nation navigated their way through this period?

This study of Berg's *The Goldbergs* is particularly interesting now. In 2010 a cable network called Jewish Life Television (JLTV) began airing reruns of *The Goldbergs* in a segment with other Jewishly related nostalgic pieces from the time, such as the *Jack Benny Show* and the *Soupy Sales Show*. Notably, for this intersectionality analysis, *Amos 'n' Andy*—an ethnic minority show also grown out of radio and both controversial and widely popular among Blacks, Jews, and other Americans, as the first Black television serial, is not included in the JLTV lineup. As discussed below, that is likely a good thing.

Then in the fall of 2013, ABC began airing a new television sitcom that was also called *The Goldbergs*. The family portrayed in this show is white-coded, assumed to be Jewish with only light and occasional Jewishly related references. The show is situated in the 1980s; the characters are loud and often act in comically unbecoming ways. Its location in a suburb of Philadelphia is unproblematized. As opposed to Berg's unsuccessful 1950s attempt to move her television Jewish family to the suburbs of New York, the 2013 show presumes suburban placement as obvious for their television Jewish family. Berg's form of assimilation portrayed in the early *Goldbergs* might have often been presented as comic, but they were always upstanding people and neighbors,[4] with Berg attempting to run the series as socially acceptable, if even Jewish. Popular culture has changed a great deal in these sixty years. In this chapter we will use an intersectional approach to examine this phenomenon and why Berg's attempt ultimately failed at that historical moment.

Setting the Stage

In order to undertake a Jewish feminist intersectionality analysis of popular culture, we must begin with a reminder that at midcentury, the United States was in the midst of an intense ideological struggle. In this postwar moment, news of racial and cultural genocide in Europe was shocking the nation. The United States then entered into a new kind of war with a new enemy. We began a cold war with emergent communist countries just as we finished a hot war with fascist ones. Yet many US methods replicated those of the ideological regimes we demonized, including cracking down on those potentially dissident at home. As we developed a portrait of the spacious new suburban vista, the lives of many real people were being constrained. Thousands lost their livelihoods during the Red Scare. As a "kinder and gentler" form of anti-Jewish genocide than Nazism, additional attempts to eradicate Jewish difference were conducted through the Red Scare. Jews were disproportionately targeted, as were African Americans, Puerto Ricans, native Hawaiians, and "homosexuals." The history of *The Goldbergs* stands firmly within this national history. Nowhere was US society immune from the very real ideological tug of war, least of which the entertainment industry. Philip Loeb, the first character to play the family father, Jake Goldberg, was blacklisted during the Red Scare. Berg and company fought the blacklisting of Loeb. It is a fraught story, though ultimately under McCarthy era pressure Loeb was replaced. The character Molly's "expansive" move to the suburbs was enabled in part by caving to the crackdown, by sacrificing the dissident Jake (Loeb).

At this historical moment, US women were being asked again to redefine their identities. Male soldiers were returning home from overseas and needed the jobs these women had recently been asked to perform during World War II. Economic opportunity became available to some in a partial financial boom. In the mid-1950s, news of Christine Jorgensen's "sex reassignment surgery" was splattered across the popular US press as well as the medical literature. This was a historical moment when aspects of one's identity presumed to be as immutable as one's "sex" were suddenly open to change, shifts, switches.[5] Across lines of race-class-"sex"-gender roles and sexuality, religion, ethnicity, cultural identities long held to be "facts" were morphing, and the facticity of such facts were called into question. As part of the managing of such changes, there was a move to shore up such identities, to fix them in more permanent ways. Many of the new versions of identity crossing in this era were fueled only through complex processes of reessentializing identity categories and the communities themselves created in and moving across lines previously held to be impermeable.[6] How do the Goldbergs and their attempt at life in the suburbs factor into these dynamics? An intersectional analysis of the exploration of the move from the minority, ethnically infused Bronx *Goldbergs* to the relatively sanitized suburban Haverville (a ville/town for the "haves") can help us figure this out.

As both a radio production and in the Bronx segment of the television show, the title proclaimed: *The Goldbergs*. Under this explicit minority ethnic marker,[7] attention is drawn to the family's Jewishness. Weber recognizes that the primary theme of the earlier radio show was about the acculturation of immigrants in the United States.[8] However, as the show moved to television, and the set of the television show moved from the Bronx to the suburbs, aspects of this acculturation process shift. Particularly for the purposes of this intersectional investigation, the Jewish specificity of the show's content becomes confusedly masked in the suburban phase.

World War II was over. As opposed to earlier developments of working-class suburbs to house relocated workers near new industrial zones, middle-class suburbs were new on the US landscape.[9] *The Goldbergs'* relocation is a step *up* the class ladder. With the assistance of government loans and mortgage programs, many European-heritage Jews like the fictional Molly flocked to these new areas, architectural embodiments of a postwar nationalist ethos of what it meant to be "American."[10] Berg herself remained an urban dweller. However, as in Berg's show, in real life many who survived the Red Scare then thrived through governmental largesse by taking flight from the nation's cities to its new suburbs.

Amos 'n' Andy, Berg and Hansberry: Clarifying the Costs of "Success"

Some might argue that the US Jewish large East Coast migration from the cities to the suburbs was successful, for this is when new pockets of Jews moved into the middle class and increasingly became accepted as naturalized "Americans." Within this frame, the failure of Molly Goldberg to adapt to her new environs appears inexplicable. Yet, the achievement story leaves out the range of losses incurred in this grand historical moment for the nation at large, and for the Jewish community in particular.

Around the time when *The Goldbergs* went off the air, *Amos 'n' Andy* also stopped airing. *Amos 'n' Andy* is also made possible in the historical context of minority migration to urban areas, in this case of many southern blacks to northern US cities.[11] Many African Americans protested the "low class" and crude dialogue in the show. Berg was at least Jewish herself, though she spoke with no immigrant accent and had gained quite an elite class position. The framers of *Amos 'n' Andy* were white men. It is true that Black characters played most of the parts by the time of the television show. However, like many more acculturated Jews who did not appreciate the low-class, immigrant portrayal of the Goldberg family, many African Americans wanted a more "uplifting" public image of African Americans portrayed if they were going to be seen outside the African-American community (meaning open access via US television). Like Berg's work, *Amos 'n' Andy* could not weather the changes of this historical moment in the United States, despite the show's long record of success. Let us look at a different medium to trace distinct Black and Jewish urban-suburban transitions (which we will also need to challenge as only separate phenomena).

A few years after the demise of *The Goldbergs* and *Amos 'n' Andy*, Lorraine Hansberry created her first play, *A Raisin in the Sun,* for which she won national acclaim.[12] Much of the publicity, however, touted the play as a masterful depiction of the (US) American dream. After all, the family history is one that emerged from slavery, migration north, urban poverty, finally to the promise—as with *The Goldbergs*—of "success": a house in the suburbs. And yet, *A Raisin in the Sun* is really more about the cracks in the so-called American dream. It exposes the ways in which the dream, hinging on that move from poverty to the middle class, from urban apartment dwelling to a house in the suburbs, is raced, classed, gendered, and sexed. The family's new white neighbors proclaim the right to live freely among people like themselves (other whites). The struggles, contradictions, and xenophobia made explicit by Hansberry were lost on much of the viewing public wanting to see yet another affirmation of the "other" turned acceptable.

While chronologically earlier, politically *The Goldbergs*' last season takes off where *Raisin* ends. *Amos 'n' Andy* producers did not attempt this suburban transition before it went off the air. However, by 2014, ABC began a new television sitcom, Black-*ish*. Here the heterosexually headed Black family does live in the suburbs where they are basically accepted. The struggle concept for the show is whether this means that the family has lost its credentials as Black. For her time, Hansberry more explicitly showed us the cost of getting the suburban house and gives us a hint of the costs to be incurred by showing us the white racist majority in the new "golden berg" (golden town) neighborhood. In comparison, if somewhat less self-consciously, in the final season of *The Goldbergs*, we get to watch episode by episode what happens when "others" attempt to join the flock to the new white middle-class suburbs. Attempting to appeal to a television audience, however, Berg did not politicize the similar issues and xenophobia her characters confronted in their new neighborhood. She attempted to approach them with humor, sentimentality, and goodwill. Yet even Gertrude Berg could not avoid the struggles and contradictions, any more than she could successfully navigate them.

Contradictions: Upbeat Episodes, Real Issues, and a Crashing Show

When the television show changed its locale, it also changed its focus and target audience. We must then ask: when Molly gave up the famous Bronx (read: Jewish) trademark, what else did she lose? In the larger house, the characters loose some sense of intimacy. Certainly, the separated houses of the suburbs affect a kind of isolation. Despite many shows involving neighbors, Molly certainly loses the intimacy of her tenement window community.

But more, the downward spiral of the actual show over the course of the season contradicts the flow of the individual episodes. Generally, in the Bronx segment, episode narratives focused inward to the Goldberg's largely Jewish world. Some portray family dramas, as when their uncle's son might not make it to synagogue with him for Yom Kippur services, or when son Sammy begins to date neighbor Dora and the family is concerned that he remain in school before getting married. Other episodes are meant mainly as silly escapades, such as when Molly takes over the kitchen at their summer vacation resort. In contrast, in the suburban season, each week the show's story line generally began with the framing of an "issue." In particular, the issues arose from a focus outward. The topics usually exposed aspects of the challenges of assimilation demanded of the Goldbergs in their new non-Jewish environs. The challenges here mirror those of many American Jews, particularly those of northern and Eastern European heritage, at midcentury.

Issues addressed in these episodes included co-constructed Jewish, race, gender, class, and sexuality matters: body image and standards of beauty, family structure and intergenerational tensions, citizenship, trustworthiness, enterprising spirit, cultural practices, and holidays. The presentation of each issue begins as a challenge. The characters then struggle through associated dilemmas in which they move back and forth between emerging American suburban, supposedly ethnically cleansed, gender-neutral ideals and their cultural urban Jewish knowledges in its many identity manifestations. Within the world portrayed on the television show, their street smarts and cultural dexterity (code for immigrant low-class Jewish wheeling and dealing and the less formal mechanisms open for women within that cultural imaginary) seemingly allow them to open up space for the new Jews on the block.[13] As the episodes move toward their finales, they seem to push the boundaries of normative (raced, sexed, classed, gendered) cultural citizenship with some culturally specific contribution these Jews can make.[14] Like many sitcoms we have come to know, the final scene is always cathartic, upbeat, bearer of a moral message, a display of challenges successfully met. Despite the promise of boundary pushing suggested at midshow, however, the catharsis tends to reinstate the normative ideal. In the end, the mythology of the emerging (US) American imaginary is not challenged but reinscribed. This is why Molly didn't last past one season in the suburbs.

Let us explore this with a look at specific episodes. As we do so, however, let me note the kind of intersectional context I am using for the analysis. Antler's 2007 work on Gertrude Berg suggests an inversion of the post–Philip Roth Jewish/gender vilification of the "Jewish mother."[15] Western Jewish stereotypes of "the mother" figure had long relied on an amalgam of character traits such as sturdy, practical, smart, and loving. As many US Jews of European heritage were moving through the reassignment period (from nonwhite to honorary white, from poor to middle class), some Jewish male writers are credited with reinventing the portrayal of Jewish women in general and Jewish mothers as iconic figures in particular.[16] In their new US more "normative" contexts, Jewish mothers get renamed by Jewish men who are succeeding in US terms as overbearing, old world, interfering, emasculating. Antler's feminist and more sympathetic reading suggests that Berg bucked this trend.[17] My analysis will offer a slightly different interpretation. In order to do this, it is important to note that the male Jewish writers spearheading this gender value shift for Jewish women generally view the Jewish mother through the lens of her effect on the male child. What has had much less attention is an analysis of shifting gender and power roles when we examine portraits of the Jewish mother in the United States at midcentury via her interaction with dramatic daughters.[18]

For example, the episode titled "Rosie's Nose" proves a (heterosexually) fertile starting point. The episode begins with the adults discussing what to buy daughter Rosie (short for Rosalie) for her upcoming birthday. Their uncle wants to buy her a cashmere sweater. Molly talks Jake into buying a watch with maternalist sentimental symbolism: "seventeen jewels for seventeen years." Rosie makes clear that she doesn't want consumer items as gifts but a cash equivalent in their stead. Rosie takes the bourgeoisification of Jewish immigrants of the period yet another step. In the process, pressures to assimilate played out on the scene of women's bodies in a heterosexual milieu such as the fictive Rosalie's. It turns out that she needs money because she intends to have a nose job. The family is distraught. The drama begins. Rosie's "choice" threatens the family's boundaries. They decide that they must have given Rosie the impression that she was not pretty, a death knell for a heterosexual young woman. Their attempts to convey that she *is* pretty clue her into the fact that her brother Sam has told the elders of her plastic surgery plans. The drama is in high gear now with Rosie wailing to her mother. The adults then puzzle it through and Molly decides to see the doctor secretly and ask him (a white male displaying no Jewish ethnic markers) to join a plot to help convince Rosie not to go through with the nose job. The plan works, Rosie flees in horror from the doctor's office.

The "violence" of the nose job is averted by Rosie's complacent acquiescence to the equally "violent" manipulative disciplining at the hands of her mother (and the complicit white, presumably Christian, male authority figure of the doctor), although, since this is a television sitcom, we are all supposed to be laughing. Here we see the classed, raced, gendered, and sexed nature of the violent "persuasive" disciplining of the new suburbs, compared to the mythed "physical" violence of the city.[19] We witness the presumption of Rosie's future middle-class heterosexual marriage and childbearing. The key to Rosie's "change of heart" was reference to the fact that her children might have "her" nose and she would eventually be outed to her future husband. This is a concept commonly referred to in literature on "passing."[20] Instead of making a radical break with Jewish norms, the show concludes with a shot of Rosie's birthday celebration, where she receives the items her family originally intended to give her. Molly repeats from the opening: "seventeen jewels for seventeen years." The closing scene "safely" returns us to origins, tradition, and sentimentality.

My argument is that we can see in the suburban section of the show *The Goldbergs* the ideological dynamic at work in the nation at the time. At midcentury, moving into the 1960s, cultural identity categories were expanding, even exploding.[21] Yet each move touted as an opening was made possible by a closing; each new "freedom" demanding a new constraint. Each conception of empowerment that developed relied on a different form of disenfranchisement. Things became fluid by displacing and again firming up subtle aspects of what had once been static about them.

For example, when another episode turns to Rosie's dating, the situation stands in stark contrast to the episode of her brother Sammie's dating in the Bronx. Sammie dates a Jewish girl who lives in the Goldbergs' building (of similar class standing). She is a known "entity," and the family is connected to her family in ensuring their plans for their children. The drama is comedic at the level of the difficulty of the adults trying to talk to one another. When it comes time for Rosie to date, an unacknowledged heterosexual imperative in this Jewish and shifting class context, the family is living in the suburbs. Rosie is still in high school and comes home night after night with a different white-appearing male college student, presumably assuming her continuing climb up the class ladder through heterosexual marriage. There are many young men, and from our view as audience, each is disconnected from his home and family. Each member of the Goldberg family is impressed by the new, forward-looking attitudes of the young men, and each family member takes a liking to a different date. The drama begins. This is too much family involvement for Rosie and she comes home next with a man twice her age, twice divorced, with two children. In the suburbs, Rosie's "choices" have far outgrown Sammie's. Freedom. The drama now explodes.

The apparent expansion of "choice" in this suburban, middle-class era is seen in that the new models presented by each young man are encouraged by the family . . . up to a point. When Rosie brings home the older man, the family goes into its usual tailspin, plotting and threatening to end the relationship. Before everyone can see their plans through *for* Rosie, in the final scene Rosie comes home with yet another date, happily back to the acceptable white male college student model. Danger has been averted. The paradigm has shifted since Sammie's turn, but not altogether. Family order has been reestablished and, as in the nose-job episode, the closing scene replays the opening one for reassurance.

The argument that I offer is that *The Goldbergs* did not survive that season in the suburbs, despite a twenty-five-year track record of tremendous popularity, because the contradictions it sought to synthesize were, ultimately, unsynthesizable. *The Goldbergs* could not successfully solve their problems adapting to the suburbs because that success, in any facile way, was impossible. To succeed would have meant further assimilation and the end of what was lovable in the Jewish particularity of the much beloved Goldberg family. This was a defining contradiction for many European-heritage Jews of the era and a level of assimilation presumed later to be acceptable for the 2013 television Goldberg family.

Given our knowledge of the termination of Berg's show, from this historical vantage point, ending each episode on a happy note was, in fact, tragic. The forced happiness exposed the gulf between the ideal of assimilation and what was ultimately inassimilable in the new middle-class suburbs. With the insight of hindsight, the episode endings appear as "failed" drag performances where the performers mistake the parodic power of drag for being the "real" thing, only to elicit pity and jeers instead of identification and cheers.[22] *The Goldbergs* tried to perform an assimilated identity as "Americans," as ethnically cleansed as was the assumed new version of mass suburban culture. The show failed, their assimilation was arrested. At this historical moment, *The Goldbergs* never made it to "real" status—the mark of success coveted in drag performances.

The End of *The Goldbergs* and the Future of American Jewry

In *Looking for God in the Suburbs*, Hudnut-Beumer (1994, 1) writes, "The 1950s was a high point for the place of religion in the United States. Never before in national history had as many Americans belonged to, attended, or associated themselves with religious institutions. Not only in adherence, but also in status, religion experienced a popularity that was without parallel."[23] In the case of *The Goldbergs*' mid-1950s move to the suburbs, we can then more deeply understand an oft-noted insight: as Jews sought to become more American, they actually further distanced themselves from American norms. For example, there are almost no religious references at all in *The Goldbergs* episodes. We know the Goldbergs to be Jewish, historically and culturally. Did secular Judaism express Berg's notion of Jewish identity, or was the choice to portray Jews as nonreligiously Jewish part of a broader tendency among Jews generally at the time?[24] To address the pain and discrimination that too often accompanies "difference" in the United States, many Jews sought to divest themselves, or at least portray themselves as divested, of their "different" religious (at least, assimilation also required cultural shifts and losses as this chapter points out) associations. This move might have made their Jewish otherness stand out less in *some* ways, but their very lack of religiousness also separated them from the growing mass of religiously identified mainstream Christian Americans.[25]

This is also a time in the African-American community of exploring alternatives to Christianity in an attempt to overcome historical racism in the US context. Most African Americans retained connection to their Christian postslavery roots. However, while many are familiar with the rise of groups such as the Nation of Islam, this was also a historical moment of African Americans searching out Hebrew, Israelite, and Jewish ancestries. Some also reached out to the more organized Jewish mainstream with various results.[26] For the Euro-heritage Berg and this US postwar moment when Euro-heritage Jews are moving in fits and starts into a more acceptable (meaning white) US identity, (Euro) Jew is the Goldberg's racial marker, and no wider Jewish racial diversity is acknowledged, despite the growing ranks of non-Euro Jews in the US.[27] The class move to the suburbs is part of the attempt to whiten the television family. However, in an attempt to remove a central marker of their otherness/Jewishness, *The Goldbergs*, as so many actual Jews did, created altered sexed, raced, class, and gendered markers of otherness for the many Jews who could not comport to the new US assimilated standards.

So what became of the "Goldbergs" of our nation? As more Jews played out the fictive Goldberg migration on actual new suburban landscapes, did they do any better than Molly in her encounters with "otherness?" Certainly not all Jews in the United States were urban dwellers and moved to suburbs at this time. They were, however, impacted by these shifts in norms and expectations by and for US (mainly Ashkenazi) Jews. Let us consider the situation of Asians in the United States, a group often referred to as "the new Jews," while remembering that "Asians" and "Jews" are not necessarily separable groups. For example, author Gish Jen (1996) presents a tale from half a generation later in the suburbs when her character Mona, a child of Chinese immigrants, converts to Judaism in her very Jewish new suburban neighborhood.[28] Mona's experience in the (by then) more Euro-Jewish middle-class suburbs of New York City calls into question what became of the "Goldberg children," children of families that created these new golden bergs/towns. As yet a later version, Jen Chau (2004) suggests that the melding never really worked. In Chau's case, as a mixed Chinese/Euro-Jewish child raised in New York, though the norm became more Jewish than in *The Goldbergs*' time, the "people" never really became any more able to accept difference. Despite the ever "happy" endings of early sitcom style, *The Goldbergs* did not really point us in that direction either.

The years 2014–2015 must be the beginning for exploring US minority groups possibly "making it" in the suburbs. After the 2014 start of the two sitcoms, the *Goldbergs* (set in the 1980s) and Black-*ish* (set in the current period), ABC started off its 2015 season with another minority ethnic show: *Fresh Off the Boat*. This sitcom, set in 1995, shows a Taiwanese family's challenge to adjust/assimilate when they move from Chinatown in Washington, DC, to the mainly white town of Orlando, Florida. The racial themes are explicit here as well, though again, they are set in comedic fashion.

Berg herself explored some issues of Jewish-Asian relationships. In an interesting development, after the closure of *The Goldbergs* with their last season in the suburbs, Gertrude Berg returned to Broadway to perform in the Leonard Spigelglass play, *A Majority of One*. As a play, in contrast to what many would argue was possible on a nationally syndicated television show, the messages were more complex and more politically boundary pushing. Gertrude Berg played Mrs. Bertha Jacoby, a Euro-Jewish woman in her late fifties, living in Brooklyn. For Berg it was back to the city and the ethnic shtetl, to some degree. But in some ways this recentering in a minority ethnic milieu allows the play to be more overtly political than Berg was on television. Mrs. Jacoby is described as in her "late-fifties, well held-together, with a clean face that has known many woes but remains cheerful."[29] Their neighborhood is starting to have "colored" people and Puerto Ricans moving in. Propaganda of such a "threat" to property taxes was precisely the cultural formula that was used to encourage many Euro-heritage Jews, at that historical moment being redefined as honorary whites, to leave their urban dwellings for the suburbs . . . with mixed outcomes.[30] A neighbor comments that it used to be a "very good neighborhood, years ago." And years ago they also did not allow Jews to live there. The neighbor's prejudice is called into question by Mrs. Jacoby's son-in-law, Jerry. Her daughter seems to have married up, at least Jewishly, like we are preparing for Rosie of *The Goldbergs*. Though Jerry is Jewish, he has made it to an official position in Washington in the State Department. He gets a promotion and must move for a time to Japan, and the young couple decides to bring Mrs. Jacoby with them.

There is similar drama as we are accustomed to in *The Goldbergs*: though Berg is the star, she is often suspect now as of a past generation. On this journey she brings her Brooklyn, minority-ethnically marked ways and causes all sorts of trouble in a world where she is criticized for not knowing the "right" (read upper-class and nonmarked white/Christian) ways of "America." Yet, of course, it turns out that Berg's character and her "native wits" (again, read lower-class gendered pushy bargaining) prove more valuable for the international deals being cut. In the process she develops a close tie to a Japanese businessman and they end up shocking the "progressive" Jewish younger generation with their interest in marriage to one another across cultural and racial lines. At first the Berg character presumes the impossibility of such a union. Once back in her own mixed ethnic context in Brooklyn with its own rules, however, Mr. Asano (played not so threateningly by Sir Cedric Hardwicke) comes for a visit and the two are promised to one another.

The interracial union is at once daring and was nearly shunned. It is also presented as the "progressive" thing to do and an example of interracial peace at the start of a historical moment of intense interracial uproar. Is this union possible because Mr. Asano is Asian and not African American? Because he is not presumed to be Christian? Because the character is not American at all and is protected by the international trope? Because the boundaries between normative Japanese of that historical moment and Euro-heritage Jews did not threaten the emerging mainstream Jewish investment in "whiteness?" I would argue that it is also more palatable in that he "happens" as well to be wealthy and refined (in many ways still a "marriage up"). Finally, despite my comments on the likely mixed-race future of the living Jewish children of characters such as Molly Goldberg, because the couple is in their late fifties, their miscegenation poses no real "threat" of mixed-race children.

Many of the mixed-race unions between Euro-heritage Jews and other people that characterized the generation of the "Molly Goldberg" children did not actually fare that well. The suburbs might have suggested a world of safety to the parental generations, and what the children did with that safety in real life was take real risks of the sort that threatened Molly and Jake in the fictional suburban moment of the sitcom. Rosie's sexual experimentation beyond the boundaries of the "new" yet acceptable might have been thwarted, though in real life many Euro-heritage Jewish young women did engage in interracial unions. For those whose explorations yielded children, the results were "mixed." It is this historical moment that creates "movement kids"—children of parents starting in the 1960s era of sexual and racial exploration, many multiracial, who have been coming to voice in the last decade or so.[31] But the stories, often expressing much pathos, of self-aware movement kids in many ways still "speak over" the untold numbers who do not have such a narrative. In fact (as will be discussed in later chapters), many Jewish families at that time pressured their daughters to end their interracial unions. Middle-class European-heritage Jews were among those most in favor of abortion. (Note: abortion is allowed in Jewish legal tradition.) Many Jewish women who brought their pregnancies to term from interracial heterosexual unions were pressured to terminate their parental rights with their mixed-race offspring (as will be discussed later in this book). Once these mixed-race Jewish children were put up for adoption, social workers and adoption agencies found it difficult to place them with Jewish families.[32] On the one hand, the US Jewish community likes to pride itself on its leadership stance during even the earliest days of the civil rights movement (indicated by Berg as both Molly Goldberg and Bertha Jacoby). On the other hand, the real-life Rosies who stepped too far "beyond the pale" were not generally embraced; more painfully perhaps, nor were their children.[33] We are at a new historical moment when more Jews of color in the United States are speaking up—and we need to articulate the centrality of an antiracist Jewish feminist agenda for our time. I will attempt such an articulation in the conclusion of this book.

For now, let us note that Gertrude Berg's television attempt to smooth out the rough edges of 1950s northeastern suburban cultural tensions were hindered as much as many actual people's attempts to become "ordinary Americans." Episodes began on a high note, often not fully meeting the challenges presented along the way. As with real people setting out on new frontiers in a newly gendered, raced, classed, and sexed landscape, *The Goldbergs* ran into a dead end. The failures of the suburban segment of the show were reflective of the lived limitations in that historical moment.

Conclusion

The changing status of Jews in the United States, perceived as a community, at this historical moment was both product and producer of intense ideological transformations and contradictions. As this discussion of *The*

Goldbergs' original trajectory demonstrates, portions of the Jewish community were both crossing a race/class line at this delicate moment, and in other ways they were not making it over that line. The basic politics of the US Jewish community today continues to be constructed and constrained by these midcentury dynamics: about the relations among those who made it over the "line" and those who did not, those conceived as part of the new collectivity and those marginalized.[34] The question, posed by that fatal suburban season of the show, as to what opportunities for Jews as political agents are opened up and which narrowed within differing paradigms of assimilation, is as significant today as it was half a century ago. Perhaps others will extend this analysis as the 2014 *Goldbergs* show develops.

Chapter 4

Ritual Encounters of the Queer Kind

A Political Analysis of Jewish Queer Ritual Innovation

Introduction

In this chapter on Jewish feminist intersectionality analysis in the area of sexual and gender justice, I seek to bring the quite intellectual pursuit of political philosophy into play with the not-necessarily-so-rational aspirations at work in many people's spiritual needs. Here I hope to honor spiritual strivings while still holding us responsible for their political and theoretical merit. To do so, I propose staging an encounter between Jewish queer interests in feminist ritual innovation, particular revolutionary thinkers/activists, and certain currents in lesbian and queer theory popular in the secular academy within an intersectionality frame. Specifically, given the focus on sexual and gender justice, I examine an example of an idea for a Jewish coming-out ritual discussed over time in the Jewish Queer Think Tank. Using the contributions of contemporary queer, intersectionality and other radical theorists, I attempt to articulate one possible function of ritual as identity-producing, revolutionary performance.

I argue that by using the work of intersectionality theorist Shane Phelan, we can avoid the essentialist presumptions of GLBT identity common in US secular culture encoded in the language of "coming out." Once we establish queer identity as a multiply inflected social construction in need of constant reconstitution, we can make use of the anarchist notion of preparation for determining the role of ritual in such reconstitutions. In this context, we will examine Augusto Boal's contributions on the political potential of theater to enable certain self-conscious reconstitutions. If we think of ritual as a kind of theater, we can take seriously the roles of participants as actors in a ritual performance. To clarify the radical potential in this move, I utilize Judith Butler's theory of performativity where sex, gender, and sexuality are not understood as inherent traits but as identities produced through their very enactments. In sum, I will argue that mutually constitutive intersectional queer theory, along with the help of certain core anarchist concepts and Boal's projects in radical theater, can be employed in intersectional feminist-situated and queer Jewish ritual innovation. The goal here is to keep our spiritual journeys grounded in, rather than serving as a refuge or flight from, politics. In this way I suggest bridging an all too common secular-spiritual divide in the service of the democratic pursuit of making possible what seems impossible about our radical visions and aspirations.

Jewish Queer Innovations: A Coming-Out Ritual?

For those doing Jewish intersectional race, class, queer, and feminist ritual innovation, it is clear that their queer politics and their feminism inform their engagement with their Jewishness. I think, however, that the "sense" in which this "informing" works has thus far been undertheorized, communally limiting its contribution to a sexual and gender justice agenda. In this way, even for those involved in queer and feminist ritual innovation, the "stuff" of intense critical and intersectional queer and feminist theory often remains too separated from the ritual engagement. I would like to think about the "encounter" of intersectional theory and spirituality more explicitly. In this chapter, I hold the yearning for ritual accountable to our knowledge base as intersectional critical theorists. In this mainly feminist Jewish queer analysis, I largely seek to conduct a close reading that will assist us in our work to avoid a primary concern in intersectionality studies: essentialisms. In order to do so, I will take up a close read of an example of essentialism in one such ritual encounter: new rituals that deal with the spiritual yearnings of some queer Jews, and directly use some aspects of queer theory to do so. My aim here is to take seriously the desire for ritual of some queer Jews in our diversity, appreciating the role of the sacred, without losing touch with developments in intersectional secular queer intellectual projects (made by many of the same queer Jews).

For many years, I was privileged to serve as the coordinator of a group which its members call the Jewish Queer Think Tank (JQTT). The JQTT was originally formed as a project of Jewish Activist Gays and Lesbians (JAGL), a New York City–based political activist group. The JQTT met quarterly to examine issues of concern to Jewish sexual minorities in the context of both the larger queer and Jewish communities.[1] After about four years of meeting together, some members brought up the issue of queer Jewish rituals. Eventually, the group responded to the call of one member to create a "coming out ritual." This member's desire for such a ritual, and the group's affirmative response, may be seen as part of a growing awareness and movement on the part of feminists and queers in our diversity to address aspects of our lives, relationships, and life paths that need to be acknowledged, marked, celebrated, and explored spiritually—or recognized publicly as sacred—aspects that have been left out of Jewish practice historically framed by elite Jewish men.

Jewish elite men have rituals that mark moments on a life path they have experienced as important: circumcision, bar mitzvah, marriage, death, and so on. Many cultures have developed rituals to mark such life-cycle events, with Jews practicing their own versions of these rituals in specific ways, according to the customs of the local Jewish communities in which they occur. Geographical, ethnic, racial, and other differences are central to the array of rituals that have grown over time, all considered by their own communities as Jewish. Feminists have noted that any number of experiences that may be considered important historically for many women (e.g., first menstruation, first girlfriend, childbirth, miscarriage, becoming a senior, divorce and other separations, etc.) have gone unnoticed in the ritual cycle of elite male-defined Jewish communal life. Feminists have begun to create new rituals, and adapt old ones, to bring the sacred into the cycles of their bodily and collective lives and/or to make sacred the significant moments of their life paths in our diversity. With the expansion of rituals stimulated by Jewish feminists, we increasingly find queers exploring similar terrain as part of larger Jewish feminist sexual and gender justice aspirations.[2]

It is probably no coincidence that one of the first areas a self-defined queer Jewish group might begin its exploration of rituals concerned with sexual and gender justice would be related to the notion of "coming out." In contemporary US culture, what has been identified as the coming-out experience has been foregrounded as the central defining moment in the mainstream in the lives of people who consider themselves GLBTQ. Many people came (and are coming) out under extremely difficult, if not life threatening, circumstances. For many, coming out was/is a pivotal experience in their lives. In the absence of any existent ritual in traditional Jewish life to accompany such an event, it is understandable that some Jews might want one. Without communal affirmation, this intense experience occurs in isolation, often isolating many individual queer Jews from the larger Jewish community.

Developing coming-out rituals has also been important to Jews who have long been queer identified. There are queer Jews who now look back to their earlier experience and wish there had been some communal way to acknowledge these moments and processes, to honor them, to celebrate them. When Jewish feminists began engaging in ritual innovation, many discussed the power of such work as not only to respond to present-life situations, but as a means to help heal injuries experienced in one's past, and also in the past of one's community. Jewish feminist involvement in ritual innovation was also part of a feminist sexual and gender justice agenda of societal transformation. We increasingly now hear of Jewish feminists and queers envisioning the power of ritual adaptation to address individual and communal needs as well as current and historical yearnings for repair, rejuvenation, justice, redemption, and fundamental social change.

The beloved member of the JQTT, J., who brought up the idea of a coming-out ritual had originally imagined a ceremony where all the people who had come out in a given year as gay or lesbian would be welcomed by those already out within a particular community. This vision turned on its head the homophobic push to isolate and pathologize gayness. Further, in the Jewish mystical tradition, liminal moments are understood as inherently powerful; they are both dangerous and imbued with transformative potential. J. recognized coming out as a liminal time and sought to address the discomfort that liminality often stirs without normalizing the moment or turning it into something static. Part of how this might be achieved is through the communal aspect of Jewish ritual, using the multiracial, cross-generational, and cross-gender and sexual makeup of the Jewish queer community. The diversity inherent in any particular Jewish community can serve queer needs in an expanse of their particularity in this context in helpful ways. For example, seeing ourselves across a spectrum of age, gender, race, circumstance, and positionality within the Jewish queer community reminds us that we are all in process. It also opens possibilities for mentoring across difference. Role models and mentors play significant parts, particularly for minorities within any given community. In the context of new rituals for queer Jews, the dynamics may be multifaceted, that is, those who have been out longer serve as role models for those more newly out, and the current political context of those newly coming out for those in the ritual who have been out longer.

Coming out has often been described as a transition, a "finding oneself," "coming home," or "finding one's community." Some experience their queerness as a fought-for political development, or a shedding of cisgendered, hetero-patriarchal indoctrination. In the various cases, many queers who are coming out experience, or fear, excommunication from their community and/or being turned out of the home. If we were to ritualize the coming-out experience in a communal rather than individual or private way, we might work to problematize this interesting dynamic in which many people feel acceptance or achievement and exclusion at the same time. What might we do if we want to use ritual to address this phenomenon and help to transform it? As an act of empowerment, we in the JQTT asked specifically: What could a ritual of "welcome" look like? In the JQTT discussions, we explored images in Jewish tradition and language used in Hebrew for welcoming. The Hebrew word for *welcome* is *Brucha Haba'a*. The literal translation of this phrase into English is actually: Blessed is the one who comes. We find that the very word for welcoming when translated into English has multiple meanings for queer Jews in the United States. A Jewish queer "welcoming" ritual in the specificity of a Jewish language and tradition can serve to welcome, as it suggests making sacred coming out and the (potential or actual) pleasures of sexuality and transgender living for Jews who simultaneously live within the systems of signs of contemporary US queer culture.[3]

We thought the event could be a welcoming ritual, with words and Hebrew songs of blessing to cradle it. We discussed moving into a circle formed by those already out surrounding and embracing a smaller circle comprised of the newly out in our community. For a moment in time the newly out would experience looking out to a world populated by loving, accepting activists. The ritual creates a time and a space in which to see a world of mentors, path breakers, and communally engaged queers in relation. The time and space of the ritual disrupts the other times and spaces in which the newly out all too often face hostility and/or incomprehension, in which they too often see a heterosexual, cisgendered (include here often white/European-heritage, male, able, presumed to be middle class, etc.) world in which they have no place and are destined to be separated and marginalized, alone.

The discussion and the play of images at the JQTT meetings were sincere, heartfelt, and important. We were engaging with Jewish traditions and histories, exploring aspects that have come down to us in our place and time as empowering, and those aspects that have been used in, or as justifications for, the oppression of women and queers and those not within current hegemonic white/Euro-heritage/Ashkenazi norms. For example, the man who proposed the coming-out ritual offered the imagery of the "living waters" in Jewish tradition, which could be reclaimed and used in ritual to symbolize "the fullness of life after the death of the closet." He was responding to a water ritual common in Judaism referred to as *mikvah*. Traditionally this ritual was used to cleanse the soul and prepare the body for the holiness of such experiences as the sabbath or sexual relations. As one example, observant women must go to the mikvah after their menses, and the ritual is a requirement before their husbands will have sex with them again (following the period of sexual abstinence Jewish rabbinic tradition has developed during a wife's menses). Many women have found this ritual very spiritual. This mikvah ritual and its imagery has also often been used in the Jewish cisgendered, hetero-patriarchal control of women's bodies and their (presumed hetero)sexuality and cisgender. We could reclaim mikvah and its symbolism and reconnect it with our sexuality and gender nonconformity in new ways.

Before further exploration of mikvah and other rituals, however, we need to address certain more theoretical aspects of the phenomena. From our work together in the JQTT at that time over the course of more than a year, it became clear to me that we needed new rituals as part of the transformation of Jewish life as well as part of disrupting the notion that heterosexuality, masculinity, whiteness, Ashkenazi heritage, being born to Jewish parents, and cisgender conformity are normative. But we must also be careful how we go about constructing these new rituals, whether they be related to mikvah or any other aspect of Jewish tradition. We must ask deep questions regarding just what sorts of ritual innovations will, in fact, be disruptive of heterosexual, cisgender, and other nexes of normativity. We must be cautious not to replace traditional essentialist notions with new ones. In this spirit, I want to subject the very notion of a coming-out ritual to critical inquiry. What I am about to write, therefore, is not a critique of the individual JQTT member or any one person's particular desire for this form of ritual innovation, but of a larger phenomenon of ritual innovation.

Creative Jewish Queer Rituals: The Challenge of (Be)Coming Out

A coming-out ritual may serve as part of a wider project to end heterosexism and transphobia in the context of Jewish and other social justice work to end racism, classism, colonialism, imperialism, and myriad forms of co-constructed injustice. Depending on the context, however, a coming-out ritual may also risk reinforcing a number of problematic ideas about, and practices involved in, queer lives. The coming-out paradigm was developed as part of gay liberation.[4] As Phelan (1994) points out, the notion of "coming out" has tended to presuppose an inner, or inherent, essence of gayness.

Much of the narrative of coming out presumes that being gay "is," in an uncontested manner, simply part of some human beings. This understanding is grounded in a view that being gay is an ahistorical phenomena; it is an individual essence. As many queer theorists have discussed, however, being gay is historically situated and culturally constructed. In contemporary US terms, coming out is often gendered, raced, classed, Jewed, as well-operating in different ways in various and overlapping communities. In an effort to challenge the potential essentialism in the coming out narrative, Phelan writes that coming out as gay is, instead, a process of (Be)coming out. What she means by this is that coming out is not simply the expression of an a priori state or orientation, formerly hidden and now exposed. Rather, coming out is a process of "creating oneself" as gay.[5] Over time, in a combination of individually and collectively politically salient situated processes, we create queer culture, cultivate new epistemologies, interact with racist, Christian hegemonic, heterosexual, heterosexist, cisgender, and transphobic societies in myriad ways, developing our very identities as queers—as similar and different as we may be from other queers and those who consider themselves in particular relation to queers (e.g., those who identify not as queer but as bisexual or trans, gays and lesbians, nonsexual people, those who are polyamorous and/or men who have sex with men).

What happens when we submit ritual innovations to such an intersectional philosophical critique? Specifically, what possibilities are opened when we take Phelan's intersectional theory seriously in the work of creative ritual development? In what manner can Phelan's insights assist us in critiquing the welcoming ritual discussed above? Are there ways to tap into the welcoming kernel of that ritual that do not play into hegemonic understandings about identity? Can we think about a coming-out ritual that does not reinforce an essentialist, ahistorical notion of homosexuality (or other identities)? Will we be able to develop rituals that do not presume that coming out is only (for some) or at all (for others) about now making public a formerly private or inherent state of being? How can we have a ritual that brings the power and empowerment of the sacred and of community to the process of (be)coming out? What kinds of imagery could such a (be)coming out ritual employ?

I want to be clear, my purpose in asking these questions is not to set myself up to answer them definitively. I am not interested at this point in mapping out *a* (be)coming out ritual on my own and outside of a concrete communal enterprise. I would be particularly skeptical of such an effort, especially in an academic guise as I sit here on my own in the library. The JQTT continued to work together on this very topic as numerous queer Jewish synagogues/*havurot* (fellowships), communities, and groups of friends do similar work. At this juncture I am interested, however, in pointing out certain issues from an intersectional perspective that may be of service to communities engaged in such a project of ritual innovation (in ways that might be of assistance not explicitly in queer spaces only, but for the variety of our life-cycle and experiential needs).

To begin, being informed by Phelan's contribution, we could say that a strict dichotomy between those "coming out" and those "out" may no longer make sense. That in a particular ritual there can be a circle clearly composed of "those out" and one of those only now coming out seems less possible and less attractive if we take into account the complexity of our lives as queers, the continual processes of (be)coming out and conjuring our diverse queer selves and communities. In naming the cloudiness of the once clear "out" and "newly out" distinction, it is not that we should suppose that everyone is the same. However, if coming out is a (be)coming out, then everyone is always in the process of constructing their sexualities, genders, and multiple vectors of politically relevant aspects of our identities. This suggests that everyone is always (be)coming out even as we are all likely to be doing so rather differently, have been consciously doing so for longer or shorter spans of time, attaching different significances to it, prioritizing it differently, and so forth. Some of us never felt the experience of "coming out" sexually or in terms of gender nonconformity at all, though most of us face challenges every day regarding coming out, being out, and all manner of (be)comings. For many lesbians, beginning to relate to other women sexually was a gradual process involved in becoming feminists, and living and working within feminist communities. Yet even for these lesbians, setting up single or joint bank accounts, holding hands while out for a walk, or demanding family status in hospital visits with partners all require decisions of (be)coming out. Similarly, a woman newly being in a public relationship with another woman or a trans person and who identifies as multisexual will likely have concerns about others obscuring her identity as bi/multi/pan-sexual. In noting that we are all part of a (be)coming out process, is there still a way to honor the needs of those to whom this process seems newer (and in answer to the JQTT member's original framing of the need for the ritual)?

Second, if we take seriously Phelan's concept that we are all always in the process of (be)coming out, then there would not necessarily be some fixed group into which we could be welcomed. There is, instead, a group of individuals in different manners and in different phases of constructing themselves as queer and constructing queer communities. How does this insight transpose the concept of welcoming altogether? Who needs welcoming in this case? By whom? For what? Is it also possible to see different groups with shifting memberships during the course of a ritual? The new questions of "who, by whom, and for what" may need to be answered in multiple ways. Depending on the answers to the questions, specific individuals might find themselves in different categories at different points in the ritual. One's identity and role are likely to morph as the ritual unfolds. I wonder how different rituals may recognize and respond to the particularities of different individuals in the variety of their present needs. Asking questions of this nature might enable a coming-out ritual to be more democratic and multilayered than one in which the groups are distinct and fixed because they can aid in the development of a ritual experience in which all are participants in making queer community.

A concrete example may be found in another coming-out ritual explored within the JQTT. Originally unrelated to the work of those of us in the JQTT, the New Jersey Gay and Lesbian Havurah (NJG&LH) developed a coming-out ritual for its own community. Some of the members then utilized their Havurah experience to do workshops with other groups of queer Jews interested in developing such rituals. One member of the group, David Rogoff, also led a workshop using their ritual at the Conference of the International Association of Gay and Lesbian Jews. After various experiences with the ritual, the Havurah had an opportunity to perform it together as a community for a second time. David was also a member of the JQTT. At that point he brought materials from the different versions and workshops and worked on the ritual further in the JQTT.

The NJG&LH's and other groups' coming-out ritual is a beautiful collective piece of work being adapted over time. It is sensitive, artistic, and performance oriented. The ritual draws deeply on aspects of Jewish history and liturgy, reclaimed in creative and moving ways. It is grounded in a good deal of diversity within contemporary Jewish queer lives. One of the most significant aspects of the ritual for the purposes of this section of the paper concerns the ways that it manages to exemplify Phelan's conception of coming out as a (be)coming out. The central portion of the ritual involves a series of shifting locations, transformations of the tradition in the service of queer Jewish experiences that acknowledge the many facets of coming out and the process-like manner of (be)coming throughout one's lifetime. There are sections devoted to "coming out to ourselves," "coming out to family and friends," "coming out at work," "becoming involved in the gay community," "coming out in the Jewish community," and "coming out in the larger world." Through the combination of choreography and multiple sites noted to localize newly created blessings, it is clear that each section will be comprised of different subgroups of participants. There are many coming outs, some more relevant than others in our lives at a given moment and more open to multiple aspects of diversity among Jewish queers such as class, race, ethnicity, relation to rabbinic tradition, immigrations, Hebrew familiarity, and so on. At different points in our life journeys, we will find ourselves in the company of changing groups of people, supported by or distant from shifting groups of others. Among additional portions in the New Jersey ritual, there is also a mournful yet encouraging section dealing with "hope for those still in the closet."[6]

In the JQTT, we also spoke with David about the ways that such (be)comings do not usually occur in any one or linear way. The different aspects of coming out enable individuals and communities to work on new challenges for them over time. There can be no "culminating" point in the process of (be)coming out, no "final" sphere to conquer. Similarly, the "hope for those still in the closet" needs to involve all of us in constantly pushing ourselves and drawing others further out of the closet, and the many closets that seem to develop over time. The notion of (be)coming out breaks down the simple dichotomy of those closeted and those not. These insights may be helpful for other versions of (be)coming out rituals. Even when multiple sites of coming outs are incorporated, there can still be a tendency to employ a separative and or linear imaginary, so that coming out is symbolized as a process for one vector of identity that follows a particular path and "ends" with a section suggesting "now you are out," as if to say that "now your identity/community/justice-building work is done."

Let us explore another example of a ritual in order to push this point further. There is a group of people in a circle, each with their arms clasped around another's waist to make a strong barrier.[7] In the center of the circle are the persons newly "coming out (however self-identified)." They are asked to loosen up and move around the circle, bumping into the people making the circle. Those forming the circle are singing songs with a quick, tense tempo. (For a Jewish ritual, the singing can be in one or another Jewish language, though those from other communities can sing in their own languages.) Those inside cannot get out; they come to feel stuck, closed in. At the prompting of a ritual facilitator, those making the circle change the shape of the ring and instead form two lines to suggest a pathway. The line may curve and shift. Those inside are moved to begin to walk through the path of people. The singing changes to the use of cacophony. There are many songs at once: sad, upbeat, poignant, nostalgic, newly written for the event, choppy, funny, traditional prayers, children's ditties, and so forth. As the people are walking through the path, the singing changes again to more harmonized-rhythmic chanting. (Some readers may have experienced semi-spontaneous transitions such as these in drumming circles.) Those at the back of the line forming the path can move forward in order to keep the path spreading out, twisting and turning. After some time, the facilitator prompts those making the path to stop elongating it. This allows the walkers to "emerge" from the path, at which point all are called to sing and dance together. The singing becomes jubilant with many voices singing together. Jewish celebratory songs may be mixed with tunes from secular artists known in our multiracial/ethnic, queer and feminist communities, bringing parts of our identities together.

There are aspects of this ritual that are intense and moving. The music can be chosen to help set a mood, evoke experiences, and connect participants to different emotions. At the start of the ritual, those newly out recall the trapped feeling of being in the closet. The early part of the walk suggests the confusion many people feel when first coming out and at the many moments life presents. Then things move a bit more smoothly; we find a stride—at least at some points in our lives. The road shifts in unexpected ways but we are also getting more familiar with our surroundings, developing relationships, and building coping, resistance, and survival skills. Participants build momentum and finally emerge, "come out." They are now joined by the others. The experience is cathartic and participants feel exalted. All sing and dance joyously like at any *simcha*, happy occasion.

Think how this ritual also relies on linear imagery of identity formation, as the finale occurs when the individuals are "out." Think how clearly it distinguishes between those who are in the closet or newly coming out, and those who are already out. The ending of the ritual homogenizes queer identity, mixing everyone together as if they are now all the same. And yet the twisting pathway suggests that the way is not simply linear. Ecstatic aspects can be combined with acknowledgment of destruction to note that experience and change are not linear (it is common in many Jewish rituals of celebration to also include a marker to oppression). Occasionally some people forming the lines of the path may choose to (or be called to) run through path as well. Some who had been inside the circle may come to feel empowered to hold up part of the communal path. The last portion of the ritual can be amended from just all dancing together to certain types of Jewish circle or other Jewish-style dances. The facilitator can call different individuals and groups into the center and back out to the communal circle in order to respond to differing needs and acknowledging multiple subcommunities beyond "the newly out and the already out."

In discussing some examples of particular rituals and ideas about them, I do not intend to suggest that these are all the options. There are, there will be, and there need to be many "(be)coming out" rituals that work for different individuals and diverse groups in changing contexts. There are likely to be many empowering aspects of any one ritual, and many opportunities to reassess a group's needs, rethink the implications of imagery employed, and redesign the rituals. These rituals can be a time to focus on the creative, constructionist, contingent, and fluid nature of queer sexualities (as well as imbricating identities). They can be a time to play collectively with the dialectic of meaning, community, risk, expression, sex, desire, race, passion, gender, sexuality, beauty, violence, and power that is both operative and also impossibly possible. These musings bring us to some deeper questions regarding the very function of ritual. In the following section, I will bring together social theories that may assist those interested in intersectional queer ritual innovation that is consciously political. In light of these questions regarding queer and feminist Jewish creativity with ritual, I seek to articulate in what ways we might reinterpret the, or one possible, function of ritual itself. Ritual, important in the spiritual life of individuals and communities, can also be understood as fundamentally political. As part of the development of new queer and feminist Jewish rituals, we may be able to understand ritual more broadly as a clear and directed aspect of revolutionary social change.

A Political Function of Ritual: Anarchist Preparation

Religious participation is often criticized for taking up the space of political activism within a vastly oppressive social system. But is this necessarily so? Can religion, spirituality, searches for the sacred, and ritual (in the context of this article, in particular) be a part of fundamental political change? How might we think of ritual as an aspect of social transformation, rather than a practice reinforcing the status quo? Without serious attention to such questions, intersectional Jewish queer, feminist, and other modes of ritual innovation run the risk of confining the very set of experiences they seek to liberate. In order to answer these questions I propose looking to the anarchist notion of preparation.

As noted in chapter 1, Marxism popularized and brought us to a form of identity work that separated out one aspect of identity to privilege in analysis and political work. In addition, orthodox Marxists-Leninists have traditionally prioritized activity that would bring about their vision of a full-scale revolution in society. Many have understood this revolution as existing within a bounded period of time. In this understanding, there is a prerevolutionary period, the revolution, and a postrevolutionary time. The function of the revolution is to radically alter the social relations in a given society. As such, it is speculated that the postrevolutionary time will be one in which social relations are then equal and democratic. Anarchists have their own version of this concept of revolution. They generally work with socialists, communists, and others toward *the* revolution. They do, however, place more emphasis on the relationships between the means of bringing about such a revolution and the revolution or the aspired to postrevolutionary time themselves.

Turning orthodox Marxist-Leninism on its head, anarchists suggest that revolution needs to happen on multiple levels of human existence beyond the one privileged identity, and that the notion of a quick, sudden revolution should not necessarily be the exclusive focus for a revolutionary.[8] Certainly, we need fundamental transformation, but we also desperately need to *prepare* ourselves for living democratically in a way that is informed by multiple aspects of our communal experiences. Experiences of, and experiments with, social relations that are different (even dramatically) from those at present enable us to live these alternative social relations as they become more possible on a grander scale, or in more localized contexts.[9] Engaging in the work of preparation, we learn how to practice democracy.[10] As we have also learned all too well in intersectionality studies, we also often learn that there are mistakes or lapses in our visions that perhaps only living them out can show us. Participating in small-scale, radically democratic projects empowers us *now* for the work we will be doing on into the future. Taking on the tasks of egalitarian relationships across numerous politically salient identities and production now (without waiting for *the* revolution) allows us to explore the possible in the impossible structures of our current social relations as they are co-created. (See Ochs 2007; on B'not Esh see Feld 1999 and Ackelsberg 1986; on *havurot* see Prell 2007 and Weissler 1989; on Jewish Renewal see Weissler 2010).

One of the more inspiring and concise discussions on reinterpreting the (im)possible can be found in Emma Goldman's critical essay "Anarchism: What It Really Stands For." Perhaps most interesting for our purposes, for example, is that in response to critiques of anarchism as "impractical, though a beautiful ideal," Goldman (1969, 49) references playwright Oscar Wilde, saying that "a practical scheme . . . is either one already in existence, or a scheme that could be carried out under the existing conditions; but it is exactly the existing conditions that one objects to, and any scheme that could accept these conditions is wrong and foolish. The true criterion of the practical, therefore, is not whether the latter can keep intact the wrong and foolish; rather it is whether a scheme has vitality enough to leave the stagnant waters of the old, and build, as well as sustain, new life." Wilde and Goldman see how accepting what is said to be "the" reality before us stifles us with impossibilities. These radicals of the theater world have vision enough to see multiple realities, even those that are yet to be created, transforming the impossible into the very possible.

When anarchists and small communitarian socialists (as have existed in the kibbutz movement in Israel, for example) have discussed preparation as part of the strategy for making possible the impossible, they have usually used the examples of syndicated labor movements, learning cooperatives, worker-run factories and business, and/or small-scale egalitarian communes (Ackelsberg). I would like to suggest here that ritual can also be a form of preparation. Through play, imagination, and accessing spiritual dimensions, we create microrealities in ritual. If our visions of fundamental social transformation remain in the more orthodox Marxist/Leninist mode, we are likely to foreclose possibilities for the change that ritual innovation is designed to open up. In this sense, the anarchist perspective becomes more helpful for queer Jews and others interested in intersectional and creative ritual development.

For our purposes in this chapter, let us examine how such a discussion might affect (be)coming out rituals. The processes of "coming out" referred to here as (be)coming out are part of a revolutionary process of disrupting heteronormativity and transphobia and making possible/possibly queer lives. The traditional Marxist-Leninist model for revolution throws us immediately back into a more stylized and static "coming-out" phenomenon. In this view, it might be said that in queerness, as in all revolutions, there is a closeted time, the explosive moment of coming out, and then a life as one who is out. Such a linear view of the revolution of coming out misses the process orientation and multiplicity of constructionist layers discussed above with reference to Phelan's notion of (be)coming out. The anarchist understanding of revolution allows more for the complex, temporally shifting, and constructionist view of queer life as a process of (be)coming out. As there is not necessarily one simple revolutionary moment, with a clear-cut before and a clear-cut after, queer's lives are ever in process of creating alternative realities in our diversity. (Be)coming out more closely resembles the anarchist processes of experiments in radical democracy and alternative social relations over time. In (be)coming out, we acknowledge that there are many modes of possible queerness and "outness," more than we might even be able to imagine in our current historical context. The anarchist view encourages us to keep working at opening possibilities.

Rituals which situate a clearly demarcated group of "out" queers welcoming a separate and clearly demarcated group of those now coming out are likely to reinscribe a separative understanding of queerness and a progressivist, linear notion of coming out, with its time before and its distinct time after. They are likely to reinforce the static notion that one is either out or not, one of the welcomers or one of those being welcomed. Exploring the radical potential in the anarchist view of revolution that acknowledges the uneven, cocreated, often circular, messier realities of (be)coming more egalitarian can therefore be important to those involved in Jewish queer and other forms of ritual innovation. It assists us in avoiding an unfounded investment in the future as "better," common in modernist progressivist narratives and political thought. In anarchist fashion, F., another member of the JQTT, worked with us on the idea that ritual is not only something you create to occur in a given time and space, but also about recognizing and "imbuing action[s] and object[s] with intention and meaning." By taking on aspects of the everyday as having ritual potential, and not only the extraordinary such as the Marxist-Leninist revolutionary moment, we can exercise our capacities for transforming the co-constructed micropolitics of domination. Resonating clearly with an intersectional approach and anarchist notions of spontaneity, this aspect of the JQTT's work in Jewish queer ritual innovation played with the empowering potential of more flexible and less contrived modes of ritual innovations.

There are many ways to ritualize mundane moments that make sense in the context of queer Jewish lives. For example, it is a common Jewish practice to put a mezuzah on our doorposts. The mezuzah establishes identity, community, and our spirituality of connectedness. Physically, a mezuzah is a small case hung diagonally in a doorjamb, which includes a scroll with the words of a central prayer referred to as the *sh'ma*. In the *sh'ma*, we are asked to identify that which we know to be our most sacred knowledges. With these knowledges we are called upon to pay attention to all comings and goings, to love what we know as our God (however we might define that now in our diversity) with all of our heart, all of our might, and all of our soul. We are called upon to carry our knowledges through the generations. Often Jews more observant of rabbinic practice will reach up to touch a mezuzah in a doorway as they walk through, and then kiss their fingers (as the practical method of "kissing" the mezuzah, which would tend to be placed too high for most people to kiss directly). In a Jewish community there are usually mezuzot on the many doorposts in buildings. The mezuzah helps makes conscious for us moments of liminality, of crossings-through.

Can we queer this concept in an intersectional context? Can we use the common Jewish practices involved with the mezuzah to infuse aspects of our also co-constructed queer, mundane lives with the power of the sacred and political transformation?

What if we were to explore certain core themes of what are our most sacred truths for each of us in multiracial, cross-class queer Jewish communities, those which we want to remember to carry with us through the many spaces of living? How do we want to change the world by example? How can we teach alternatives to those around us so that they may affect others who may impact others? What knowledges do we want to be in touch with as we move through the locations in which we are more and less out, where we work on different aspects of the struggle to end anti-Semitism, homophobia, racism, classism, transphobia, sexism, and all mutually constituted oppressions? Could we imagine mezuzot on all doorposts in queer places we go and in the various arenas of our daily lives? We can reach, or look, up to our imagined mezuzot when we need to focus as we walk into a meeting in which we anticipate that our lifestyles will be challenged, into a dance club in which we want to enjoy *and* want to make empowering choices, into a gathering with family members who might be unaccepting of us and/or our families. We can transform the traditional act of kissing the mezuzah into a way to stay aware of our own knowledges of righteousness, to remind us to keep our heart, minds, and arms open, to stay aware of when we need to protect ourselves and others and resist injustice.

In this case, we can transform a traditional practice to help us have intention in our lives, as we attend to our relations in the world, in our work of social transformation. As intersectionality and anarchism suggest, the transformative potential of rituals can be found in micropractices based on our mutually constructed communities, in performing acts that help us keep our eye on the prize in trying situations. Ultimately, whether it be in communal and elaborate rituals or individualized acts that we imbue with the sacred, let intersectionality take its cue from the theatrical experiences of Goldman and Wilde. In any number of motions, actions, roles, and performances, ritual may therefore also be seen in this context as a form of political theater. To clarify this concept, let us turn to a discussion of the work of Augusto Boal.

Ritual and the Tradition of Political Theater

Augusto Boal is a Brazilian radical and performance artist. Developing theater in the tradition of Brecht,[11] Boal understands drama as a specific tool in revolutionary praxis. Theater, like religion, has often been seen as an escape from reality in such a way that diffuses potential political energy on the part of the oppressed. Boal and others seek to transform the cathartic tendencies often at play in theater into direct action. In his work, Boal often refers to theater as the rehearsal for the revolution. In guerrilla theater, role playing, forum theater, the joker system, and other imaginative theater exercises used by participants involved in a theater of the oppressed use actors, ordinary people, setting, and style to enhance people's capacity to see the contradictions of the multiple co-constructed systems of hierarchies in which we live. They use dramaturgical techniques to develop people's critical capacities and their imaginative potential. Through the exercises, happenings, and events people become actors, political actors. Within and from the theatrical projects, people take action on the multiple issues confronting their lives and the lives of their communities.

What does this have to do with the encounter between intersectional queer strivings for spiritual fulfillment and expression, and an exquisitely cynical or in many ways postmodern queer theory? Regarding Boal's notion that theater is a rehearsal for the revolution, a postmodernist might critique Boal's retention of the notion of revolution as too modernist, still stuck in progressivist and totalizing paradigms.[12] This is a significant critique. Perhaps another way to see this, however, is that Boal is too humble. Perhaps, the rehearsal for the revolution which Boal sees in radical theater is part of unfolding revolutionary aspirations, as we examined above among anarchists. Invoking Langston Hughes (1994) within an anarchist tradition, we might say that the radical transformation of society need not be deferred.

One of the main strengths of Boal's work is the way that it engages ordinary people from any variety of communities in some of the most radical forms of direct action. Experiments with political theater also enhance these differing people's capacities to act individually and collectively in changing their life circumstances. Situating this work within the anarchist tradition, let us address the situation that there is not some postrevolutionary moment that looks so different from now. There will not be a postrevolutionary moment that any theorist or practitioner can predict before living out the processes involved in the multilayered radical transformations. Boal's theater techniques are developed to encourage insight, dialogue, feedback, problem solving, critical self-examination, and community building across difference. These are necessary in the difficult processes of social transformation with multicultural and multi-issue coalitions and movements. Similar to the anarchist notion of preparation, Boal writes that "only out of constant practice will the new theory arise" (1985, 79). Working with Boal's techniques, we can find an alternative to futurism and progressivist narratives, coming to see that the experiment with alterity is likely to be what alterity is. Alternative social relations are not some specific thing that we know not of now, but experimentation and play with alterity is the experience of alterity itself. To put it another way—similar to the argument in chapter 2 on Kincaid, on the lack of an Archimedean point outside colonialism—there is not some "real" reality outside the theater.[13]

It is interesting that in Boal's work we can see aspects of the various concerns thus far discussed in this article. For example, as a political activist, Boal discusses the spiritual nature of his work. In his view, new modes of theater are necessary for the democratic imperative to help free our spirits and our spiritual impulses. We can use theater to combat alienation and the deadening of our souls that occurs under the mutually constitutive systems of oppression in which we live. Through Boal's work, we can see that he understands both the rituals of theatrical development, and the theatrical elements of ritual. His work is an art of challenging the reality of what generally is considered the "real" and the unreality of that which is fictional and/or not yet real. He recognizes that a central limitation of what we tend to call reality is that it is confined to what is "supposedly already known" (1985, 76). In his theater, reality is about creating what seems impossible, about opening up the unknown, the untried, the unexamined, the unexplored. Finally, bringing us back to Phelan, he explores what it means for theater to be "change and not a simple presentation of what exists: it is becoming and not being" (1985, 29). In the context of mutually constitutive intersectionality's insistence on multivalent co-constructionism, the anarchist idea of preparation and Boal's work in political theater, we can now see that this is also where queer theory has much to offer queer Jews and all those interested in radical ritual innovation.

Ritual Innovation and Performativity in Queer Theory

Boal is a player, an actor, creating a stage, a theater of our mundane existing locations. He and his troupes enact dramaturgically and expose the contradictions of multiple and cocreated systems of exploitation. As one example of his method, by working in everyday settings, the actors enable people to see these settings in new ways, and jump-start ordinary people out of the taken-for-granted quality of even their most minute, and often presumed to be distinct, social relations. Boal's players purposely make what seems to be normal and separate no longer so. It is only a small step from here to Judith Butler's notion of performativity.[14]

As a key aspect of queer theory, Butler suggests that the self is a social construction and that, therefore, every identity is a performance. In contrast to notions of the eternal Jewish self, for example, this theory suggests that Jews are those who perform Jewishness. Jewishness is what is performed as that which is Jewish. To give a concrete example, Jews are not *expressing* our identity as Jews when we wear a Jewish star (*magen david* or shield of David), presupposing some essential Jewishness about us that is now publically revealed. Instead, wearing a Jewish star is a performance of Jewishness relevant in particular historical and geographical contexts. Wearing a Jewish star is an act, repeated by many and part of myriad related acts, which creates a Jewish identity. Jews are people who may ritualize moving through doorposts; Jews are people who may put up and kiss mezuzot. As with the need to transform Jewish identities and practice according to the vast diversity of our lives, queer Jews might reclaim these performances, as examples, in the process of living diverse queer lives and ending racist, heterosexist, and transphobic oppression. In Nietzschean fashion, when Butler says that there is no "'doer' behind the deed" (33), in this context we can take her to mean that there is no Jew who puts on a Jewish star or kisses a mezuzah, a doer who acts out Jewishness. Instead, it is the acts themselves that constitute the (queer) Jew. What does this mean for ritual? Boal wrote that "theatre is action" (1985, 155) and developed "theatre as politics, not just political theatre" (2001, 336). In a related fashion, Butler, rather than seeing a performance as "about" life, helps us to see that life is the performance. Concomitantly, ritual is not about creating a space outside of life or society. Life in society is itself a performance. Ritual may be used as a (somewhat) conscious alternative performance, as the Jewish queer imaginary mezuzah serves to enhance our intentionality. For Butler, a subversive form of parody is one that does not stay on the level of parodying an original, but one that is a parody of "the very notion of" originals (175). Similarly, the JQTT discussed what sorts of ritual performances expose supposedly "nonritual" acts as performances as well.[15] Shoring themselves up as they walk through the door, the cowboy, the observant Jew, and the coquette each enact a ritual of preparing themselves, their identities, strengths, and weaknesses at that moment at which they walk into a room. What might be the radical potential of breaking down the distinction between rituals as theatrical and the rest of life as "real?" In the queer appropriation of kissing the mezuzah, a Jewish sexual and gender outlaw comes into the confidence to face a difficult situation, making what might have previously been an impossible stance of courage now very possible. Alternatively, if in a communal ritual the participants act as empowered selves, this is not merely a quaint skit. A ritual that involves participants acting as empowered is a performance as "real" as all the disempowered performances the actors play every day. We may have learned to be disempowered selves by being taught, expected, forced to act as disempowered selves over time. Similarly (while I do not intend to invoke behavioralism here), as part of the revolutionary process, we can in part learn to be empowered selves by acting as empowered selves. Like any revolution, in intersectional and anarchist understandings this doesn't happen suddenly and fully as if there is only one vector being transformed. We need practice. We need to pass through many doorways, finding many imaginary mezuzot as we prepare ourselves for alternative worlds of social relations. Specific acts in which we play the roles of empowered selves, specific rituals that create opportunities for us to engage with ourselves and others as empowered selves are some of the many excellent modes of "preparation" for living more fully as empowered selves within and beyond a ritualized experience.

Ritual, Revolution, Performance: Issues of Repetition

Butler suggests that the reason certain acts appear as natural within a particular culture is that those acts present themselves as originary. Further, these acts achieve the effect of being natural by the repetition of their performances within a social system dependent on numerous intersecting performances. One might well ask, then: how is change possible under these circumstances? If what is considered normal becomes so through the repetition of acts, then to disrupt the repetition makes it possible to resist normativity. If the dominant understanding of the relations of multiple aspects of identity is recast in differing sets of relations, the separative mode of identities is called into question. Not repeating, enacting alternative performances, and other mechanisms can serve to disrupt the flow of events that sustain a presumption of the separative and the natural. The radical potential of a Jewish feminist and queer ritual is the possibility of just such a disruption.

It is important to note that the radical potential of this notion of disruption does not have to wholly topple a unitary hegemonic idea or practice. In order to be part of deep social change in intersectional context, a particular counterperformance need not succeed in stopping the oppressive performances for all and for all time. The question to be asked is not whether performances either change the status quo fully or not. Such an either/or notion of revolutionary work too easily leads to despair and reinstates us in the world of impossibilities. On the other hand, in an intersectional mode, it might be more helpful to develop alternative performances that expose the natural and separative for their constructed nature, and/or those that begin to enable further empowering performances. On this point Butler is likely to agree with intersectional and anarchist reinterpretations of the relationship between what is seen as impossible and that which is possible. Aspirations, resistance, and creative alternatives crumble under the crushing force of the *impossible*. But a disruption of the repetition brings the otherwise impossible notion of fundamental change back in relation with the possible. As Butler notes in her preface to the Tenth Anniversary Edition of *Gender Trouble*, she does not write of denaturalization "simply out of a desire to play with language or prescribe theatrical antics in the place of 'real' politics, as some critics have conjectured (as if theater and politics are always distinct). It was done from a desire to live, to make life possible, and to rethink the possible as such" (xx; Butler also discusses the possible and impossible in 2012).

The notion of repetition plays a significant role in Butler's understanding of essentialized identities, normativity, and their possible disruption. Questions regarding repetition are also interesting for those involved in theater and ritual innovation. One reason performance art has been seen as "not real art" is that a performance "event" cannot be repeated in the same way twice. But who is to say that Karen Findley's wearing a dress made of meat-steaks outside the Miss America Contest transformed consciousness any less than a (re)production of Shakespeare's *The Merry Wives of Windsor*?[16] Repetition is part of what makes ritual, Jewish and other religious/communal rituals in particular, so powerful. Knowing that your communities have engaged in these, or similar, acts over thousands of years carries great weight for many people (though often such views of historical continuity are inventions of particular communities). This weight can often contribute to what feels so grounding about long-practiced rituals. This weight can also be part of what might feel burdensome about certain oppressive aspects of ritual. Within this context, any innovation in a ritual might be experienced as radical. But those involved in creative ritual work often struggle with whether or not new rituals (or new aspects of old rituals) are sufficiently radical if they themselves are not repeatable. Some new rituals are developed for one-time purposes. Other developments are intended to supplant traditional rituals altogether. As a radical proposal in ritual theory itself, I do not think the political potential of a ritual innovation rests on whether or not the innovation is repeatable. In the case of a (be)coming out ritual, for example, the JQTT discussed many options.

One might envision a (be)coming out ritual in a particular community as a one-time performance. A participant might then take the idea on the road and do workshops, training others through the example. One can incorporate a (be)coming out ritual during the celebration of the Jewish New Year or new moon. The new year and new moon have long symbolized renewal and growth. Situating a (be)coming out ritual at these times relies on the power of the traditional Jewish calendar. Some have suggested that such a ritual can be scheduled during the US Coming Out Day/Week and a Trans Day of Remembrance. This option is still situated in a repeatable yearly cycle, but one that ties Jewish needs into the development of secular queer culture. A (be)coming out ritual may happen one time in your life. Something of this nature may be introduced into a regular cycle within a community. A community may decide to hold a (be)coming out ritual among its repertoire to be conducted as deemed necessary. Some communities might like the ritual repeated the same way each time. On each occasion, particular communities might like to develop new versions. Some individuals might be present performance after performance. In other cases the changing makeup of the community participating might give the ritual its freshness.

The point is that not one of these choices is right or wrong. Butler is careful to warn us that "subversive performances always run the risk of becoming deadening clichés through their repetition and, most importantly, through their repetition within commodity culture where 'subversion' carries market value" (xxi). For our purposes, we might say that subversively new rituals cannot be packaged and reperformed without attention to context. Instead, communities ought to be encouraged to ask questions regarding what will make this ritual most transformative for them at the time. Relying on anarchist plays on spontaneity and planned programs, like those in the JQTT, others might come to see that the variety of ritual innovations possible can even give traditional blessings, liturgy, and prayer deeper meaning.

Moving On

This chapter, like the book as a whole, addresses work in process, a movement in creation. Queer feminist Jews and others—alone, in pairs, small groups, and large communities—are taking ritual seriously as part of queer spiritual life, celebration, and liberation. I applaud the creative and revolutionary work being done and in this chapter have made a call to keep our new ideas and practices in the religious/spiritual realm in mutually empowering relation with ideas in secular and intersectional self-consciously political theory. With the assistance of secular critical theory, let us take a moment to return to the specific idea of reclaiming the mikvah for queer Jews. A group of queer Jews may develop a mikvah ritual for a one-time experience, or repeat it cyclically. In the traditional version, a person going into the mikvah is naked and checked carefully for any hairs or particles on the body that would come between the woman's body and the water. Women have often found this process humiliating. Transfolk generally cannot even use traditional *mikvas*. Queers and all women could use the mikvah as a time to reconnect to our bodies, our genders, our sexualities, and our skin coloring and racial heritage, turning what has often become the legalistic "checking" into a celebration.

Jewish queers often express the need to redefine the spaces and textures of what have hegemonically been designated as holy and profane. Although some might find this unappealing or too controversial, a group might purposely include wearing or dipping into the water something that would have commonly suggested impurity. Ritually dripping a drop of lubricant into the water would make the mikvah halachically (in Jewish law) unkosher (unsuitable for ritual use), but participants might see it as a way to enliven the "living waters" with a symbol of queer (and hopefully safe) sex. For those who have lived through this age of AIDS, such a moment of purification which points directly to queer sex could be particularly empowering. As another idea, in the traditional ceremony the individual takes three dunks, reciting a blessing and completely submerging oneself in the body of water. As a group ritual, a community may reclaim the three submersions. Together they could rewrite the blessing to address three aspects of import to the group. Each submersion could be named, with all invited to dunk for two of the three, and one specifically reserved for those newly coming out in some sphere of their lives. In this way, linkages across members in a diverse community and in the processes of (be)coming out can be explicitly acknowledged while also attending to the special needs of those newly (be) coming queer. Nehirim (http://www.nehirim.org/) is an example of a Jewish queer space that has worked in various ways with reclaiming mikvah. Experiencing freedom with one's body, the visible physicality of what we mark as race, ableness, gender, and sexuality in the context of the ritual can be part of the process of doing so in many aspects of one's life beyond the intentionally ritualized time/space. Facing others in one's communities while experiencing one's power helps enable one to tap into power in life and situations beyond the religiously ritualized moment. Dealing directly with issues of oppression and liberation in the context of a group ritual can enable active engagement with the politics of oppression and liberation in society at large. How else can we utilize ritual innovation in the service of our spiritual needs as well as the process of revolutionary social transformation?

To bring the discussion to a temporary close, I would like to take conscious note of the import of the very Jewish mode of answering questions with questions. For future work, we might ask: What repetitions are central to the oppression of queer Jews in particular? What presumptions of "nature" must diverse communities of queer Jews dislodge in order to live more freely as Jewish queers? What kinds of ritual performances can disrupt these repetitions, in different contexts and in different ways? What sorts of performative disruptions can denaturalize that which is natural and considered discrete aspects of identity and oppression in the sociocultural context in which queer Jews live, make meaning, participate in community, and therefore constitute an ever-contingent and historically specific universe for different queer Jews? Do specific groups—such as lesbians, bisexuals, trans people—have different needs from other groups? Do aspects of different queer lives challenge Jewish normative rituals in particular ways? In what ways do languages, nationalities, races/ethnicities, abilities, size, mental illness, nonconformity, class, and change in all of these matter for queer Jewish and other potentially radical ritual innovation?

By posing these and other questions and by opening a dialogue in terms slightly different from both the GLBTQ normative coming-out narrative and uncritical ritual makers, Jewish queer ritual innovations can serve as a productive encounter between the spiritual and the secular in many of our lives as a manifestation of intersectionality theory. Informed by queer theory coming from the secular academy as much as learning from and deep involvement in Jewish communal life, can those of us involved in ritual innovation do our work? If ritual is to be one aspect of making the impossible possible, I am hoping that through engagement with these different sets of questions, queer Jews (in our diversity, as well as any others) may develop concrete rituals that they find spiritually fulfilling and politically revolutionary. I have used the specific example here of coming-out rituals discussed over time in the Jewish Queer Think Tank and performed in different ways by various JQTT members and others. I intend, by assessing the potential political function of ritual itself, that the work of the JQTT might have wider application as well. It is my hope that questions which continued to arise for us in the JQTT may stimulate further questioning regarding essentialism for others in their own overlapping communities.

Chapter 5

Jewish Feminism, Race, and a Sexual Justice Agenda

Introduction

Jewish feminism, as feisty and creative as it is, does not exist in a vacuum. As has been argued throughout this work, viewed from the context of intersectionality theory, Jewish feminism does its thing amid numerous constricting and generative trends, historical legacies, and any moment's current conditions. Jewish feminist developments in the area of sexuality have been shaped by multivalent cocreated discourses, including those regarding gender, Jews, race, class, ability, nationality, immigration, and sexuality that have been constraining and productive simultaneously by related discourses that have seemed "progressive." In all, Jewish feminist engagement with sexuality in the last century has been quite active and intense, though it has not steered a straight course nor has it completely been able to leave the "constraints" in the so-called dustbin of history.

A helpful entry point in discussing specifically US Jewish feminist engagements with sexuality is the national response to the mass of immigration from Europe at the turn of and early part of the twentieth century. This focus on a defining moment for Eastern-Euro Ashkenazi Jews is crucial to exposing how Jewish feminist sexual and reproductive justice agendas are rooted and continue to be located—for all that is fabulous and all that is problematic—within this raced and culturally specific historical frame. Until we are better at naming the raced and classed nature of how we got to where we seem to be on the frontiers of Jewish and feminist sexuality explorations, we will be limited in our work for sexual and reproductive justice.

Northern European, Ashkenazi Jews have not always been the main group of Jews in the United States, although the Ashkenazi legacy has become hegemonic. This chapter will look at the origins of Jewish settlement in the United States to critically examine issues of sexual and reproductive rights and justice issues for a diverse feminist movement today. This chapter also lays the groundwork for the next chapter. From here, we can explore a more focused case study of reproductive justice in a Jewish feminist context in chapter 6.

Race and the Jewish Immigrant Angle

To consider all Jews in the United States as having a European immigrant narrative seriously obfuscates the history of US Jews. Among the first Jews to arrive in what eventually became the United States were probably Israelite-heritage slaves brought forcibly from Western Africa. These were not the immigrants of Emma Lazarus's 1883 sonnet that was eventually adapted and made part of US history, as the inscription on the base of the Statue of Liberty. The research on this remains scant and is in much need of development.[1]

The other known early group of Jews to arrive in what we now refer to as the United States were Portuguese Jews (practicing Jewish ethnic Sephardi traditions). This second group probably overlapped with the first group for a long time (Brettschneider, 2015). While there were likely a few other Sephardi Jews here before, as early as 1654, it is documented that a group of twenty-three Jews arrived in New Amsterdam. They were fleeing Portuguese Inquisition activity in the territory Portugal had conquered in Brazil (taking the area back from the more "tolerant" Dutch). It is interesting for contemporary scholars that the group contained women as well as men, suggesting that the group intended to settle here.[2] Most from that particular group did not stay, though in general the history of the Portuguese Jewish community has been studied more than the Jews of African heritage in the United States, leaving a historical record for academics. In fact, Emma Lazarus was a Sephardi Jewish poet and political actor of Portuguese ancestry, whose family settled in the United States during the colonial period.

The next group migration of Jews to the United States came from Germany in the mid-1800s. At a time when immigrants from Germany were moving to the new territories here more generally, approximately 150,000 Jews came to the United States from a range of regions, many of which were later unified into what we today refer to as Germany. Often the story of this immigration refers to economic conditions. However, from an intersectional perspective on matters of sexuality in a heterosexual context, Jewish feminist scholarship demonstrates the importance of codeveloped restrictions on Jews regarding marriage at this time as well as a primary factor in the immigration.[3]

The since the early 1900s, the majority of Jews in the United States have been of Eastern European descent. Over a period of approximately forty years, millions of poor Jews from this region came to the United States. This development changed much in the history of (US) American Jewry. Given tremendous growth of the community in such a brief period of time, when the United States was also coping with many non-Jewish immigrants from similar regions, US Jews became a focus of public opinion and policy in ways that Jews were never focused on previously in US political and ideological life.

Race, Jews, Sexuality, and Eugenics in the United States

In response to the millions of new immigrants on these shores in the early twentieth century, most fields of public and academic discourse were mobilized to respond to the "shock," "manage the problems," and plan for the future. Though the United States had always had an underclass comprised of various groups and a fear of workers standing up against the tide of capitalist "progress," this mass Eastern European immigration set the nation on edge in new ways. With more access to new technologies and faith in science, more pockets of "knowledge" could be brought together for an attempt at a systematic response to a human flood "threatening" to wash out the shining qualities of the US national character. The United States needed the people power and cheap labor of these new immigrants, but these people would also have to be housed and fed; they might be seen on the streets before or after work hours, need some degree of education for themselves and their children, and would inevitably "multiply like rabbits" . . . geometrically expanding the enormity of the threat they posed.

Turning to science, immigrant women's sexuality and reproductive habits became a focus of interest to Christian white elite Americans at this time. When the IQ test was developed, minions of researchers went to a likely place they could gather a large data set from a relatively captive population: Ellis Island. Subjecting Jewish and other immigrants to newly developed IQ test experiments in English, researchers quickly proclaimed Jews, Poles, and most of the others in the data set "feebleminded." Because this flawed research suggested such a high percentage of the feebleminded in these grouped populations, researchers quickly concluded that this feeblemindedness was genetic. This meant that not only did US policy makers, health facilities, housing boards, and other legal venues have to confront what they perceived as the challenge of the masses of feebleminded Jews before them, but—since the feebleminded were "infamous for reproducing"—plans had to be made with haste regarding the real threat of potential future generations of the "unfit."

Jewish women were targeted in plans of hygienic and eugenic campaigns. On the hygienic front, their cultural, domestic, sexual, and reproductive habits were studied and reformers set out to (re)train them. Jewish women, among others, were likened to animals and their habits were seen as "naturally primitive." Thus, the hope was that new scientific techniques could be used in their human training, and the training would allow them to be counted among more human company. For this Jewish women needed education, guidebooks, carrot-and-stick incentives (which included many state-sanctioned severe punishments) to "learn" how to keep themselves, and their homes, families, food, neighborhoods, and workplaces clean. Germ theory was being newly adapted and applied in the US-immigrant-rich context. Reformers set about their project to save the populous from infection by "germs" all too easily spread by the new immigrants. Again, though many populations of the new immigrants faced similar fates, Jews bore a special burden for fighting their infectious habits as their Polish, Italian, Russian fellow populations were, at the very least, Christian (even if so many were Catholics).[4]

Eugenic discourse flourished in the effort to slow down the growth of this lascivious and infectious population, and limit its effect on the national scene.[5] In similar ways with sometimes differing motifs, Jewish men and women were seen as sexual perverts, prone to unnatural (yet innate) behaviors such as masturbation, lesbianism/homosexuality, excessive voluptuousness and desire, wanton procreativity, and irresponsible displays of affection of all sorts. The response by reformers was to constrain Jewish women's sexuality as much as they could. In disproportionate numbers, Jewish women found themselves among the imprisoned, institutionalized, and the subjects of social worker reform. Their sexuality was seen as powerful and dangerous; they were more likely to be deemed hysterical and thus "protectively" placed in the custody of the state, health "care," and criminal "justice" systems.

We need to see the multiple modes of eugenics at work. In the case of early-nineteenth-century Eastern European Jews, as with many other communities, it was not only views about and policies targeting this population. In complex ways, the multivalent pressures of assimilation, such as discussed in chapter 3 on *The Goldbergs* and television as an example of popular culture, inspired many Jewish immigrants of this time period to aspire to participate in the increasingly hegemonic presumptions of how to protect oneself and one's family, how to become a more accepted "American."[6]

Thus, these eugenic trends also found a home among many Jews, and Jews participated widely in the dissemination of beliefs regarding, and cures to, these ills. For new Jewish immigrants, the idea of science as savior was persuasive. Social reformers did often appear to be able teach Jews much sought after "modern" ways. Many among the immigrant community did wish not to be considered feebleminded and dangerous, but to be proper "Americans." Jews wanted to make a contribution to their new home and leave behind what was cast as the clannish, unclean, primitive ways of ancestors in Europe. New, clean, shiny, healthy, educated, social reformers, and their message seemed the antidote to the confines of patriarchal traditions, overbearing parents, and small-minded shtetl mind-sets. Similarly, along with their engagement in communist, socialist, and anarchist movements, Jewish women and the Jewish community became disproportionately engaged in activism for contraception and abortion rights because these were seen as good ideas, especially for the urban poor.

Many writers have discussed the ways that by midcentury the US Jewish community, commonly associated then with Eastern European immigrant roots, underwent a race- and class-based reassignment in the taxonomies of US hierarchical thinking.[7] As discussed in chapter 3, doors stood somewhat more open for Jews to enter middle-class professions, and the perception of the community as a whole went from "other" and nonwhite to the possibility of "American" and white. Many Jews were cautious, as the costs of leaving behind aspects of what was Jewish in becoming "American" seemed great. At the same time, many wanted their second-class, suspect, and sexually/racially "other" status to end. A common American mode for ending discrimination against "others" is to try to wash out what is "other" about them. As we saw in the analysis of the work of Gertrude Berg, like our earlier twentieth-century feminist forebears, there was much that was appealing for Jewish women in this midcentury bargain.

It is not easy to resist the attraction of a potential rise in socioeconomic status, access to education, better housing opportunities, and loss of a despised public image of one's group. Thus, desires for freedom and things that suggest freedom brought many rather willingly into new versions of what might be considered a Faust-like bargain. Freedom in the United States comes in a package resembling monied, white, heterosexual, gender normative, Protestant people and cultural norms. Jewish exotic, wild, alluring, Semitic sexuality (rooted in European anti-Semitism, a fiction as much a creation of "America," as it reflected anything about actual Jewish experience) was slowly eclipsed by a fictive image of a whitewashed suburban housewife and the preparation of Jewish girls for such a "free" and "successful" future. Few actually can survive such whitewashing. Few can emerge seamlessly refigured. Certainly not everyone accepted the bargain in the first place. Not everyone thought they even had a shot—certainly if the class ladder seemed too crowded for you to climb it, if your coloring was just not white enough, your body shape too Jewish to pass in good Christian company, your hair just would not stay straight, your desires would not be properly caged.

Jewish Feminist Push Back Against/Complicating Eugenic Targeting

It is these tensions that create the conditions for more contemporary US Jewish feminist explorations regarding sexuality. For some, assimilation in these ways is deemed neither possible nor desirable, and these women have to find alternate paths to freedom, community, self-esteem, and fulfillment. It is not a criticism to point out that these very aspirations place these US Jewish feminists firmly within the historical moment, moving onward from such midcentury developments mentioned above. This is the promise to Euro-heritage Jews generally in the bargain for reassignment. Many still caught the winds of change and were enthused by the hope of promises of freedom. What were some of the issues specifically?

Lesbians and gender queers are significant examples, as discussed in chapter 4. A significant arena we will focus on here is birth control. Jewish women of all sexual and gender orientations and skin colors had been primary targets in eugenic campaigns earlier in the century, before Nazis made *eugenics* such an explicitly nasty word. Many people who were deemed "progressive" social reformers were part of the eugenics movement. Margaret Sanger's work to create a movement for birth control was driven largely by eugenic conceptualizations, and she clearly allied herself with eugenic groups. At the same time, birth control was simultaneously appealing for many women—to the degree that new technologies might become available to change the inevitability of large families, the dangers and burdens of both pregnancy and childbirth without much agency. Jewish radical free-love activists such as Emma Goldman participated in the new birth-control movement precisely because it also held promise for women's sexual freedom, even as the movement was making headway in large part through people and ideas seeking to limit Jewish birth rates for eugenic purposes.

In each era—early twentieth century, midcentury, and more contemporary times—we find Jewish women and feminist organizations at the forefront of reproductive rights campaigns as expressions of our insistence on sexual freedom. This work has largely had two primary tropes: increasing access to limiting births, and increasing births. Usually reproductive rights issues such as legalization, safety and choice in birth control, and abortion are in the camp to limit births.[8] Sometimes the work to enhance safety, such as protection from sexually transmitted diseases, falls within larger movements to limit births or to enhance them. For example, some options for birth control, such as condoms, are also promoted as safe sex methods. Addressing (often racially disparate) environmental hazards on women's reproductive capacities is also a matter of safety as well as a concern in reproductive justice circles for rights to have and raise children.

There has been a very high level of Jewish involvement (individual and organizational) in the US reproductive rights movement, such that it is a relatively mainstream issue in the US Jewish community today. It must be noted that in Jewish law as understood among contemporary global north Jewry, abortion is not prohibited. The health of the mother is generally understood to come first in any conflicts. Additionally, in Jewish tradition practiced by the majority of US Jews, foetuses are not considered "people." Referencing this cultural difference is an important resource in exposing the Christian particularity of the anti-choice movement and its rhetoric. For example, not only Jewish women's and feminist organizations, but large mainstream Jewish communal organizations in the US have placed access to safe abortions at the top of communal priorities in public health and community education, as well as decisions about which candidates to back in election years, and much lobbying activity. This work is as important for women and all those interested in family planning, as it is in interrupting explicit and implicit Christian normativity in the United States.

At the same time, the mass movements in the United States for access to birth control and abortion (movements in which Jewish individuals and communal organizations have played a leading contributing role) have been criticized by other minority groups for taking over the agenda of the reproductive rights movement. Jewish women and communal organizations seemed to have turned the eugenic origins of birth control and abortion, largely aimed at controlling Jews' reproduction and Jewish women's sexuality, into apparently unproblematic matters of freedom and gender justice. The days of poor and racially stigmatized European heritage Jews being primarily targeted for forced sterilization, institutionalization, and sexual surveillance have been significantly slowed due to that midcentury racial/class reassignment discussed in the chapter 3 on *The Goldbergs*. Other minority groups, such as Mexican-, Native-, and African-American women have not lost their target status to the same degree and thus a reproductive rights movement that focuses on the "right" to limit births remains unseemly.

Many women are still targeted for forced sterilization programs, are disproportionately under state surveillance, and are subject to punishment for their sexual lives and reproductive activity.[9] Thus, diminished social justice work on these issues in the mainstream reproductive rights movement is seen as evidence of a callous collusion with continuing racist eugenic practices. Somewhat of a split has emerged between what is often referred to as reproductive rights and reproductive justice (Smith 2005, West 2009). Jewish feminists and the US Jewish community at large remain in the forefront of the mainstream reproductive rights movement. Many Jewish feminists are proud of this. Simultaneously, many are also aware of the fraught history of the "right" to limit births, its base in raced and classed eugenic discourse, and are active in justice movements to end the continued practices of forced sterilizations. Many Jewish feminists are proud of this as well.

Jewish Feminism in US Reproductive Rights/Justice Activism

Let us take a moment to briefly review the historical role of Jewish feminists and the Jewish community at large in US reproductive rights and justice activism. Jewish organizations have long been at the center of the reproductive rights movement in the United States. Since the early nineteenth century, Jewish organizations have been leaders in this arena.[10] Jewish women immigrants from Europe were known for effectively reducing their own fertility rates before the start of the US birth control movement. Considering birth control important, Jewish women were active in the fight against the Comstock Laws in the United States, which sought to prevent citizens from talking about birth control (Silberman 2009).[11] Activists such as Emma Goldman (Ferguson 2011, Goldman 1969) and Rose Pastor Stokes (Zisper and Zisper 1989, Stokes 1916) distributed literature and lectured on the importance of contraception, courageously defying the anti-obscenity laws in effect at the time.[12] Many Jewish women got their information about birth control, health, sex, and family issues from the *Jewish Daily Forward* and other newspaper advice columns, socialist in orientation and written primarily in Yiddish, as well as from many pamphlets (Gonzalez 1997).

During the 1920s and 1930s, newly middle-class volunteer organizations such as the National Council of Jewish Women (NCJW) were frontrunners in the founding of birth control clinics across the country, then referred to as Mother's Health Bureaus (Rogow 1993). In 1932 the Brooklyn Maternal Health Center opened, operated by NCJW volunteers, expanding to three clinics over the years. By 1946 the Brooklyn Maternal Health Center linked up with Planned Parenthood, founded in 1916 (Wardell 1980), and by 1955 the Planned Parenthood committee of Brooklyn had taken on full responsibility for the clinic.

Reproductive rights activists organizing beyond Brooklyn, the Detroit NCJW section also opened a Mother's Health Clinic in 1926. The Detroit clinic was the first birth control clinic between New York and Chicago. Predating the NCJW clinic by almost forty-five years was the Young Ladies Aid Society, which became the Chicago Women's Aid and consisted primarily of Jewish members. In 1923 the Chicago Women's Aid opened a birth control clinic and sustained ties with Planned Parenthood from 1928 to 1947 (Hoggart 2000).

Despite Margaret Sanger's involvement with race-based eugenics leaders and projects that targeted Jews (Ordover 2003), many Jewish women worked closely with Sanger in the US Birth Control Movement. For example, in addition to activists such as Goldman who campaigned with Sanger, two of Sanger's assistants, Anna Lifschiz and Fania Mindell, were Jewish immigrants.[13] In addition, Jewish women directed and staffed the Birth Control Clinical Research Bureau (BCCRB) in New York in 1923, which would later be called the Margaret Sanger Bureau. Fortunately, there was a legal loophole that allowed doctors to prescribe birth control if they deemed it medically necessary.[14] The BCCRB operated five days a week with extended hours for working women, for example, allowing over five thousand women to receive treatment in 1929. The BCCRB also offered training sessions that taught doctors to fit diaphragms. Lena Levine later directed the BCCRB and helped Sanger with the founding of Planned Parenthood (Boman 2001).

Over the years, many mainstream Jewish organizations that started out as charitable groups or in support of Israel expanded their focus into reproductive rights. For example, at their 1968 convention, five years before *Roe v. Wade*, B'nai B'rith Women (BBW)—now known as Jewish Women International—called for the right to safe abortions. After *Roe v. Wade*, the 1974 BBW convention adopted a platform, "The right of a woman to plan her family through free choice must be guaranteed. Antiquated laws restricting family planning and contraception information, or forbidding abortions should be abolished" (JWI, 2013). While other racial and ethnic minority communities were also mainly concerned with the right to have children, and keep those that they birthed, large Jewish organizations of this time mainly continued the primary focus of the conceptual terrain of women's reproductive choice on contraception and abortion. The BBW stood by this platform when *Roe v. Wade* was threatened in 1989 with a Missouri case, *Webster v. Reproductive Health Services*. At its 1981 convention, Hadassah— a large American Jewish women's Zionist organization—encouraged all of its members to join abortion-rights advocacy coalitions. A wide range of Jewish women's groups long engaged in the fight for reproductive rights endorsed the Mobilize for Women's Lives Rally that was held in Washington on November 12, 1989, to defend a woman's right to choose an abortion. Among the many Jewish groups across class lines endorsing the rally were the National Council of Jewish Women, Hadassah, and the BBW.[15]

Mainstream US Jewish organizations continue to lead the way in reproductive rights struggles. For example, under the Affordable Care Act (2010), corporations are required to cover contraceptive services. However, in 2014 the *Burwell v. Hobby Lobby* ruling gave for-profit corporations the option to refuse their employees contraceptive coverage based on the owners' religious beliefs. Some versions of Christian belief forbid contraception and/or abortion. The American Jewish Committee (AJC)[16] filed an amicus brief against Hobby Lobby, arguing that women's ability to function as equal members of the economy depends on their ability to regulate their own fertility. In addition, the NCJW was one of eight Jewish groups that filed an amicus brief for this case, noting separation of church and state.

When the reproductive justice movement emerged, it became apparent that what had long been referred to in the reproductive rights movement as "choice" was different when race, ethnicity, class, gender, and other politically salient factors were taken into account. Women whose lives were impacted by different aspects of reproductive oppression sought out a more inclusive and transformative approach that reflected the experiences of their communities. Reflective of Jewish feminists' agenda in the early years of the reproductive rights movement, the reproductive justice movement combines reproductive rights with social justice issues such as economic justice, education, and immigrant rights (Kimala 2010, and with Native issues in particular and environmental factors, see Hoover et al. 2012). The overarching goals of reproductive justice are for women to have the right not to have children or to have children, and the right to parent those children they chose with dignity in safe environments. Some Jewish feminist groups have begun to note how the rights movement needs adjusting and are realigning their aims. For example, the NCJW held a national conference in March 2013, where reproductive justice was a main topic of concern. The NCJW, Jewish Women International (JWI), Religious Action Center of Reform Judaism (RAC) in association with Women of Reform Judaism (formerly the National Federation of Temple Sisterhoods), and the Religious Coalition for Reproductive Choice all collaborated to create a reproductive justice supplement to a Passover seder. The supplement retells the story of Exodus as it applies to women's lives and struggle for reproductive justice today. (The biblical Exodus story an ancient incident of eugenic sterilization given technologies of the time.) For deeper change, however, the reproductive justice movement is still fighting to be at the center of women's rights and advocacy organizations, including those led by feisty Jewish feminists, as well as by Jewish feminist and mainstream organizations.[17]

Whither Jewish Feminist Sexual and Reproductive Justice?

What is the recommendation for a future agenda here? Jewish feminists have been leaders in ritual innovation on a range of feminist and queer aspects of life. Sexual justice has been a core inspiration for much of this work. In addition, Jewish feminists must work to bring together groundbreaking developments on both sides of the reproductive rights and reproductive justice projects as part of a larger feminist vista of sexual justice.

In the past twenty years, however, our engagement in aspects of a movement to not only limit births but also to enhance fertility has been no less fraught (Shanley and Asch 2009, and Thomsen 2013). One of the tropes of eugenics was called "positive" eugenics, focusing on enabling populations deemed worthy to have more children and make the birthing process safer. Again, one can see the dual nature of such work: shouldn't all well-meaning people want to work for women's health, to ensure that pregnancies are wanted, to enable safer pregnancies and births? There has been a fine line between highly problematic right-wing efforts and "progressive reformist" ones in the developments in these arenas and their political success. Many times the subject of such work is not "women" and the realization of their full humanity, but care for potential foetuses and the angelic "unborn" (Berlant 1997). Living women often lose out when ideas about foetuses and the rights of the guiltless unborn are pitted against them. Many of the "new reproductive technologies" such as ultrasounds, genetic testing of people and foetuses, in-vitro fertilization, and surrogacy have passed the "culture police," due to how they have been able to fit into and promote fundamentalist Christian antiwomen agendas.

At the same time, Jewish doctors and scientists of all genders, and ordinary Jewish women as subjects have again been in the lead on the research and use of these techniques. Damningly, these movements for the freedom not to "have" children have somehow been divorced from the movements of other minority women to "have" children (such as the movement to end forced sterilizations and other moves to curb "overpopulation"). Again, this development places Jewish feminist and general Jewish communal leadership in certain facets of the reproductive rights movement seemingly at odds with other feminists and efforts engaged in this social justice area. Plenty remains to be done on a reconfigured agenda where Jewish feminist and larger Jewish organizations (with by now much organizational strength) can play a part in new action areas for sexual and reproductive freedom.

Another example of the multilayered role of our historical routes to contemporary Jewish feminism in the area of family planning relates to adoption practices on a social justice/sexual justice agenda. Jewish women are involved at a slightly disproportionate level in adopting children and definitely in "adoption rights" activism.[18] While this topic is the subject of its own in chapter 6, a few words are called for in the context of this chapter on Jewish feminism, race, and sexual justice. Moves to allow single women, older women, working-class women, women with some disabilities, and women (and others) outside the heterosexual norm to adopt children have spurred US Jewish feminists to their historic activist selves. Included in this agenda has been the initiative to remove the ban on "transracial" adoptions, seen from that vantage point as a remnant of Jim Crow anti-miscegenation racism. All of these aspects of adoption activism are figured in US legal parlance as "fair access" issues, a conceptual framework with which liberal Jews are historically quite comfortable. The frame of "fair access" makes sense to a population that wanted access to the goods and bounty of a nation that thinks of itself as abounding in riches. Being denied access to the "goods" which the nation has to offer (in this case, children) is a marker of discrimination, and Jewish feminists proudly put ourselves on the front lines of work against discrimination.

Similar to the other reproductive rights issues mentioned above, these aspects of the adoption rights campaign are hauntingly severed from parallel recognition and justice movements by those who, as communities, have not undergone "reassignment" from "other" to (even provisional) "member." A simultaneous movement exists to call attention to the fact that adoption policies focused on access in the ways named above gain ground at the direct expense of other minority and poor women (Roberts 1997 and 2002). The pool of children to which adults seek to gain access comes from somewhere. Easier access to adoption has been made possible by clearing a path toward terminating certain parents' rights. It is no coincidence that the groups disproportionately found among the early terminations are poor women, women of color, and third world women, who in this example are generally not Jewish (and if mixed, have not largely been Jewish-identified and supported by Jewish institutions). The domestic growth of a prison nation, with skyrocketing numbers of women in prison and on parole, has meant more children than ever before are in the foster care system.

The movement for adoption access has tried to move children from foster care to adoption available with greater "ease" and swiftness. Publically, the rationale for this is to assist youth languishing in problematic and temporary foster situations. Speeding up the foster care to adoption pipeline also makes it far more difficult for poor women and women of color and all in the criminal justice and welfare systems to hold onto the parental rights to their children or to fight to keep their children in foster care and out of an adoption track (Ronnell 2004). Again, options for future agendas for Jewish feminists abound, including closing the gap between these two social justice movements in which Jewish feminists and large Jewish communal organizations play such central roles—as activists, lawyers, policy makers, researchers, social workers, community organizers, comrades, birth parents, and potential adoptive parents.

In all of this, it remains fatally misleading to assume that the Jewish feminists involved are now "reassigned" and "are" white and middle class, whereas the "other" feminists are poor and people of color who are not Jewish. We are at a crossroads in Jewish feminism, where we must recognize the politics and costs of the racial positioning of Jewish feminists who understand themselves as and/or are often perceived as "white." Our image of our communal selves must come to include—and be transformed in the process—the millions of nonwhite/Ashkenazi/Euro-heritage Jews and those related Jewishly among us.

We must take note of the large numbers of those Jewishly identified and related who do not identify as Ashkenazi, white, and/or of European heritage. According to demographic studies—based on combinations of mainstream sources such as the US Census, the National Jewish Population Survey, and the Institute for Jewish and Community Research Study—about 20 percent of the approximately six million people in the United States who identify as "currently Jewish" are in this category. There are about another one million people not identified as part or all white/Ashkenazi/Euro-heritage among the groups identifying as having a Jewish heritage—16 percent of over four million people (perhaps not practicing now, or children of Jewish fathers not raised within Jewish communities)—and "connected non-Jews"—about 10 percent of two and a half million people (such as non-Jewish spouses in families raising their children as Jews) (see Tobin, Tobin, & Rubin 2005, 23).

There is much Jewish multiracial and multiheritage engagement in feminist movements for sexual freedom, despite the fact that much of Jewish leadership (individually and institutionally) remains largely Euro/Ashkenazi-heritage/white-light skinned. Jewish feminist leadership in certain aspects of work for sexual justice does not fully reflect the range of multiracial Jewish feminist experience and activist potential. We can work together to reshape the nature of our work in sexual justice movements in ways that directly reflect also how Jewish women of color face antifeminist and raced-sexual profiling in the United States today. In the following chapter and the conclusion, we will explore some examples in more detail.

Chapter 6

Reproductive Justice

Costs of Increased Adoption Access

Introduction

It is time for us to look into a matter of reproductive justice in an intersectional Jewish feminist context. As a work of intersectionality, this chapter's focus is on ways that race and ethnicity are politicized and created by the state in imbricating ways with other politically salient identity signifiers such as sexuality and gender where Jews (and Jewish feminist aspirations) are directly involved. I look at apparent progressive victories for women, GLBT adults and frequently Jews (in the other categories as well) regarding adoption and ask at what costs such apparent achievements have been attained.

This chapter focuses on increased adoption access by bringing down barriers to transracial placements and swifter foster-care-to-adoption timelines (through the Adoption and Safe Families Act or ASFA). As noted in chapter 5, large-scale US reproductive rights activism has often focused on making safe and legal the ability of women to limit births though knowledge, contraception, and abortion. Earlier in the 1900s, Jewish women did have trouble with forced sterilization and being able to raise the children they birthed. This issue did not, however, make it onto what became the large-scale reproductive rights agenda. Because of poverty, displacement, and language barriers, Jewish women were often not able to parent their own children. As in many poor and minority communities, webs of neighbors, extended family, and communal institutions were used often for informal foster and adoption purposes. Still, the medical establishment and the state did take an active role in that Jewish women were subject to involuntary sterilization, and institutionalized without their consent for activities (among others) such as being what was considered sexually "queer," promiscuous, and having too many babies.

Over time, a new vision of reproductive justice emerged from within movements of women of color and their allies to focus on barriers for women to getting pregnant, birthing children, and being able to raise the children they birth (Price 2010, Silliman et al. 2004, Hoover et al. 2012, West 2009). At the time that Jewish women were among priority targets in this sphere, the infrastructure of social work and foster care that we have today was not in place the way that it became later in the century. Adoption was not formalized until after World War II. The system of often community-based orphanages, which frequently served a function similar to foster care (temporary support of children whose guardians could not take care of them) was morphed into increasingly systematized and policed foster care and adoption. When Jewish children were adopted by strangers, records were regularly altered to hide the Jewish background of the children or placement with a Christian family was extremely unlikely. Adoption of Jewish children, even if of European background, was considered a cross-racial and cross-cultural match, as European Jews were generally not considered white, their Jewishness making them other in numerous co-constructed ways in Christian (US) America. Also, at this time, stealing Native American infants to be raised as white Christians was still all too common (Brettschneider 2006).

Complications in developments regarding expanding practices of transracial adoption since the 1990s are situated firmly within this arena. This chapter argues that the primary cost of increased access is the capacity for Black women, generally not Jewish in this context, to keep existing families intact. Latinas and Native Americans face similar circumstances. However, in the adoption world, there is a longer history of placing Latin@ and Native American children in transracial situations because, like many Euro-Jewish-heritage children, they could often be passed off as white. Increased access is true for primarily Christian white-coded and monied adults, in this case where in particular many GLBTQ people and/or Jewish adults seek to mobilize their privilege (however unconsciously) for such access. However, Black women, across sexualities, disproportionately pay the price to increase the adoption pool.

Characteristic of feminist theory in the later second wave, and critical race theories of the same era, was eschewing the notion of a hierarchy of oppressions. As we have noted in intersectionality studies, as identity-related progressive and radical theorists and activists analyze power, emphasis can be placed on the mutual construction of multiple identity markers instead of (1) either a focus on one axis of power and oppression (such as race or gender) and (2) ranking differential modes of oppression in relative terms. This has been a helpful move in the examination of, and efforts at challenging, inequalities in power. At the same time, however, as individuals, groups, and citizens, we continually face attempts to separate, categorize, and rank humans in our interactions as we ourselves constitute the state. This chapter looks at navigating the precarious balances of power we are constantly forced into in society, despite the theoretical and activist attempts to unthink these very paradigms.

For this exploration I use a case study of the racialized power dynamics in changing US adoption law and practices. There are multiple hierarchies of human worth operating within this arena.[1] Here I focus on the constellation of legislative moves, mostly in the mid-1990s, which not only turned more women of color into "birth mothers" (women who have relinquished their parental rights to children who are then entered into the adoption market), but also explicitly gave more white-coded women, GLBTQ people, including Euro-heritage Jewish women and GLBTQ people at this historical moment in the United States, access to the children of this expanding class of women. Included in the 1996 Personal Responsibility Act (commonly referred to as Welfare Reform)[2] was a little-known provision that expanded transracial adoption options. (In the US, "transracial adoption" almost exclusively refers to a case of white-coded adults adopting children coded as "of color.")[3] There is much to be said in favor of transracial adoption, and I personally am a Jewish European-heritage, light-skinned adoptive mother of African-American children. At the same time, however, I argue that this particular piece of legislation needs to be seen as part of a multipronged attack on women of color—through antigay legislation, anti-immigrant policies, intensified drug criminalization, and welfare cutbacks. Here is a rich, albeit extremely troubling, example wherein women, perceived as a group, and GLBT folk (through progressive efforts to end restrictions on GLBT people adopting) were portrayed as "winning" rights while the rights of specific women and queers racialized as "other" in the law were being restricted. Jewish women are not included in most academic studies of this phenomenon; however, Jews adopt in the United States at a slightly higher rate than their percentage represented in the general population. In addition, due to their continued overwhelmingly liberal politics on domestic issues, Euro-heritage US Jews in the current political context, often coded as "white" in academic feminist work, are generally actively supportive of the progressively framed transracial adoption, and this practice is widely supported in the US Jewish community.

In this chapter I will examine the case study as an intersectional critical theorist, doing applied theory most explicitly in this chapter of this book. I ask, How do a range of intersectional critical theories (feminist, Jewish, queer, race, class-based) assist us in challenging power in our concrete relationships within bureaucratic and legislative state systems? How can we mobilize such theories within mundane frameworks that demand our separation and ranking? In short, how can we make practical use of intersectional critical theories about power that refuse to separate and hierarchically order the worth of humans while resisting existing state systems that require exactly such separation and ordering?

Setting the Stage

While discrimination remains intense, in the late 1990s many queers and historically "less desirable" groups of women such as single, older, and Jewish women were being told that their chances for adopting children were getting better. The moment was being framed as an era of equality and freedom for queers and other "others" interested in forming families with children. Primarily, however, it was gay men and lesbians being referenced, not bisexuals, trans, and other queers. Most people are unaware of the anti-Semitism operating that presents significant barriers for Jews to adopt in the United States (Brettschneider 2006).

Also, while there was some opening at this time for adults of color to adopt children, this was mostly an opening for white-coded adults. Being white in the adoption world increases one's market value—whether you are a birth mother, a child, or a prospective parent.[4] Euro-Jewish adults seeking to build families in this historical moment had an investment in naming themselves, and accepting the coding by others, as "white." Before being eligible for adoption, a child is placed into foster care while the state determines the capacity of the prospective adoptive household as a family unit. Children are entered into foster care for many reasons, for example, if their parents or guardians are unavailable or unable to take care of them as a result of unexpected illness or an accident. Parents can also become suddenly unavailable to parent if they are incarcerated. Children may be placed in foster care after being removed from parental care if such care is deemed inadequate. Black children are more likely than white children to be placed in foster care—even when combined with other predictors such as abuse allegations, child disability, parental substance abuse, and Medicaid benefits (Hill 2006; Hill 2005a). There are similarities here of the disproportionate scrutiny and penalizing judgment to which Black women today and Euro-Jewish women historically have been subject. But the formalization of these processes, in the combination with the legislative moves to be discussed, have transformed the terrain significantly since Euro-Jewish women were the primary targets of these penal controls.

Since the late 1980s, throughout the country, moves have been made to bring down barriers for queers and others wanting to adopt children who were previously degraded in the adoption market.[5] A 1997 study of Americans' views about gays and lesbians found that a majority supported adoption rights for gay and lesbian couples. There are states that still expressly discriminate against lesbians and gays in the adoption process. As of this writing, in many states gay couples, on a case-to-case basis, must go through a judge in order to adopt. On the other hand, there are sixteen states that have made joint gay adoption legal: Arkansas, California, Colorado, Connecticut, DC, Illinois, Indiana, Iowa, Maine, Massachusetts, Nevada, New Hampshire, New Jersey, New York, Oregon, Vermont, and Washington. Same gender couples can currently complete a "second parent same-gender adoption" in the following sixteen states: Alabama, Alaska, Delaware, Hawaii, Iowa, Louisiana, Maryland, Minnesota, Nevada, New Hampshire, New Mexico, North Carolina, Oregon, Rhode Island, Texas, and Washington (LifeLong Adoptions 2014). Studies show that the profile of gay and lesbian adults adopting are disproportionately white and monied. Monied Euro-Jewish gay and lesbian adults made use of this development more often than acting against it.

Unfortunately, in the United States, too often rights and capacities for some come at the expense of rights and abilities for others. This opening for women in "less desirable" adoption categories, as well Jews and gays and lesbians, directly involves a war on minority communities. In 1996 the US Congress passed a related set of laws—laws banning queers from marrying, and laws regarding immigrants, and welfare. These laws, in conjunction with earlier federal antidrug laws, constituted the legal context of the expansion of particular adoption options.

The most important feature of these interlocking legislative moves for the current discussion is a little-known provision in the welfare law changing the legal tenor for transracial adoption. Further, in the mid-1990s, new legislation changed foster-to-adoption precedents and explicitly eased the way for creating interracial families through adoption.[6]

Under the 1996 Interethnic Adoption Provisions, agencies that receive federal funding can no longer use race and ethnicity to deny or delay a foster care or adoptive placement.[7] This Provision was followed up in 1997 with ASFA, which expressly sought to eliminate delays in foster care to adoption procedures. While targeting Jews for differential treatment in US adoption practices is not legal, many agencies are private, Christian, and distinctly biased against placing children with Jewish adults. Additionally, despite the law, many workers in state-level social services mobilize their anti-Jewish bias, barring adult Jews from placements. With the proliferation of small agencies, brokers, and connectors, as well as the Internet to help connect individuals to organizations beyond geographic confines, Jews have slightly more agency in adopting in the United States than they have had previously in history (Brettschneider 2006).

These laws were characterized as gains for marginalized groups within the adoption market (women, gays and lesbians, and Jews) or more broadly as a progressive victory as a blow against racism. There has also been a correlating dynamic threatening women of color—straight or queer. During this time, the state attained wider access into the lives and autonomy of women of color.

Antidrug Legislation

By 1996, 1980s mandatory drug sentencing brought women of color, in particular, into the prison-industrial complex at faster rates than before. Although these laws were touted as new effective measures to target major drug dealers, the laws were used more frequently for small-time drug offenders, including women in the criminal justice system, in unprecedented ways, and the rates of women in prison for small drug infractions skyrocketed.[8] The racial differential in the 433 percent increase breakdown (between 1986 and 1991) of this overall figure is staggering: a 241 percent increase for white women and an 828 percent increase for African-American women. Of particular concern for this paper is also that the average age range of the women impacted falls within prime childbearing years, and prime years for many women mothering young children.

The state's increased involvement in the lives of African-American women resulting from the enforcement of new drug infraction laws also increased the state's involvement in these women's families, including increased interruptions to these women's capacities to parent. Since 1991, the number of children with a mother in prison has more than doubled. As a result of the 1980s drug laws, Black women have been more likely than others to have the soundness of their families called into question, and more Black children are now likely to have their mothers deemed criminals. More than half of all mothers in state and federal prisons are Black, and

Black children are over seven times more likely to have a parent in prison than are white children. Further, more than 6 percent of children in foster care have been removed because of parental incarceration. By the 1990s, the "War on Drugs" had enabled the state to increase the pool of potentially eligible adoptive children at the expense of their Black mothers' rights.

1996 Welfare Reform

In 1996, Congress passed the Personal Responsibility and Work Opportunity Reconciliation Act, also commonly referred to as "welfare reform." The intent was to change welfare as we have known it in this country, generally seeking to drastically reduce the number of clients on welfare.[9] Many facets of the act targeted women and mothers. The act brought the state further into the lives of many women of color, in particular, who are disproportionately poor and also poor women of color who are mothers. Black women held a disproportionate place among those kicked out of the welfare system, resulting in increased economic hardship. With the poor already under state surveillance, welfare reform increased the state's involvement in qualifying and classifying families, disproportionately Black, as adequate or inadequate, in part due to a decrease in the resources available to families that help them to qualify as fit. Thus, since welfare reform, more women of color have had their children forcibly removed from their custody.

1996 Defense of Marriage Act

Although gays and lesbians are often perceived in mainstream media to be "white," obviously they are among all communities. This problem of erasing people of color operates in multiple ways. The 1996 Defense of Marriage Act (DOMA) and its overturn in 2013 was a case in point. DOMA stipulated that marriage consists only of a legal union between a man and a woman. While DOMA was a setback in GLBT rights and was said to signal an era of a retraction of GLBT family rights more broadly, it further increased barriers to financial stability and state involvement in the lives of Black lesbian mothers particularly.[10]

The existing US gender gap in wages means that female same-gender couples are disproportionately economically disadvantaged compared to different-gender couples and male same-gender couples. Further, studies show that as a group, lower-income Black lesbians would most likely benefit in legalizing same-gender marriage. This is due to the prevalence of Black lesbians with children, and particularly with high rates of civil service employment (meaning those working in jobs that do have health care and other benefits, given that many jobs—especially for the poor—do not carry benefits). The passage of DOMA, which meant continuing to bar same-gender couples from marriage and its related benefits at the federal level, most directly hurt Black lesbians with children by denying health care and other benefits for children and partners, significantly disadvantaging them economically. This increased the likelihood that families headed by Black lesbians would be involved with the state welfare system. The effect of retracting DOMA remains to be seen and studied. But we have lived with more than a decade of the impact of DOMA, which this chapter takes into account.

1996 Immigration Laws

Since September 11, 2001, the forced registrations, arrests, and detention of immigrants, targeting populations of Muslims, Arabs, Middle Easterners, and South Asians in the United States are aspects of the evolving methodology of strengthening the military industrial complex more generally. Laws passed in the mid- to late 1990s to limit the mobility and choices of immigrants were only sporadically enforced, and resistance to them had nearly succeeded in getting them overturned, when the events of September 11 occurred. After that day, not only were these laws not repealed, but they were both stepped up and more systematically implemented.

The growth of the immigrant population in detention came as a more recent extension of the boom in the criminalization of the public resulting from domestic "wars" on drugs. Post–September 11 antiterrorist laws have also been used to more effectively police domestic peoples of color.[11] Again, these developments, supposedly cracking down on illegal immigration, brought more women of color into the prison system, dismantled families of color, and increased the state's access into the lives of women of color and their children.

The Adoption and Safe Families Act

On the heels of the transracial adoption provision of welfare reform passed in 1996, the 1997 Adoption and Safe Families Act (ASFA) provided a set of state adoption timeliness measures for placing foster children in permanent homes. However, from the perspectives of the families whose children are removed under these measures, ASFA (combined with increased access of adult whites to children of color) was highly oppressive. Increasing access to children for some, especially in the context of ASFA, also means severing ties of existing families, often painfully and problematically. Race here remains a significant factor, making ASFA's impact—compounding the transracial adoption provision's effect—racially unjust.

Among the implications of 1980s drug laws and the relevant 1996 legislation named here (regarding welfare, immigration, and same gender marriage) have been that women of color generally faced increased challenges economically and in their capacities to keep their families intact. ASFA then increased the state's interest in terminating parental rights and removed support services from family reunification efforts. Created by the Interethnic Adoption Provisions of the 1996 Welfare Reform, ASFA increased the likelihood that children of color would be included in the expanding eligible pool that gay and lesbian and other previously excluded white-coded adults, such as single women, older adults, and European-heritage Jews could adopt.

Since ASFA, the number of children in foster care whose parents' rights have been terminated increased from 10.7 percent (1998) to 17 percent (2007). At the same time, states did not report much innovation in reunifying families. This decrease in support services comes at the greatest cost to Black families and children because it directly decreases the likelihood of Black families, in particular, attaining services that would help them qualify as eligible to keep their children with them. In comparison with whites, Black children and families receive fewer and lower-quality services in the child welfare system: fewer foster parent support services, contacts by caseworkers, access to mental health services, and access to drug treatment services (Hill, 2006).

Not only are Black families more likely to be separated by foster care placement, but Black children are less likely to be reunified with their biological families. Once their children are placed in foster care, Black women are more likely to lose them. The state is more likely, and timelier in efforts, to reunify white children who have been placed in foster care with their biological parents than it is with Black children. Even when parents demonstrate the same job skills, substance abuse problems, and have received the same services, the Black families are more likely to be broken and kept apart.

Significantly also for this study, the increase in average sentencing stays since the early 1990s (given new drug and anti-immigration legislation) converges with ASFA's provisions that seek to accelerate timely adoption processing. States' new decreased time-frames for seeking termination of parental rights creates a distinct disincentive for child welfare workers to do meaningful and individualized case-planning. This is then especially so regarding needs of children in foster care with an incarcerated parent. Thus, between 1997 (ASFA's passage) and 2002, parental rights termination proceedings of incarcerated parents more than doubled.

Legislation from 1996 Onward: Linking the War on Women of Color and New Efforts Supporting Transracial Adoption

Formal adoption is a recent development, which began as a strictly race-matching escapade (despite all the forging of documents this required!).[12] As part of a new movement against racism in the United States, in the post-1960s era, many "white"-coded progressive adults (this included a number of newly white-coded Jews) sought explicitly to adopt nonwhite children. There were of course many different understandings of what these white adults were doing. Some understood themselves as "just" building their families, now simply without regard to race. Some sought to personalize their political commitments against poverty in racially marginalized communities by raising racially minority children. Many sought to challenge efforts at creating mono-racial families, long at the core of race-based genocide in this country, with the adoption apparatus mimicking this process.

In the 1970s, the new experiment of transracial adoption had mostly come to a halt. Many cite the public statement made by the National Association of Black Social Workers discouraging the practice, as they assessed the new trend in adoption as yet another form of cultural genocide.[13] For many progressives, the NABSW analysis was at the core of shifting attitudes favoring same-race adoption placements once again. However, in racist (US) America, policy and practice dominated by the elite is not usually first motivated by minority communities' needs, as expressed in their own voices. Politics is a complex business. The move away from transracial placements was sought by a number of prominent public figures in the Black community. It also clearly served to reinforce white supremacist concerns against racial mixing.[14]

In the 1980s and early 1990s, transracial placements in adoption were either expressly discouraged or implicitly avoided in most states and by many individual agencies. 1996 was a historical moment in the aftermath of *University of California v. Bakke,* and many other efforts to undo policies and practices that had emerged which named racial difference for the purposes of ending racial discrimination. At that moment many white folk, claiming to speak for progressives generally, began to make public headway in the effort to yet again "ban the ban" on transracial adoption. I have no doubt that many who led this fight sought justice as they understood it.[15] It also must be said that such efforts helped pave the way for new versions of anti–women of color legislation. Included in the 1996 Personal Responsibility Act was a change in the law regarding transracial adoption.[16] The multipronged attack on women of color—through DOMA, anti-immigrant policies, intensified drug criminalization, and welfare cutbacks—included provisions making it easier for white adults to adopt the biological children of women of color.

Many have described this move as a renewal of the white savior strategy to end "the race problem" in the US. This understanding of the race problem recognizes the incredible disparity between the lives of people according to race, and the tremendous disadvantages faced by those within minority communities. Long a staple of Christian/white identity construction, the more white/Christian one is, the better off one is. In this analysis of the race problem, however, the equation is not merely empirical. This is to say that wealth, health, status, agency, and other important differentials that fall into a racialized hierarchy are not simply matters one can quantify—and then leave room to critically untangle the web of racism that has brought us to this day. Instead, in this view, white/Christian identity is *essentially* understood to be associated with more dignified humanity. The twist has long been that various groups have vied for, and been sought out for, designation in this group, as many would argue, including many European-heritage Jews. To be *white* then meant one *was* better off. After years of analyzing the failure of civil rights to affect equality in the US, many have revived the essentialized notion that the problem is not discrimination against Blackness—but Blackness, or other minority status, itself.[17]

This movement drew on historic policies denying women of color's reproductive rights (in many ways differently than the denial of elite women's reproductive rights).[18] Related to DOMA, and in conjunction with anti-immigrant and antidrug laws, the 1996 welfare reform sought to solve the race problem by whitening as many Black and other minority children as it could. Taking children of color away from their bio-families and making it easier to place them with white families was a strategy to solve the "race problem" by a new mode of cultural genocide.[19] The thinking was: if raised by "good" white families, Black kids can *be* white, and thus avoid Moynihan's notion of generational cycles of poverty and loosening of moral stature.[20] We can see the continued anxiety that being better off and not living a base-line existence suggests the loss of black identity in ABC's 2014 sitcom Black-*ish*. In this case, the television family is heterosexually biologically related and all black, but upwardly mobile and currently living in a middle-class suburb. The challenges faced by the fictive Goldberg family discussed in chapter 3 are not over in assimilationist US society.

What is often missed in analyses of the tripartite set of laws targeting minorities through the hand of the INS—post–September 11 folded under the umbrella Department of Homeland Security, drug enforcement, and welfare workers—is the ways these laws turned so many more minority women into the "birth mothers" of adopted children than in previous history. At this historical moment, Jews as a group, even presumed to be Euro-heritage, are being coded less frequently as racial minority, for all the actual racial complexity in the adoption world on the ground.

Conclusion

US law notes that separating children from their families has been part of longer-term genocidal policies against Native Americans. Historical analysis demonstrates a similar situation for Jews in the United States. However, a similar argument that severing ties between biological African-American families and making the children available for adoption to white people also constitutes genocide has been far more controversial.

As we found in urban areas of the 1900s with Jews, the method of removing children from homes in certain communities to whiten them was a favorite in the 1800s with respect to Native children. Legal efforts at whitening Native Americans operated by forcibly removing their children and placing them in "good Christian" homes and Christian boarding schools. As this was prior to the racial reclassification of many Euro-heritage Jews, though few in number in the United States at the time, Jews as a group absolutely would not have qualified as operating "good" homes. It was also quite effective in terms of devastating Native communities, cultures, identities, and modes of survival. Separating children from their families has largely come to be recognized as part of longer-term genocidal policies against Native Americans. US law acknowledges this situation to a large degree. The 1978 Indian Child Welfare Act states clearly that "an alarmingly high percentage of Indian [*sic*] families are broken up by the removal, often unwarranted, of their children from them by nontribal public and private agencies and that an alarmingly high percentage of such children are placed in non-Indian [*sic*] foster and adoptive homes and institutions" and requires placing Native children in Native homes.[21] However, when Dorothy Roberts (2002) argues that similar trends in severing ties between biological African-American families and making the children available for adoption to white people also constitutes genocide, many people—including many progressive white people in the adoption world—cannot hear the argument.[22]

We cannot predict specific, comprehensive, or linear outcomes of the 1996-plus legislation that made it easier to make transracial adoptive placements in the new Christian millennium along with the demise of DOMA. In what ways is it good, or not, for the children? In what ways is it good, or not, for communities of color? What potential avenues are opened for interrupting racism or broadened for reinscribing racism, even if in new ways? How are queers factoring into these new racialized systems? How are queers and women and Jews (and those who are all) as groups helped and harmed, and how are we differentially affected depending on race and class? How are homophobia and efforts to resist heterosexism and anti-Semitism still at work in the constantly changing adoption world?

It is clear, in the meantime, that there is a relationship between new versions of a war on women of color and the budding market in transracial adoption that is considered good for those in previously discriminated against groups of prospective parents in the adoption world, such as women, GLBT, older people, Jews, and all those that cross these groups.

The combination of DOMA (until its overturn) and increased access, particularly for GLBT adults across the categories of Jews, women, and so on, to form families appear as contradictions. These two signal trends seem paradoxical only if one uses a monoracial, white lens that folds US Jews (assumed to be all Euro-heritage) into this framework. When the experiences of Black lesbians, for example, are included in the analysis, these apparent contradictions recede. Both together form a portrait of barriers for Black women, of any sexual and cultural orientation, to form families and to keep their families together. Increased access for GLBT adults and other formerly marginalized prospective parents in adoption circles, to the extent that it comes through increased access to transracial adoptive placements and/or swifter foster care–adoption tracks, mainly benefit white and monied GLBT and other adults, who are the vast majority of adopters. Black women bear the brunt of the burden for such increased access.

Touted as progressive victories in foster care and adoption practices and access, legislation of the late 1990s also comes at great costs. Black women, who are disproportionately responsible for Black families, are also increasingly disadvantaged economically. More Black women than previously in history are engaged in state welfare and surveillance systems through welfare monitoring and increased criminalization with newly designed drug and anti-immigration laws. The expanded pool of potentially adoptable children, praised by white liberal advocates, is disproportionately created by severing the ties of Black families. For purposes of increased access in adoption, many Euro-heritage Jews have (consciously or unconsciously) opted for attempting to be on the white side of the Black/white divide that is still all too operative in the United States today. While there is not a one-to-one correspondence between white-coded adoptive parents succeeding in their aspirations to adopt children and each case of a Black woman being thwarted in her fight to keep her bio-family intact, the larger system trends suggest at the very least an important linkage. As Jewish feminists, as well as other feminist and queers explore their "expanding" access in adopting, it will be important for ordinary people and scholars to continue to closely mark the correlation of the cost of such changing access. It is in all of our interests to redirect current policies, beliefs, and practices to support Black women in strengthening their families, as many of us seek to grow the capacity for all families to become stronger.

Conclusion

Jewish Race Segregation and Jewish Feminism

Introduction

On an *erev* Shabbat, our home phone rang a number of times. The caller was insistent and we weren't answering. My older daughter realized the calls were from her sister's school. She was afraid; she was afraid her sister was in trouble.

At the time, my younger daughter attended the Abraham Lincoln School, a local public school. Contrary to the way the children there are taught the story, I explain that Abraham Lincoln did not free the slaves. Abraham Lincoln was the president of the country when everyone who worked so hard for so long brought legal slavery to an end. Still, it is a source of pride and inspiration for an African-American child to attend a school attempting to make good on Lincoln's legacy to end racial slavery and hatred. We still face that battle. As Michael Brown in Ferguson, MO knew, and as relayed in the stories of my then-nine-year-old, racial hatred and its deadening consequences continue to be part of the daily landscape. But why was my kid in trouble that day at the Abraham Lincoln School, and what does it have to do with Jewish feminism?

It turns out that the incessant caller was a senior Lincoln School administrator, Mrs. Oleary. There was a "small incident" at school that day. Mrs. Oleary overheard a boy say something to my daughter (which I refuse to repeat) that "accounted for" why her skin is brown. Mrs. Oleary wanted to assure me that she does not approve of such language and that appropriate action had been taken. I asked what kind of appropriate action and was informed that the boy's parents had been contacted and the parents were disciplining him. This privatized course of action for a public school on an issue as systemic as racism did not seem appropriate to me, but that's only part of the story.

Mrs. Oleary wanted me to know "that sort of behavior is not tolerated" at the Abraham Lincoln School, and that the issue had been taken care of. When she used the word *tolerated* my brain waves reorganized. I then understood something that had been going on that afternoon, which until that moment I had not yet grasped. My daughter had been agitated after school and saying something like, "I am not tolerated at school." She was also afraid of how much trouble she would be in at home for how much trouble she had been in earlier at school. Mrs. Oleary said, "I have no idea how she could have gotten that idea. I was very careful to explain and I asked her if she understood what I was saying."

What had happened? An incident had occurred that day in school and, among other things, my daughter was hauled into the principal's office, heard phrases like "not tolerated here" and "could be suspended for this," and she assumed it was *she* who was in trouble. What might be helpful to relate at this point is that pretty much all the teachers and other professionals in the Lincoln School are white women (as they are in most of the US). Almost all the kids are brown skinned of one sort or another. My daughter had friends at school, liked her teachers, and felt known and loved by her principal. On any given day she will have had some fun, learned a thing or two, and have been a somewhat successful product of the civic training elementary schools are intended to provide. There are many facets to a life; she was, and continues to be, these years later, the target of racist, sexist, and homophobic harassment daily. My sixteen-year-old African-American daughter is consistently subject to anti-Semitic stereotyping. Back to this story . . .

When I told Mrs. Oleary of my child's understanding of the incident and its aftermath, Mrs. Oleary was defensive, explaining herself, rather than inquiring about my daughter's well-being. Yes, Mrs. Oleary is white, and by this time I was getting frustrated with her. It was *erev* Shabbat in our home—the home of the rabbi in the only synagogue in our city and of the only known/out Jewish child at the Abraham Lincoln School.[1] Segregation. In response to Mrs. Oleary's repeated defensive semirhetorical query, "How could she have thought that?" I eventually huffed something to the effect that we live in a racist society where African Americans are taught at an early age to be responsible for other people's racism.

With that, she finally replied to what I was actually saying by referencing a distant relative who has two Black children. Having established her credentials, she could thus assure me that she totally understood what I was saying and could feel what my daughter was feeling. I got off the phone relatively pissed off, and realized I needed to check in with my kid who had experienced yet another racist incident and was afraid that it was she who was in trouble.

Interestingly, my daughter no longer seemed as agitated about the event as the ever-vigilant Mrs. Oleary. Despite all the posters in the school about bullying and hate speech, incidents such as this were (and remain since) a regular occurrence for my daughter at the elementary school (and then at her middle and high school). Mrs. Oleary randomly overheard one exchange between two children in the hallway that day and swooped in like the great white hope—calling over and over on a Friday night, yet referring to the situation as "small." I assume she meant well. I came to feel that she actually didn't have many tools with which to address her legitimate concern about racism or what presented itself as a deeper reality (my daughter's confusion, the repetition of racist acts) when she tried to take action. She did not understand how her well-intentioned attempt at an antiracist intervention created additional stress. She did not apparently think for a moment about how, by telephoning over and over on *erev* Shabbat, she was shattering one of the child's rare moments of peace from her pretty constant struggle in a racist society.

When my kid talked to me (not the first time) about the many interactions among which this particular incident is but one example, she explained that her teacher says, "The boy does things like that to her because he likes her." Wow. Among other things, that means the teacher was aware that such things occur more regularly than this supposedly one-time significant, yet "small," incident.

It is important to note that I liked this teacher a lot. Still, I was angry about the teacher's response, which excuses boys and lets them off the hook for heterosexual violence against girls. As a feminist, I understand that the teacher is actively teaching girls to expect, accept, and even be flattered by such abuse. The teacher participates in how boys grow up without many touchstones of accountability or a critical self-awareness of their privilege and its violent outlets. Perpetuating this dynamic narrows girls' options for developing a critical framework in which to put their individual icky experiences in a social context of power dynamics. When a teacher tells individual girls that boys are abusive because they like you, it deprives girls of the camaraderie of bonding with other targets of heterosexual male violence and finding their own ways to push back and develop agency.

At the time of this incident, I had been preparing a presentation for a group of Jewish feminists on the state of antiracism in Jewish feminist academic work. Feminism has given me many tools to help my daughter with parts of what had happened that day, but then I asked myself what *Jewish* feminism would have to offer my daughter in this story. Where were we, Jewish feminists, for her? What did our academic work have to offer her to get through this one racist incident, to get through a day, to get through the third grade? I would like to conclude this book on Jewish feminism and intersectionality with my provisional response.

Again, the point of this work is not to focus on the absence of Jewish material in the general feminist intersectionality literature. Instead, it is to do the work of Jewish feminist intersectionality itself. In these chapters I have presented a variety of ways to approach this field, situating the examinations within different major areas of feminist theory: subfields of feminist theory such as diaspora theory, popular culture, and sexual, gender, and reproductive justice. I bring this series of explorations to a close here with a pointed argument as to why critical race work is inherent in the Jewish feminist project. It is not an optional item to add to one's political to-do list, not a choice as to when one has time to be an antiracist worker. It is central to any work of Jewish feminism, however one identifies racially.

Naming the Problem: Jewish Feminism, Antiracism, and Racial Segregation

As has been demonstrated throughout this work, there have been many important works by Jewish feminists that offer, and help us all to develop, different antiracist analyses. Many of these works are not positioned as specifically Jewish feminist work.[2] There are also many Jewish feminists who care deeply about racism, many of whom are actively engaged in general anti-racist projects, or support critical race studies as an academic field.[3] We can also find an increasing incredible collection of writing in which Jewish feminists are doing anti-racist work *as* Jewish feminists.[4] As important as this writing and activism are, and are to me personally, race and racism are still not sufficiently on the radar screen of what is currently published as Jewish feminist work.

As rich as Jewish feminist intersectionality work has been (even if not using that name), if I scan book indexes and tables of contents of Jewish women's and feminist books, magazines, and journals, unfortunately most of the work contained there does not place race as a principal aspect of analysis, nor does it incorporate others' works that do so as central to framing its own projects. While I would still hold that Jewish feminists are among those generally to be relied on in antiracist struggles,[5] a gap remains here that is crucial to our need for Jewish feminism itself. There is too wide a gap between the good intentions and hard work of so many Jewish feminists against racism on the ground, and the lack of serious and critical attention to race in what is generally published as academic (and other) Jewish feminist writing.

This gap is a problem. This gap is dangerous. It is not a problem because I want this movement that I care about to "look good" to others. It is not dangerous because we risk losing "allies" to have when Jews are attacked. Fundamentally, for me, the chasm between real-life antiracist commitments of so many Jewish feminists and the absence of antiracist analysis within most of Jewish feminist writing is a problem because I need Jewish feminism to help me be in the world. My being in the world, among other excruciatingly important things, is hindered by racism, and if Jewish feminism can't help me with that, then Jewish feminism is failing me.

Obviously, this is not just about me; it is about all of us. Specifically, Jewish feminism needs to be able to speak clearly to matters of racial justice and injustice for the Jews of color among us. More broadly, Jewish feminism must be held accountable for critical race work for all Jews and for all of us—Jewish and non-Jewish or not-so-Jewish. The fact that too much of what is produced as Jewish feminist published work does not engage race or clearly operate in a way that is informed by antiracist scholarship is dangerous, most profoundly because racism is deadly.

In the rest of this concluding chapter, I want to analyze some of the problems associated with this current fact that Jewish feminist work is operating without a central antiracist analysis. I will end with what I hope are some clear statements as to why antiracism is crucial for Jewish feminism. With a continuing focus on racial segregation, I'll start with some things in the US domestic sphere, and then move to the international level.

Jewish Feminism and Race in US Jewish Contexts

We might say that gender is always a factor in Jewish studies. As a feminist, I suggest that gender is operating, even if not consciously, as a paradigm in the work of Jewish studies colleagues. One role of Jewish feminism is to make gender a conscious category, to unthink patriarchal presumptions regarding gender, to do new Jewish studies projects in which feminist experiences, methodologies, and insights are the motor force.

Similarly, race is always a factor in Jewish studies and Jewish feminist work, if even not explicitly. If race is always a factor in Jewish feminist work, then what is my problem? Race in this case, as in the gender example above, is implicit, and thus not sufficiently critically analyzed. Most contemporary Jewish feminist work unconsciously assumes a position of whiteness. It does not usually interrogate what is so white and Euro/Ashkenazi about itself, how that came to be, what part that plays in systems of injustice, or what options that opens for justice. And so while I say that race is a facet of Jewish feminist work, for the most part this work is not answering our needs for critical race work and analyses that aren't only about Euro Jews, Ashkenazi sensibilities, and whiteness.

Let me fill in some information.[6] Demographers continue to find it difficult to "count" Jews, and statistics on them as being Jewish means different things to different people. As mentioned earlier, from 2000 census data estimates were that 20 percent of the US Jewish community is comprised of non-Ashkenazi, Euro-heritage, and people of color (in US parlance). From my anecdotal experiences, this number is far larger than either Euro/Ashkenazi or even many Jews of color imagine. Still, the number does not take into account the estimated two million people of color in the United States who have a Jewish person in their family tree or who have some Jewish ancestry but don't identify as Jewish in ways recognizable to demographers of Jews. Why is it that most Jews do not know this? Why don't most activists and scholars of color, Jewish or not, know and comment on this? We would find any analysis of the United States lacking that ignored the approximately 15 percent of the population identified as African American. Why is this large segment of US Jews generally not seen—by Jews, and by other feminists who are generally doing such excellent intersectionality work? To try to answer this, we have to take seriously this problem of US Jewish racial segregation, bringing us into deeper parts of this invisibility.

Sexism and Heterosexism

Who is seen, who is counted? Aside from the thinking on Yom Kippur (the annual day of atonement) that states we are all seen and accounted for, if you are not involved in a heterosexual marriage with a Euro Jew, you are often nearly invisible within the human Jewish world. US progressives can make this situation worse by taking this Jewish public self-portrait as a given. Even in my undergraduate university classes, there are students who know to query the presentation of any community as only comprised of heterosexual, normatively gendered, raced, and classed members.

Yes, the organized US Jewish community is fairly obsessed with the intermarriage rates of Jews, with how many Jews are and might potentially be "lost" to the Jewish community through outmarriage. This is a heterosexist paradigm. The dismantling of DOMA or the 2015 SCOTUS Supreme Court decision did not change the structure. It is a cornerstone of the sexism that we Jews have on our own and also that is internalized from dominant US Christian heterosexism and sexism. Yet, despite such high levels of Jewish "outmarriage," in progressive circles, Jews are often still presented as problematically "tribal." (Note the inherent and racial confusion of criticizing this group now seen as "normative" as also more "primitive" or reactionary.)

When it comes to explicitly interracial matters and "outmarriage," US Jewish demographers do on occasion note how many Jewish men—assumed to be coded white—tend to marry Asian women and other women of color, for example. As Jewish feminists, we can discuss the idea that in this phenomenon Jewish men (in a generalized sense, of course; this is probably not descriptive of any particular individuals) are attempting to sooth their Jewish anxiety regarding masculinity by being placed as finally white men because they can attract women of color. Since the demographic discussions are framed in the context of "outmarriage," however, the women of color are paradigmatically non-Jewish. It does not occur to those having these discussions that any number of the women of color married to Jewish men are themselves Jewish. Other race work also lacking here is unpacking the presumption of the whiteness of the men. Further, by including a feminist and queer perspective, we can see that the so-called soothed male anxiety occurs through a heterosexual and specifically raced power dynamic.[7]

When seen through a feminist race critical lens, the small attention Jewish demographers pay to this dynamic actually highlights other dimensions of Jewish racial segregation. The rest of the world of people of color is presumed to be so segregated from meaningful Jewish life as to not warrant analysis by most Jewish demographers.

Don't Know Enough Jewish Feminists of Color?

Let us look more directly at this notion of Jewish racial segregation as a key blockage to building a richer, antiracist Jewish feminism. In doing so we will find that there is a combination of forces at work that must be addressed, including high levels of anti-Jewish views operative within some communities of color. I present this concluding chapter as a difficult challenge, however, in particular to myself and to my Jewish feminist friends and comrades. On the one hand, there is racial segregation in the US Jewish community. At the same time, however, we must clarify a dynamic in which reference to such segregation is also mythologized in order to serve as an excuse for perpetuating the segregation.

Most US Jewish spaces are overwhelmingly comprised of Euro-heritage and usually Ashkenazi people. If you are not the kind who counts heads when you walk into a room full of Jews, give it a try. In addition, in discussions about diversity, this fact of racial segregation also leads many white-identified Jews to excuse the re-creation of Jewish communities as white because individuals can then say, "Well, I don't know any Jews of color." Does this sound familiar? Jewish feminists have long confronted conference organizers, for example, who construct all-male panels in Jewish settings, and have rejected the facile "We didn't know any women doing work in the field." While the gender constitution of panels may not have changed sufficiently, it is increasingly less acceptable to justify it by saying one doesn't know of any women or feminists working on Jewish topics.

Whether you are Jewish or not, how many Jews of color did you invite to speak at your last event (especially if the event was not on race issues)? When I ask Jewish feminist friends and colleagues why our projects, organizations, and tables of contents continue to lack the presence of Jewish feminists of color, I still hear that my friends and colleagues do not think they know enough Jewish feminists of color. Certainly true in wider feminist circles, a form of racial segregation exists in Jewish communities as well, which leads to such thinking. The work Jews have to do on this score (and people may find resonance here with other communities as well) has two parts: (1) to take into account, and become accountable for, the apartheid, the incredible racial segregation of US Jewish communities; and (2) to do some myth busting about the idea that so many Euro/Ashkenazi/white Jews don't know any Jews of color.

Jews of Color and People of Color with Jewish Ancestry

Euro Jews probably have a lot more contact than some people think with not just people of color but with Jews of color. The reasons many don't realize this has to do with structures of anti-Semitism, as well as with racism in the Jewish community and the United States that create the segregation in the first place. Why might this be so? Individually and as a community, we have a primary model of race segregation, and when many Euro/Ashkenazi

Jews come into contact with what is constructed as Blackness (in US terms), we push it away (even when, or especially when, it is noticed in ourselves).

In chapter 5, I noted that there is a legacy of African-heritage Jews in the United States from as far back as the early slave trade. Vibrant residues of this legacy continue in the United States and across the Americas. Many African-heritage Jews participate in more mainstream rabbinically related Jewish communities. In addition, many African-heritage communities in the Americas claim Israelite heritage. They have tended to operate in a more *toraitic* mode (from the Torah or Jewish Bible) than a rabbinic mode (from the Talmud of the Babylonian exile). Either way, they have largely been shunned by the mainstream rabbinically related US Jewish community (Bruder 2008, Parfitt 2013, Dorman 2013, Jackson 2013, Brettschneider 2015). Over the years, some people of color with Jewish backgrounds have found their way into Israelite heritage—rather than Jewish—communities because of the racist presumptions that Jews are white or of Euro-heritage, growing out of and reinforcing Jewish racial segregation.

The United States of the 1950s and 1960s

Jewish involvement in the US civil rights movement can actually be seen as an example of such race segregation. While it is important to recognize, examine, and continue the intense Jewish involvement in US civil right struggles (Schultz 2001), it is equally important to be clearer about the ways that Jews did not meet our goals in civil rights movements. As discussed in chapter 3, for instance, around the time of the height of Jews' involvement in civil rights, we also find that the number of biracial children born in the US began to skyrocket, as did the number of biracial kids put up for adoption. Rarely noted, however, is that the high number of unions yielding such biracial children put up for adoption were heterosexual unions between Jewish women and Black men—by which is meant Euro-Jewish women and non-Jewish (mostly) Black men.[8]

Why did this occur? Because so many of these children created outside the bonds of marriage were perceived by the Jewish women as unraiseable in their worlds as they knew them. Jewish social services have long attempted to place children born to Jewish mothers with Jewish families. However, social workers at the time placed almost all those children with Black—by which is understood basically Christian—adults because they could not find Jewish—by which they meant Euro, white enough coded—families to adopt them. Responsibility for this phenomenon should not be assigned only to the individual Jewish women and their families of origin; it is also structural, built into the institutions and thinking of the US Jewish community and the United States more generally—including social workers and adoption agencies discussed in chapter 6.

While more mixed-race Jewish individuals and families are making their stories public, we still know very little about the life experiences of the many women and their children from this period. The little that we know regarding the women, however, appears as a wealth of information, compared to what scholars know about the mixed-race offspring of Jewish men.[9] We know almost nothing about the children born to non-Jewish women of color out of heterosexual unions with Euro-Jewish men—by which it would be assumed that the men, though Jewish, in this case would be coded white enough. Though I'm not certain of my personal stance on discussions of those considered "lost" to the Jewish community through intermarriage, I do know that absent racism, the Jewish community would include these children in our obsessions about our shrinking numbers. Think, for example, of all those reclaimed as Jews since the Reform and Reconstructionist movements overrode the "matrilineal descent only" policy used in most of modern Western Jewish history. Think, for example, of the potential openings in these conversations if we included these heretofore ignored mixed-race offspring in discussions of patrilineal descent as a claim to Jewishness (a subject in my work in progress on Jewish feminist political thinking).

We could also be as interested in all the people of color with Jewish ancestry in the ways US Jewish communities tend to like to find the Jewish ancestry in folks such as Madeline Albright (whose Jewish parents converted to Christianity in Europe in the 1930s, during the Nazi threat). I find the story of Madeline Albright and many like her important, complex, and interesting. I realize and generally support that the Jewish community has invested a good deal of energy and resources trying to lay claim to the Jewishness of Europeans who are apparently Christians. Have you heard of the projects that explore the Jewish roots of Black Caribbeans? Probably not, as I do not think I have ever seen any.

A personal story: While my full-time job is in New Hampshire (UNH), I taught additional classes at Lehman College to bring in extra cash over the years we lived in the Bronx. At the University of New Hampshire, I usually have all-white classrooms or a few token nonwhites. At Lehman I had a single white person or two in classes populated by students of color. For many years at UNH, I thought I didn't have any Jewish students. At some point I realized that I had a number of students who had one Jewish parent, usually the father, who live with their families in New England. The students do not understand themselves as Jewish, but might occasionally note to me that they have a Jewish father.

Though it took me a while to "see" these folks, I came to understand that I *could* see them (was able to) and could *see* them (that they could be intelligible to me) because I had a framework (unconsciously) from the broader Jewish community that is concerned with outmarriage, and that this context is unmarked as raced white. As Jewish feminists, we talk about different forms of access to (US) American privilege, and sometimes acknowledge that as access to white race privilege. Here is an example of a Jewish feminist sensibility formulated through white privilege.

Over time I realized that I had no framework for, and only a semiconscious historical knowledge to give context to, the similarly Jewish legacies of my nonwhite students at Lehman at the time. In my classes at Lehman College, many African-heritage students, particularly Jamaican and others of Caribbean heritage, told me that they have Jewish grandparents or other Jews in their families. I would come out early in a semester as Jewish with my Lehman students as I tend to do with my UNH students, a characteristic otherness in these contexts that I use as one of my tools in the classroom to teach the concept of otherness. My coming out as Jewish brings out the Jewish stories of my generally non-Jewishly identified students. Among these stories, I began to hear in the Lehman classes that the Black and Caribbean students who had Jews in their family lines also knew more or less about their Jewishness, though—like my UNH students—most do not identify as Jewish or talk about it as much.

Why aren't these wonderful youth of color the poster children for US Jewish communal outreach efforts? Perhaps many would not like to be "the face" of anything, or specifically Jewish outreach. Mostly, however; they are not the face of outreach because US Jews do not pay a whole lot of attention to people of color as a potential "us," even if it might yield hoards of Jews to fight about in the demographers' debates. Segregation is so operative within our community that Euro Jews do not even see the many existing actual or potential Jews of color in our midst.

Moreover, I wonder how cool might it be if the Jewish community did begin to invest resources, energy, intellectual curiosity into the Jewish roots of people of color if Jewish feminists were at the forefront. What if Jewish feminists began to urge this move within the US Jewish community, write grant proposals, begin oral history projects, use and adapt sophisticated Jewish demographers' paradigms to explore the roots of and routes to and from Jewish life of the many people of color in the United States with Jewish ancestry? I would like to think that a feminist-led investment would then yield very different insights and responses from the typical ways Jewish institutions take on new projects.

Talking about the lack of recognition people of color with Jewish heritage does not even address the issues of racism and lack of recognition of people of color who identify and live as Jews currently. I have heard and witnessed too many incidents of individuals of color actively participating in a Shabbat service in a synagogue only to be asked during Kiddush if they are there with a Jewish friend, or other comments demonstrating that the other congregants assume the people are not Jews. My older daughter did a tikkun olam social justice project for her bat mitzvah featuring many Jews of color in our communities responding to a question related to her torah portion (the project title was "A Multiracial Jewish Response"). While viewers marveled at the project, many white Jews asked about the Jews of color anyway, presuming they were not Jewish. The examples are repeated endlessly by Jews of color.

Jewish Feminism and Race in International Context

What does it mean to think about antiracist engagement as a core aspect of Jewish feminism? While most of my Jewish activities are in and about the United States, it is important to take an international view in answering this question as well. There is a world of Jews across every continent and region who do and do not look a lot like most of the other folks in those regions.[10] I assume that most of us, as a US Jewish community and as Jewish feminists, have a lot to learn about different communities across the globe. Learning more and making sure we come into increasing contact with Jewish diversity from around the globe is important if we care about Jews and racial justice.

If we are working to center race in Jewish feminist work, leaving out an international view is a problem for many reasons. If we want a vibrant Jewish communal life, we cannot afford to maintain current levels of separation among the world's Jews. We *all* experience loss, although differently, when we homogenize Jewish experience and do not have global, multiple Jewish experiences as part of our self-understanding, our telling of our histories. European Jewish history does not have to be the central story of the US Jewish community.

To explain that a bit more, let me name a somewhat more familiar Jewish feminist concept: if we keep doing Jewish life, history, and community building as if only Jewish men exist and existed, then we are missing approximately one half of the Jewish world. The story we tell as "our" story is lessened, and it is skewed. We not only want to have Jewish women in a picture that has historically depicted Jewish men, for example. We not only want to have Jewish women's historical experiences being told. We not only want to have Jewish feminism's understanding of a history that has in so many ways used a patriarchal frame. Jewish feminists have said it is not only (though crucially) about *adding* one-half of the Jewish people to our collective living, but we also claim that in a *feminist* adding, we will fundamentally transform what we know to be Jewish.

Not all cross-cultural or cross-group analogies work, but I think this one does: If we keep telling European Jewish history as *the* Jewish story, then we are both missing the majority of Jewish history and the story we tell is wrong. To the degree that we are telling only a part of the story in such a way that makes the story incorrect, then such telling also is part of systems of injustice. Further, if we can start telling more of the Jewish story beyond the European/white/Ashkenazi one, then I am certain it will transform what we know, think, are, and can be as Jewish.

While I seek to make a clear call for an international inclusion that is transformative, I also want to bring up some notes of caution regarding the impulse to globalize when we want to do Jewish racial diversity work. Justice work rarely comes in a neatly wrapped package. Because I want us to do this globalizing work, I also want to share some warnings about doing it that I have noted in my experience. For now my cautions regard two central concerns: (1) avoidance behavior and (2) colonialism.

Avoidance

One concern I see when Jewish communities in the United States "go global" in response to a call for racial diversity regards what I will call "avoidance behavior." In my experience in US Jewish communities, the shift in gaze outward, internationally, is often (though of course not solely) a deflection from taking on racial diversity challenges in the US Jewish community. Thus, the move to look at Jews around the world in non-European places is not only a positive development, but functions also as an avoidance move. Redirecting a group's view internationally can be about shying away from what may be *felt* as the harder work of dealing with racial diversity in our own community here in the United States.

I have seen this shift to the international as a move generated from not being able to cope with more internal issues and power dynamics. For instance, in many US universities, progressive activists came to realize that their efforts to "diversify" their campuses—faculty or student body—were considered successful only because they recruited more nonwhite students or faculty from abroad. They found it a very different and much more difficult project to diversify their campuses with US-based nonwhite people. Similarly, part of unlearning our Jewishly created racism is learning about Jews around the globe. However, a lot of that work is evidence of a larger tendency to avoid facing racial diversity among Jews in the United States.

Let me offer some specific examples. There is much energy devoted in spurts to communities of African Jews that come to the attention of particular US Jewish communities: programs on the Abayudaya in Uganda, examinations of the DNA testing done on the Lemba priests, historical discussions of Ethiopian Jews; and migration patterns of West African Jews of the Bilad al-Sudan through Ghana, Mali, and Songhai. There are many benefits to these energy spurts. However, in my experience, community members end up taking a very distanced stance, putting on a generous and welcoming face to "visitors" (which they should). But over and over I then see that the visitors go home. The Jews of color already in the community continue to remain invisible, their Jewish credentials challenged. European-heritage Jews marvel, ooh and aah, over African dress and patterned cloth, cadence in speech, rhythm in song, cultural flourishes in interpretation. But many African-American Jews I know have trouble bringing their African-American heritage into a Jewish communal setting and having it accepted as a "legitimate" Jewish history and expression. Policing the borders of Jewishness among a diverse group of US Jews causes tensions that globalizing does not solve and can further mask.

Is this gospel rendition of liturgy an appropriation? Is the US slave experience for African American Jews permitted to be told as at all, if not directly, a Jewish part of a communal Passover seder? Is that Mexican custom an "import" for the Chicana Jew? Is it different when a Jew of color brings in something along these lines than when a light-skinned, Euro-heritage Jew does? What about synagogues with nearly exclusively Ashkenazi congregants that introduce occasional Sephardi and Mizrachi elements into a service? Euro-heritage US Jews may act the magnanimous anthropologists learning about, for example, an Indian Jewish practice in India. However, to say an Indian-heritage Jew in Los Angeles is welcome to introduce her customs and knowledge at her local synagogue may be unnerving for the individuals already in leadership in the institutions.[11] Globalizing has a neat way of not challenging the separation among racially diverse US Jews. While getting a global perspective is crucial to doing Jewish feminist antiracism work, it can help keep in place the separations and othering, both politically and geographically, already operative in US Jewish communities, including Jewish feminist communities.

Colonialism

There are ways that doing international work as part of unlearning racism as Jewish feminists can effect just the opposite of our goals of bringing us closer together in a justice paradigm and closing the distances among us across a large globe. When US Jewish institutions and Jewish feminists begin to attend to international Jewish diversity, the work may reflect ways we as a community have—relatively unconsciously—internalized the views of Western/European/US dominant paradigms. Our work often increases injustice and further others non-European Jews when it is unconsciously expressive of life inside an imagined portion of the world that acts (and in many ways *is* but importantly also *perceives* itself) as the global hegemonic force.

Among the reasons too many of us in the United States don't know enough about Jewish communities globally is that so many European Jews ended up here as a result of the moment when European global hegemony began to shift toward US global hegemony. European-heritage Jews in the United States have a historical legacy forged within a European sensibility, and now we continue to create ourselves and our understandings and practices that build on a rather deadly combination of Euro dominance with US global conceit. Thus, in general, US Jews can participate, and are complicit in colonial thinking in the ways we have integrated US/European-centered ways of thinking and organizing Jewish communal life.

What does this mean for our work? It means that a Jewish feminist antiracist project that works to end such global segregation would do well to incorporate exploration of the ways that Jews both have been *other* within the Christian, Western creation of the West and Western dominance, *and* at the same time the ways we have also internalized and participated in that very project.

To help explain more, I'll again use an analogous feminist self-criticism. We have had plenty of moments when we had to acknowledge and confront that the fact that feminists in the United States had internalized the anti-Semitism of Western patriarchy. Or, over time feminists became better able to clarify that a lot of what had come to be known *as* feminism, unconsciously particularly among communities of white feminists, had internalized certain structures of Western patriarchal thinking that led feminism to re-create many of the binaries and hierarchies of Western patriarchy, but now in a feminist form. For example, when some white feminists get wind of the concept of diversity, a common first move to address it is to "invite feminists of color in" to existing efforts. Here we see examples of attempts at ending separations function via inclusion into projects that feminists created out of (sometimes perfectly well-meaning) white feminists' experiences—instead of creating wholly new agendas, or truly transforming existing ones together with feminists of color. This serves to map white feminist experiences onto feminists of color as opposed to transforming feminism through diversity.

Similarly, US and European feminists have been called to account for the ways our efforts internationally extend Western paradigms and serve as a sort of feminist colonialism (Mohanty 1998). As many of us have learned along the way in our feminism, white feminists may critique patriarchy and know that patriarchy is an oppression—we probably all also have internalized (differently to be sure) many frameworks of patriarchy that inform our feminism—especially when it comes to issues of race and Western dominance. I am saying here that as Jewish feminists, when we turn to global diversity, we run the risk also of *doing* the colonialism and imperialism of Western patriarchy even as we think patriarchy is the thing we are wholly against. (This is the subject of my 2015 book *The Jewish Phenomenon in Sub-Saharan Africa*.) No, we do not have to—but without serious self critique, we do. I will assume the best and say that we simply do not want to do so. Thus, global Jewish feminist work that might appear to bring racially diverse Jewish feminists together can further separate us, can serve to protect the segregation in which we currently participate in both daily and more structural ways.

Why Jewish Feminism Needs an Antiracist Analysis

As Jewish feminists, we have a lot of work to do along the way to being able to make a significant difference in the ways that the broader Jewish community deepens its antiracist commitments. At present, most Jewish feminism as I know it does not have an affirmative and critical framework to address race and racism. One of the many reasons for this is the same race segregation among Jewish feminists as in the Jewish and broader US communities.

While Jewish feminists who are not of color are involved in antiracist work at higher levels than non-Jews with this profile, Jewish feminism thus far has been created in a context that does not have a racial analysis of its own. Additionally, many of us have helped create and been raised in Jewish feminist contexts that are largely Euro/Ashkenazi/white. If there are at least hundreds of thousands of US Jews of color among the approximately six million US Jews (and more who are of Jewish heritage in the US, as well as Jewishly related globally), then many of these Jews are feminists and potential feminists. Jewish feminist analysis is developed out of a combination of individual and collective experience, but it is not thus far generally developed out of experiences that are inherently informed by the basic existence of, let alone via deep mutual engagement with, Jews of color.

Having named the problem of racial segregation in Jewish feminism, I want to make sure to state clearly why I am certain it is important that Jewish feminism (and not just some among our wonderful Jewish feminist comrades) have an antiracist analysis:

1. We are sentencing my daughters and all Jews of color to Jewish death. Racism is murderous. I have a passionate view of and need for Jewish feminism as a strong and powerful tool to enable us to live. If it cannot speak to my own, my daughters', and others' explicitly raced experiences then we do not have enough to offer and we are allowing and are complicit in, this daily death . . . Jewish and otherwise.

2. Significant parts of Jewish discourse operate through obsessions with stock components of patriarchy, such as bloodlines and birthrights, and not just sex but also heterosexual sex or various forms of Jewish heterosexual panic. These are always also race issues. If we care about patriarchy and heterosexism, we have got to get on with an antiracist project.

3. Jewish feminism ought to be able to speak to important issues—and racism is one of them. If we don't have critical race analyses, then we have more work to do to develop them (as well as the internal antiracism work it will take to unpack why we don't).

4. Plenty of Jewish feminists and Jewish women are people of color. Thus, Jewish feminism is unjustly and problematically partial, as it cannot integrate these Jews' experiences and adequately address them. Jewish feminism created without Jewish women and feminists of color is not sufficiently informing to transform the general Jewish feminist project.

5. If we think that everyone needs to deal with their racism and get on with some antiracism work, and if we think that whenever people get to it, then that work will need, and be enhanced by, a feminist analysis, then all Jews are in need of antiracist analysis, Jewish antiracist analysis, and specifically a Jewish feminist antiracist analysis.

Conclusion

This is tough stuff. As much as I am addressing Jews, and Jewish feminists in this chapter directly, this book in general is also addressed to all those in progressive circles and doing intersectionality work. At present, what has been done in the field of intersectionality, in academia and on the streets, largely ignores Jews, Jewish matters of import, and anti-Semitism.

Anti-Semitism is deadly. Ask 2015 shoppers at the Paris kosher market who were attacked right after the attack on Charlie Hebdo. In 2015, one could certainly not call anti-Semitism a thing of the past internationally, given the high levels of public anti-Semitic acts and destruction globally. For those who consider anti-Semitism a thing of the past in the United States, check again. While most US Jews view that certain other minority groups face more discrimination than they do, nearly half of all self-identified Jews in the United States state that they experience "a lot of discrimination" (Pew 2013, 15). Having been raised in Jewish areas of New York City, I can still be shocked by the levels of anti-Semitism Jewish students at my university (a school with a relatively small Jewish population) face repeatedly. My children, being generally the only Jewish kids in their schools for the time we have lived in New England, face anti-Semitism regularly—along with racism, sexism, and homophobic bullying.

The lack of attention in intersectionality studies to Jewish issues of concern is unacceptable, and we need to redirect social justice efforts to include them. Avoiding Jewish matters only reinforces the status quo in many ways, including assimilationist paradigms for what we think of as the "good stuff" in the United States: freedom, equality, justice. Further, avoiding Jewish critiques of Christian privilege and Christian hegemony in the United States is proving ruinous. As progressives, feminists, queer, class, and antiracist scholars and activists, we are inching along in our efforts at dealing with straight privilege, white privilege, class privilege, thin privilege, heteronormativity, as well as hierarchies based on abilities, English language access, and nationality or culture/religion. But we are almost nowhere on the road of dealing with Christian privilege.

The Christian right grows in influence into mainstream segments of US society. Post the 2014 Hobby Lobby Supreme Court decision, particular Christian theological views regarding fetal rights and women's reproductive health are again gaining ground. The vast sums of funding from Christian right organizations put into advertising to Jewish audiences are threatening to all who care about democracy. Christian far-right groups' attempts to influence the politics of Jewish students on college campuses across the country are aimed at breaking the historic Jewish-Democratic Party affiliation. US Jews have been one of the two communities most consistently relied on as Democratic Party supporters (Jews currently at 70% self-identification and second only to African Americans) (Pew 2013, 14). Not that the Democratic Party can be relied on for spearheading consistently socially just political change, but party affiliation in the United States is taken as a marker for commitment to a set of values that intersectionality scholars likely want to bolster.

Christian right groups also seek to shift Jewish public opinion away from critique of Israeli government policy. It serves the Christian right and fatal US foreign policy for (US) Americans to continue to incorrectly think that US Jews are so powerful, steadfastly pro-Israeli government policy, and that any critique thereof is anti-Jewish and threatening to the United States. Decade after decade, Jewish population studies demonstrate that the vast majority of US Jews are critical of the Israeli government policy regarding Palestine and Palestinians (see newer 2013 statistics in the Pew report, 13). This is actually astonishing, and in jeopardy, given the flood of Christian-right money being poured into pro-Israeli government propaganda. If US Jews were as powerful as they are portrayed by both left and right in the United States, there could not be such a skewed understanding of Jewish values and actual Jews' concerns. The Christian right is not supporting US Jewish and Israeli actions to end war and injustice in Israel and Palestine. A US Christian-right agenda directly jeopardizes the values of most US Jews, and other activists seeking peace and a just transformation in Israel and Palestine.

In other issue areas both domestic and international, US Jews and Jewish groups remain at the forefront of a host of progressive to radical movements from GLBTQ, antiracism, feminist, labor, humane immigration policies, public schooling, food insecurity, environmental and sustainability efforts, war and peace, and more. The threat to free speech and public education from Christian-right creationist activism, protect Christmas efforts, antidivorce organizations, pray the gay away, and ex-gay groups is extreme. The rise in anti-Muslimists in the United States is not only a threat for Muslims and those who care about them; it is part of an effort to reclaim the United States as Christian. For these and so many reasons, intersectionality theorists will do well to include Jewish views and critiques of Christian privilege and Christian hegemony within the purview of analysis in the field.

It is my hope that this book, in its own small way, can serve by way of example how work in intersectionality studies may go about integrating into, and transforming, the field with Jewish analysis. It is also my intention that Jewish activists and scholars may find this work of assistance in efforts to build more nuanced and far-reaching mutual-construction intersectionality work on the ground and in the academy.

Notes

Introduction

1. See http://www.truah.org/. For more on Talve, she was profiled in Kaye/Kantrowitz (2007), as was McCoy. See also McCoy (2014), http://www.tikkun.org/nextgen/author/a_yavilahm.
2. Crenshaw (1989).
3. Beale (1970).
4. For some examples, see: Moraga and Anzaldua (1981), Collins (1990), and Hooks (1981).
5. Cashman (2014), Besnier (2007), Duchêne and Heller (2012), Lorde (1984), Spade (2011).
6. 1978. Available on line, for example, at http://circuitous.org/scraps/combahee.html.
7. Among other authors and these early texts, see Crenshaw (1991); Morrison (1992); Davis (1983); Williams (1991); Smith (1983); Mohanty (1988); Moraga (2000); Anzaldua (1987); Moraga and Anzaldua (1981 and 1982); Giddings (1984); Hull, Scott, and Smith (1983); Spivak (1988); and works by Alarcon, such as in Kaplan et al. (1999).
8. Among other authors and these early texts, see: Frankenberg (1993), McIntosh (2004), Butler (1999), Brown (1988), Spelman (1988), Frasier (1989), Young (1990), Scott (1999), Lerner (1972), Haraway (1991), and Gordon (1990).
9. See, for example, McCall (2005), Hancock (2007), Patil (2013), Nash (2008 and 2011), Choo and Ferree (2010), Nyong'o (2005), and Puar (2007).
10. See, for example, Davis (2008).
11. See, for example, Nyong'o (2005), Puar (2007), and McCall (2005).
12. See Smith (1983); Bulkin, Prat, and Smith (1984).
13. Among a list of works on intersectionality recently published and/or that I reviewed again for research on this book in the past year, I again found no Jewish references in an array of works: Bassel and Lepinard (2014); Beckwith (2014); Cho, Crenshaw, and McCall (2013); Choo and Marx (2010); Chun, Lipsitz, and Shin (2013); Dhamoon (2011); Hancock (2007); Jordan-Zachery (2007); Mohanty

(1988); Walby, Armstrong, and Strid (2012); and Marchetti (2014). In Grzanka, ed. (2014), p. 84, the only reference to anything Jewish is from a reprinted article I had already reviewed, which mentions "Christian, Islamic and Jewish fundamentalist discourses" in Mohanty's "The Home Question," pp. 79–86; so that the only Jewish presence can be found (1) hovering, and (2) only in a reactionary way. This is not uncommon, in a rare mention of Jewish matters, Wadsworth (2011) refers to orthodox Jewish participation in opposing same-gender marriage in California, though all other Jewish religious movements—the vast majority of Jews—have long supported same-gender civil marriage in the United States. Or see Dhamoon and Hankivsky's (2013) rendering of only a conservative Jewish understanding of the Holocaust.

14. It is not possible to include a full bibliography of pivotal Jewish feminist works. In addition to other authors and the earlier texts, see Elwell's dissertation (1982 and also 1987); see also Weissler (1998), Antler (1990), Moore (2008), Ochs (1990), Ostreiker (1982), Umansky and Ashton (1992), Prell (1999), Feld (1999), and Daniel and Johnson (1995). Plaskow's 1991 *Standing Again at Sinai: Judaism from a Feminist Perspective* helped define the field as it came of age in feminist theology. Further, see Hyman(1995), Davidman and Tenenbaum (1994), Peskowitz (1997), Levitt (1997), Peskowitz and Levitt (1997), and Baskin (2002). See also the *Jewish Women in America: An Historical Encyclopedia*, eds. Hyman, Moore, and Weisbard (1997), and the later international edition (though a proper account of Jews of color in this legacy is lacking). Ackelsberg has articles in many of these edited volumes as well.

15. Other interesting examples of Jewish feminist works related to race include Miri (2009), Ross (2000), Delman (2002), Silliman (2001), Shepard (2008), and Gray (2001).

16. Although Walker's work has a tendency to reify the separate categories of Black and Jewish (Jewish here problematically equaling white), while she herself is mixed heritage. See also Segal (1997), Brown (2000), the work of Rain Prior, and the films Lacey Schwartz's *Little White Lie* and Nicole Opper's 2010 *Off and Running*.

Chapter 1

1. Early attempts to work out the arguments of this piece were presented as papers at the 1998 Western Political Science Association Meeting (WPSA) session and the 1998 International Association of Women Philosophers (IAPh) Symposium. I would like to thank Lisa Disch for her thoughtful feedback and those at the WPSA session for the great discussion, Dawn Rose for introducing me to and helping with the Jewish texts in medical ethics, Wendy Lee-Lampshire and Uma Narayan for their thoughtful feedback on the IAPh version, and Lisa Tessman and Bat-Ami Bar On for being careful editors of the first printing.

2. As is often noted in intersectionality studies, the most widely circulated articulation of such a critique was published in 1977 as the "Black Feminist Statement" from the Combahee River Collective.

3. Plaskow (1991). We see the pain of these false choices addressed by queers in the queer Jews issue of *Response* (Winter/Spring 1997), no. 67—a phenomenon we still face today.

4. Such is the presumption of the academic journal *Race, Gender and Class*, for example. See also Gerda Lerner (1997), on this discussion. For a specifically Jewish discussion, note that in the introduction of Christie Balka and Andy Rose, eds. (1989), the editors write, "Lesbian and gay Jewish experience is not monolithic. . . . Rather, it is influenced by the vicissitudes of religious identity, gender, age, class, geography, physical ability, and other factors." *Influenced* is the key word here. Balka and Rose take their primary categories of sexual orientation and Jewishness and "relate" them to additional categories. Attending to diversity among lesbian and gay Jews is important; in this instance, they suggest that the way to understand multiple identity categories is to see that certain secondary factors affect (even a complex of) primary factors. They explain the situation of being "doubly other," whereby cultural aspects relating to sexual orientation marginalize Jewish lesbians and gay men from both Jewish and larger US life.

5. Anzaldua, ed. (1990). As an example of cross-discussion, see Norma Alarcon (1999).

6. Judith Butler, for example, is Jewish and has a significant background in Jewish philosophy. She does not, however, generally problematize Jewish issues. Moreover, in her most popular written works she often relies on Christian cultural markers. For an example of work directly taking on a Jewish subject, see Butler (2012).

7. Notably, this is less the case for racial minority feminists. Angela Davis (1981), and Patricia Hill Collins (1990), explicitly use a three-tiered model of race, gender, and class. Audre Lorde (1984), is credited for working exquisitely with even more complicated sets of identity groupings, though she did not engage in the same kind of analytic frameworks as philosophers such as those discussed later in this chapter.

8. I will be referring specifically to Elizabeth V. Spelman (1988). Although she has published much since this work, I focus on this text because it helped many other philosophers and activists so significantly and is a foundational text for intersectionality studies. Consequently, we were also affected by the problems in this work.

9. Spelman (1988, 14), and the framework for chapter 5.

10. Ibid., 48.

11. Ibid., 41. Though Spelman cites a passage from Aristotle in which he discusses a "community of slaves, male and female," she does so in order to demonstrate her central point regarding gender (i.e., the lack of "women" among slaves).

12. It is others such as Judith Butler (1990), who will trouble the feminist reliance on gender as the socially constructed version of sex. Part of the point of this chapter is that, as helpful as works such as *Inessential Woman* are, their analyses break down when additional identity categories are taken seriously. Concomitantly, although demonstrating so is beyond the scope of this chapter, Butler's extremely

important *Gender Trouble* (1990), does not hold up under the pressure from Spelman's race critical work.

13. Early in the text, Spelman refers to the Athenian distinctions as "class" distinctions. This begins to shift in the section of the chapter on Aristotle where Spelman uses her analysis to critique the racist bias of contemporary feminist philosophers; Spelman 1988, 51. Although she is not clear as to why she must choose one contemporary equivalent to the category slave, she discusses the inadequacy of both modern usages of *race* and *class*. She concludes that "'race,' is probably less misleading than 'class'" (200n44). It is interesting to note, however, that when she first shifts within the text to modern paradigms such as race, she also names class, religion, sexual orientation, nationality, and servile status as other important factors of identity, and refers to both class and race regarding slave status (51–53). Fifty-four pages into the text, she is using the term "race" (in quotation marks) on its own.

14. Despite referring to class and race in the introduction to chapter 5, Spelman (1988), 116 explains before she begins her actual analysis in the chapter: "I shall not explicitly be examining class and classism, though at a number of points I suggest ways in which considerations of class and classism affect the topic at hand. Many of the questions I raise about comparisons between sexism and racism could also be raised about comparisons between sexism and classism or classism and racism." Her topic at hand is gender and race. It is probably true that there are many comparisons to be made with class; however, issues involving class need attention to their own specificity.

15. Such a two-tiered model is schematized most clearly in Spelman (1988, 46), where she charts natures vis-à-vis biological/psychological descriptions of male/female–slave/free.

16. Thanks to Uma Narayan for helping me articulate this point.

17. In discussing Aristotle's conception of a "well-ordered political community," Spelman (1988, 42) writes: "When a people are a slave people, it doesn't matter . . . whether they are male or female." She also cites Angela Davis's account "of Black female slaves as 'genderless'" (1988, 201n51).

18. Spelman (1988, 42–43).

19. Although Spelman will note in chapter 5 that her "point is not that Black men cannot in any way be sexist to white or Black women, for indeed they can," she also makes sweeping statements such as, "But this is a racist society, and generally, the self-esteem of white people is deeply influenced by their difference from and supposed superiority to Black people." See Spelman (1988), 121. Even given the power of racism, to allow for this generalization in such stark terms we would have to consider white and Black people as undifferentiated entities with a single relationship of power, which is precisely the idea Spelman's book is intended to counter.

20. The term *Talmud* refers to two collections of teachings redacted in the fifth and sixth centuries, one in the land of Israel, and one in Babylonia. Both compilations are organized around the structure of the Mishnah (a compilation of laws and teachings from the first and second centuries CE), and contain commentary

and discussion on the Mishnah, as well as much additional material, including legal discussion, stories, remedies, and aphorisms.

21. For the context of this chapter, Alicia Ostreiker's 1996 work on biblical texts demonstrates the power of looking to other texts that present fundamental challenges to the dominant narrative.

22. I want to thank Lisa Disch and Jane Bennet for pushing me on this point.

23. See Lorde (1984).

24. Rabbinic Judaism does not define the whole of Jewry, historically or today. It does, however, remain hegemonic.

25. I am presenting a version in a Jewish framework of what Smith (1979) has referred to as a view of multiple oppressions that is not about "arithmetic," and to which Spelman herself refers in debunking the additive approach. See Spelman (1988, 123).

26. Thus, one cannot even say that Jewishness is thickly bounded as one might find in an essentialist identitarian tradition. As the categories below assume, one can "become" Jewish as well. "Proselyte" names one who has converted to Judaism.

27. I want to thank William Connolly for helping me clarify and articulate this point for a context beyond Jewish scholarship into contemporary political theory.

28. Kathy Ferguson's contribution here is much appreciated.

29. This is Boyarin's 1997 methodological claim in his use of Talmudic texts in his project. He asserts that his project has "two faces." In the introduction to the text, he writes that "Jewish culture demystifies European gender ideologies by reversing their terms, which is not, I hasten to emphasize, a liberatory process in itself but can be mobilized—strategically—for liberation" (xxi). He also aims at the goal of reconstructing a "rabbinic Judaism that will be quite different in some ways from the one we know and yet be and feel credibly grounded in the tradition of the Rabbis" (xxi).

30. This point could be supported by Narayan's 1998 critique of gender essentialism, cultural essentialism, and cultural relativism.

31. Nathins, who were descendants of the Gibeonites (from Joshua 9:27), are one of the peoples living in the land that the Israelites entered and claimed after the death of Moses. Although a conquered people, they were spared death, but were turned into a subnational caste. By King David's time, they were subject to most of the laws of Israel, but some special laws continued to apply to them.

32. The Talmud represents the rise to hegemonic power of the rabbis, a class of scholars, over the previous religious caste ordering. For an interesting example of new critical scholarship on the rise and consolidation of rabbinic power from a gender perspective, see Peskowitz (1997).

33. I much appreciate Tamar Kamionkowsky for helping me to sort through this dimension of the maze and Jane Litman for her help on the Levites.

34. In the United States in particular, many Jews identify strongly as Jews, commonly through culture and history and not as directly through religion. While Singer (2006) notes a rise in Jewish day school (full-day school) attendance,

Wertheimer (2007) found that "the number of contact hours in classrooms has continued to decline in most supplementary [Jewish] schools over the past decade" (3, 6). Many US Jews are less likely to know Hebrew and be able to navigate independently in ancient Jewish texts. For example, the Pew 2013 study of US Jewry notes that "Half of Jews (52%), including 60% of Jews by religion and 24% of Jews of no religion, say they know the Hebrew alphabet. But far fewer (13% of Jews overall, including 16% of Jews by religion and 4% of Jews of no religion) say they understand most or all of the words when they read Hebrew" (Pew Research Center 2013, 15–16).

35. Alpert (1997, 7). In the interim years, both Alpert and Kaye/Kantrowitz have likely developed and refined their views as with Spelman. This analysis is offered of these texts specifically given the pivotal role each of these books played in the development of what could be considered Jewish feminist intersectionality work using multiple identity signifiers.

36. See Rich (1980). Phelan (1994, 21) addresses a similar point. In this work, as in Phelan (1989), she delves deeply into aspects of exclusionary thinking at work within lesbian communities.

37. Kaye/Kantrowitz (1992, 127).

38. Kaye/ Kantrowitz (1992, 129).

39. In 1977, Kaye/Kantrowitz began writing a book on violence from her perspective as a woman and as a Jew. The three hundred pages of that manuscript have been edited and condensed into this essay.

40. Kaye/Kantrowitz (1992, i).

41. Kaye/Kantrowitz (1992, ii).

42. Ibid.

43. Ibid., 193.

44. Ibid., 92.

45. Ibid., 105.

46. Ibid., 97.

47. Ibid.

48. Ibid., 149.

49. For some work on these issues, see, for example, Yeskel (1996), Balka and Rose (1989), Dawn Rose (1999), and in the pages of *The Narrow Bridge*.

50. As one example, see Dekro (1996).

51. Kaye/Kantrowitz (1992, 149).

52. Ibid., 119.

53. Ibid., 121.

54. Ibid., 116.

Chapter 2

1. For example, even in her fiction, Kincaid makes a point of noting that the house in New England of *See Now Then* (134) is "built in something called a Victorian style."

2. This chapter is developed from an early attempt to articulate this argument, presented as a paper delivered at the 2010 Black New England Conference and a UNH Center for the Humanities Senior Fellow Lecture. Thanks to the University of New Hampshire Center for the Humanities and the Hadassah Brandeis Institute for research support; Jing Huang and Michael Branley for research assistance; Judith Plaskow and Lori Lefkovitz for their thoughtful comments on earlier drafts. See also Brettschneider (2012) for my other work on Kincaid.

3. I would like to thank Cassie Travers for her research assistance with Kincaid's texts.

4. An important work articulating a Jewish view in this broader context is Boyarin and Boyarin (2002). Not uncommonly, even the contributions in Mirzoff (2000) do not sufficiently bring the analyses of Blacks and Jews together.

5. See Bruder (2008) and Parfitt (2013).

6. The best example of an exception is Kaye/Kantrowitz (2007). See also the work of Dorman (2013) and Jackson (2013).

7. Biale (1986 and 2002), Boyarin and Boyarin (1993), Kaye/Kantrowitz (2007), Aviv and Shneer (2005), and Butler (2012). While diversity informs the Biale (2002), and in the US context the Kaye/Kantrowitz (2007), and Israel/Palestine for Butler, none of these works considers the African case or considers adequately the role of African heritage for Jewish diaspora theorizing. See also Beinart (2012).

8. Her British colonial education is a recurring theme referenced in her work. As an example, in *Autobiography of My Mother* (14) Kincaid notes: "At the top of the map were the words 'THE BRITISH EMPIRE.' These were the first words I learned to read."

9. As an example of this aspect of her personal biography noted in her fiction, Kincaid writes in *Annie John* (82) "As an added punishment, I was ordered to copy Books I and II of *Paradise Lost*, by John Milton, and to have it done a week from that day." Other examples can be found in various works including *See Now Then* (32, and 154).

10. For example, we see this portrayed in *Annie John* (18) with Kincaid's rhetoric: "When my eyes rested on my mother, I found her beautiful. Her head looked as if it should be on a sixpence."

11. In an example from her fiction, Kincaid writes, referring to the mother figure: "She was fierce; she had been born feeling that her birthright was already spoken for. She thought I was the person who might take it away from her." Though she continues to note: "I could not, I was not a man" (*Autobiography of My Mother*, 117).

12. A theme again in *See Now Then*, where the main character relates that her mother became angry and then became even more angry "because I would not become her. I had an idea that I should become myself" (29). We see this critical exploration of the supposed anger of an independent immigrant woman of color that also often appeared in Kincaid's portrayal of the relationship between the characters Mariah and Lucy in *Lucy*. For example, Kincaid notes: "Mariah came up to me. The look on my face must have shocked her, for she said, 'You are a very angry person, aren't you?' and her voice was filled with alarm and pity. Perhaps I should

have said something reassuring; perhaps I should have denied it. But I did not. I said, 'Of course I am. What do you expect?' " (96).

13. Suggesting that Kincaid's earlier works were more "innocent" is a creation of critics and not simply "true" of her writing and political acumen.

14. Kincaid notes: "the weak should never be in awe of the strong," which certainly infuriates the strong (*See Now Then*, 43).

15. In new diaspora theorizing, the political problems inherent in the transformation of the modern nation of Israel into a state again forms a central impetus for the negation of Zion and the affirmation of diaspora. See also Butler (2012).

16. In *See Now Then* (12), Kincaid brings a Jewish example of destruction when a minority in exile during the Nazi Holocaust comes into relation with destruction during the slave trade, conquering a people in their home lands where they are a majority population: "the murder of millions of people who lived continents away from each other; on the other hand, hovering over Mrs. Sweet . . . was a monstrosity, a distortion of human relationships: The Atlantic Slave Trade."

17. In *Autobiography of My Mother* (69), Kincaid brings these various points of loss together, noting: "It was that time of day when all you have lost is heaviest in your mind: your mother; if you have lost her; your home, if you have lost it; the voices of the people who might have loved you or who you only wish had loved you; the places in which something good, something you cannot forget, happened to you. Such a feeling of longing and loss are heaviest just in that daylight."

18. In *Annie John* (134) Kincaid describes the day the protagonist is sent away to the north by her parents: "Everything I would do that morning until I got on the ship that would take me to England I would be doing for the last time, for I had made up my mind that, come what may, the road for me now went only in one direction: away from my home, away from my mother, away from my father . . . I only knew that I felt the way I did, and that this feeling was the strongest one in my life."

19. In the introduction to *Talk Stories* (2001, 10), Kincaid relates: "I was born in St. John's, Antigua and I spent the first sixteen years of my life there. Shortly after I turned sixteen years of age, I was sent to America by my family to work and earn money to support them. I did not like any of it at all." And yet, she is clear on many of the advantages and privilege this diaspora in the promised land affords her; in *My Brother* (74) Kincaid writes regarding her brother dying of AIDS, still living in Antigua: "Had my life stayed on the path where my mother had set it, the path of no university education, my brother would have been dead by now. I would not have been in a position to save his life, I would not have had access to money to buy the medicine that would prolong his life."

20. As an example in her fiction, in *The Autobiography of my Mother* (15–16), Kincaid writes: "My mother was a Carib woman, and when they looked at me this is what they saw. The Carib people had been defeated and then exterminated, thrown away like weeds in a garden; the African people had been defeated but had survived. When they looked at me, they saw only the Carib people. They were wrong but I did not tell them so."

21. In *My Brother* (8), commenting on her language difference from her family after years in United States: "But I might have seemed like a ridiculous person to him. I had lived away from my home for so long that I no longer understood readily the kind of English he spoke and always had to have him repeat himself to me; and I no longer spoke the kind of English he spoke, and when I said anything to him, he would look at me and sometimes just laugh outright. You talk funny, he said."

22. For example, note Kincaid's view in *Autobiography of My Mother* (139): "And yet . . . it made me sad to know that I did not look straight ahead of me, I always looked back, sometimes I looked to the side, but mostly I looked back."

23. In Kincaid's works, people in general, and her people in particular, move around a good deal. Kincaid's new world began in 1492, with Europeans coming to the Caribbean and stealing people from Africa for the slave trade (*My Brother*, 165). And then more moving of kin: Kincaid's mother was from Dominica, moving to Antigua at age sixteen, the age Kincaid was when she was sent to the United States. In *Annie John* (123–127), she writes of her grandmother making a long journey to help her in Antigua when she was ill, and in *My Brother* (72), she writes of a time that her mother returned to Dominica.

24. Despite contemporary European naming of modern Israel on the continent of Asia, many African Jews and Jewishly related groups understand Israel to be part of Africa. See Brettschneider (2015).

25. What Kincaid calls in *See Now Then* (11) "the horrid something called Winter."

26. Kincaid describes this rebirth in diaspora, or diaspora ending a psychic death in the homeland, in various ways. For example, back in Antigua for the first time in years to visit her brother, Kincaid writes: "I missed the life that I had come to know. [Her life then in the US.] When I was sitting with my brother, the life I had come to know was my past, a past that does not make me feel I am falling in to a hole, a vapor of sadness swallowing me up" (*My Brother*, 23).

27. Klagsbrun (1997), 105.

28. In her comparison of Sarah and Hannah's responses to their situations, Klagsbrun (105) demonstrates how these abject women also invert power dynamics, politically turning the so-called natural world upside down, as Hannah sings, "The bows of the mighty are broken, and the faltering are girded with strength" (I Samuel 2:5,4).

29. Written after her own mother has died, Kincaid writes in the fictional *See Now Then* of the protagonist's mother when she was young (178): "she was my mother and I knew she was my mother and loved her and all of that . . ." but Kinkaid goes on to mention, "her cruelty to me, the way she left me aside when something new came up." And then later of "her dead mother lying in a coffin and being looked at by all the people she had made feel small and all those people were so glad to have outlived her and Mrs. Sweet was among them" (174).

30. Notice Kincaid's language: "The fertile soil of my creative life is my mother," in Cudjoe (1989, 402).

31. As another Caribbean feminist writer, Michelle Cliff's work is interesting to examine in relation to Kincaid's. In works such as *Free Enterprise* 1993, Cliff begins her work—on African-American women and other rebels in the United States leading up to the raid on Harper's Ferry—in the Caribbean. One of the two central characters is Annie, a Caribbean woman who fled her mother, home, and the oppressions she knew when young. She lives out most of her life then in the United States attempting to free herself and be a part of a black resistance to US racism. Numerous references are made to Jewish historical themes of oppression and diaspora in a raced context. A primary comrade for Annie is a Jewish character, Rachel, a descendent of survivors of the Spanish Inquisition who is in diaspora from Spain and then again from Latin America. These figures also embody the importance and multiplicity homes and diasporas in complex ways.

32. The three primary European powers involved in the creation of the African diaspora through slave trading in the Caribbean are Spain, France, and England. Spain's involvement is generally dated to 1502. Following Columbus's failed attempt to settle Espanola during his second expedition, the Spanish soldier Nicolas de Ovando is "credited" with settling approximately 2,500 Spaniards there. On these figures, see two of Kincaid's extraordinary essays: Jamaica Kincaid, "Columbus in Chains" (1983) and "Ovando" (1989).

33. Rodriguez (1997, 253). British colonial rule in the Caribbean is understood to have begun in 1622 in St. Kitts, settling in Antigua in 1623 (Pons 2007, 50). The English slave trade started in 1562, becoming highly organized approximately a century later (Lux 1975, 31).

34. Drescher and Engerman (1998, 99).

35. Gaspar (1993, 80).

36. Slater (1968, 12).

37. As but one example, she describes awareness as a child of the history of her people as African slaves in her description of a British girl, Ruth, in the classroom in *Annie John* (76): "Perhaps she wanted to be in England, where no one would remind her constantly of the terrible things her ancestors had done; perhaps she had felt even worse when her father was a missionary in Africa. I could see how Ruth felt from looking at her face. Her ancestors had been the masters, while ours had been the slaves."

38. In *A Small Place* (9), Kincaid actually writes that Antigua "is twelve miles long and nine miles wide." Compare Antigua, at 108 miles, to New York City, for example, where Kincaid spent the first years of her life in the United States. Manhattan is 23.7 square miles with a population of 1,611,581. See http://www.nycgo.com/?event=view.article&id=78912.

39. From her early work in *Annie John* (134), Kincaid connotes this in her fiction commenting on "the everlasting blue sky" and "the everlasting hot sun." Or in her later work, *See Now Then* (182), as "the persistent sunshine."

40. In this vein, see in particular: Jamaica Kincaid, *A Small Place* (1988).

41. On the transitions of populations and cultures in the Caribbean, see Wilson (1997), Saunder (2005), Crahan and Knight (1979).

42. In "On Seeing England for the First Time" (1991, 40), Kincaid writes of the British colonizers in her home in the British West Indies: ". . . who are these people . . . who forced me to think that the world I knew was incomplete, or without substance, or did not measure up because it was not England; that I was incomplete, or without substance, and did not measure up because I was not English."

43. For example, in her scathing article, "On Seeing England for the First Time" (1991), Kincaid writes: "In Bath, I drank tea in a room I had read about in a novel written in the eighteenth century. In this very same room, young women wearing those dresses that rustled and so on danced and flirted and sometimes disgraced themselves with young men, soldiers, sailors, who were on their way to Bristol or someplace like that, so many places like that where so many adventures, the outcome of which was not good for me, began. Bristol, England" (39).

44. In Kincaid's writing, the new is not simply all new and the relationship between new land and home land more complicated: "When I was at home, in my parents' house, I used to make a list of all the things that I was quite sure would not follow me if I could only cross the vast ocean that lay before me; I used to think that just a change in venue would banish forever from my life the things I most despised. But that was not to be so" (*Lucy*, 89–90).

45. Kincaid writes: "The reality of my life was conquests, subjugation, humiliation" ("On Seeing England for the First Time," 1991, 36).

46. In a common transposition of character, time, and place, Kincaid locates the Afro-Caribbean protagonist who has immigrated to the United States and is then living in New England as a mother and writer, set as a part of the slave trade and participant in colonial and neocolonial enterprise: "Mrs. Sweet brought her produce to market as cash crops, as manufactured goods, as raw human labor, and made an outlandish profit and wither profit she then made lyres and people who could play them and then she built a concert hall, a concert hall so large that to experience it required the fanaticism of a pilgrim" (*See Now Then*, 51).

47. We find numerous references to Jewish aspects of her life while in Vermont in *See Now Then*, Kincaid's only novel set in New England (see, e.g., 38, 39, 133).

48. Her biological father, Mr. Potter, is also then referenced in *See Now Then* (129) and Kincaid discusses her "examined" life (166). She also has the protagonist note that at the age of five "I became familiar with the idea that knowing how to read could alter my circumstances" (31)

49. "Kincaid writes: "And because Mr. Potter could neither read nor write, he could not understand himself, he could not make himself known to others, he did not know himself, not that such things would have brought him any amount of happiness. And because Mr. Potter could neither read nor write, he made someone who could do so, who could even love doing so, reading and writing" (*Mr. Potter*, 21 also 36).

50. In *Annie John* (36), Kincaid writes: "Once when I didn't wash, my mother had given me a long scolding about it, and she ended it by saying that it was the

only thing she didn't like about English people: they didn't wash often enough, or wash properly when they finally did. My mother had said, 'Have you ever noticed how they smell as if they had been bottled up in a fish?'"

51. "How unfriendly winter weather could be. The trees with their bare, still limbs looked dead, and as if someone had just placed them there and planned to come back and get them later; all the windows of the houses were shut tight, the way windows were shut up when a house will be empty for a long time; when people walked on the streets they did it quickly, as if they were doing something behind someone's back" (*Lucy*, 10).

52. Though during her time at Franconia, the cold seems to have been a marker for the complicated mimicry involved in being a colonized subject (Cudjoe 1989, 399).

53. Kincaid 2005.

54. In *See Now Then* (21), Kincaid describes the protagonist writing at her special, beautiful desk where "she would think about her childhood, the misery that resulted from that wound, eventually becoming its own salve, from the wound itself, she made a world and this world that she had made out of her own horror was full of interest and was even attractive."

55. It is also, thus, of note here that despite the centrality of media and communications to Kincaid's life work and success, she does not appear in the archives of her local newspaper, other newspapers in Vermont, or Vermont and New England Jewish media sources. Kincaid is a strong international voice, and an interestingly quiet figure. Both her work and her celebrity are covered widely in literary and popular (inter-)national interviews, yet she remains distinctly uncovered in local terms. In contrast to what became her notoriety in Antigua, her position in diaspora at least in part makes living such contradictions possible. Kincaid was banned from returning to Antigua for a period due to the publicity of the politics of her writing, and yet she maintains the privilege of a private citizen in rural Vermont.

56. Kincaid notes of the north in *Lucy* (6): "To think of it—the other my future, a gray blank, an overcast seascape on which rain was falling and no boats were in sight. I was no longer in a tropical zone and I felt cold inside and out, the first time such a sensation had come over me." On the other hand, she ends the novel *See Now Then* (182) by describing the weather in her island home as "a paradise so complete it immediately rendered itself as hell."

57. See Kincaid's *Among Flowers: A Walk in the Himalayas* (Washington, DC: National Geographic, 2005), and *See Now Then: A Novel*.

58. In *My Brother* (149), Kincaid writes in this style of ambiguity about home: "I love the people I am from, and I do not love the people I am from."

59. "I always think of myself as alone. I can't bear to be in a group of any kind, or the school of anything," in Cudjoe (1989, 401).

60. In her 2001 Introduction to *Talk Stories* (7), Kincaid compares her experiences as a new immigrant in New York City with her life back in her island home: "Young black men and women would stare at me and laugh at me and then say something insulting. That in particular did not bother me at all: in fact, I rather

liked that, it was most familiar. I had grown up in a place where many people were young and black and men and women, and I had been stared at and laughed at, and insulting things had been said to me."

61. "I spent all the time I had been away from the West Indies and from my mother building some kind of 'literary monument' to it" (Cudjoe 1989, 404).

62. This was the imagery used since the Ford's early 1900s social engineering programs turning immigrants into "Americans." The neotech backpack is a reference to the film: *Up in the Air* (2009).

63. Kincaid says that by having her own garden in Vermont she has "crossed a line," "join[ing] the conquering class," in Kincaid "Flowers of Evil" (1992).

64. This theme runs throughout much of her work. See in particular for this concept, *A Small Place* (1988).

65. In *See Now Then* (29), Kincaid has the protagonist say of her mother back on the British West Indian island where the character is from: "she taught me to read and she was very pleased at how naturally I took to it, for she thought of reading as a climate and not everyone adapts to it; she did not know that before she taught me to read I knew how to write, she did not know that she herself was writing and that once I knew how to read I would then write about her."

66. See http://www.jfrej.org and http://www.domesticworkersunited.org for archives and more information. Ai-jen Poo, lead organizer of the New York City–based Domestic Workers United earned the prestigious MacArthur "genius" grant in 2014.

67. See Brodkin (1998). A more complex portrait of similar phenomena can be found in Kaye/Kantrowitz (1992).

68. See the 2013 Pew findings on US Jews' economic standing.

Chapter 3

1. This work has been made possible with access to the media collection of the Jewish Museum's National Jewish Archive of Broadcasting, New York City. The chapter is adapted from early articulations in "Arrested Assimilation: Molly Goldberg and the Race/Class/Gender Ideology of U.S. Suburbia at Mid-Century" for the New Visions of Suburban Life: An Interdisciplinary Conference, Hofstra University: March 18–19, 2005, and "The Legacy of *The Goldbergs*" Conference at the Center for Jewish History, April 23, 2006, NYC. The author would like to thank Andrew Ingall and Joanne Jacobson for their support and for introducing the author to *The Goldbergs*.

2. On Gertrude Berg, see: Hoberman and Shandler (2003), Marc (1984), Prell (1999), Weber (1998 and 1999), Zurawik (2003), Brook (1999), and see Antler (2007) for a more complete and updated bibliography.

3. On the Jewish experience in the development of the US suburbs, see Gittleman (1978), Gordon (1959), Rand (2001), Sklare and Greenblum (1967), Adler and Connolly (1960), Diamond (2000 and 2002), Levine and Harmon (1992).

4. This is a factor distinguishing the stereotypes that are sometimes problematic in the *Goldbergs*, from the overarching problematic stereotypes created and repeated in *Amos 'n' Andy*.

5. Meyerowitz (2002). Sex here is what Butler renames as gender.

6. Borish (2002).

7. The surname Goldberg is a minority ethnic marker in the United States among Ashkenazi Jews, although it is derived from the German. I also realize that many in the United States are so unaware of anything Jewish that I do not want to overstate the cultural knowledge implicit in a name standing in as a Jewish marker. In my experience teaching outside of Jewish centers for over twenty years, I have come to realize that other even superficial Ashkenazi (let alone beyond) markers I assume are recognized as iconic in the United States such as bagels and cream cheese are not often even understood as "Jewishly related."

8. Weber (1998).

9. Lewis (2004).

10. Brodkin (1998).

11. See Ely's 1991 analysis. Thanks to Rebecca Alpert for pointing out Ely's work.

12. Hansberry (1958).

13. *The Goldbergs*, "Social Butterfly" episode, written by Gertrude Berg, first broadcast during 1955/1956 season filmed in syndication; and *The Goldbergs*, "Girl Scouts" episode.

14. *The Goldbergs*, "*Molly's Fish*" episode.

15. Antler (2007).

16. Brodkin (1998) and Kaye/Kantrowitz (1992).

17. Antler (2007).

18. The 2013 Goldbergs brings us back to older problematic gender stereotypes of the mother character. Could it be argued that all the characters are deeply flawed? Yes, though this response does not take into account the gendered and classed nature of the portrayal of such "flaws" for comedic aims.

19. Foucault (1975).

20. See Larson (1986).

21. Schultz (2001).

22. Butler (1999, 13–31).

23. According to the 2013 Pew study (15), US Jews remain less religious or consider religion less important in their lives than most Americans. Jewish association remains high, however, as Jewish identity is defined in other ways than religious.

24. Diamond (2000 and 2002).

25. US Jews remain significantly less religiously oriented, or consider religion less important in their lives, than most Americans (Pew 2013, 15). Note, that does not mean that Jews do not consider themselves "Jewish." US Jews report a strong sense of belonging to the Jewish people. The majority of US Jews report, however, that being Jewish is a more a matter of ancestry and culture (62%) with only 15 percent saying that it is a matter of religion.

26. Dorman (2013) and Fernheimer (2014).
27. Tobin, Tobin, and Rubin (2005), Brettschneider (2006).
28. Jen (1996). While not yet acceptable television, one can see the shift toward acceptance of Euro-heritage Jews in some suburbs that will not be approached in popular television culture again until 2013, in the 1980s setting, with the new *Goldbergs*.
29. Spigelgass (1959), 6.
30. For a comment regarding the geographic aspects see Massey (1993), and Levine and Harmon (1992).
31. For example, see Jones (1990), Jones (1994), and Walker (2001).
32. Berger (1978).
33. McKinley (2002).
34. Kaye/Kantrowitz (1992).

Chapter 4

1. An earlier draft of this chapter was published in the *Journal of Lesbian Studies* (2003, "Ritual Encounters of the Queer Kind: A Political Analysis of Jewish Lesbian Ritual Innovation," *Journal of Lesbian Studies: Special Issue on Lesbians and Ritual* 7, no. 2), then published separately as a book. In the context of the JQTT of the time, the lesbians refer to themselves as queer. As a matter of accountability, I will therefore utilize the term *queer* when referring to the work of the group. Those present at the particular JQTT meetings at which we discussed ritual were, in addition to myself: Eric Cohen, Tamara Cohen, Miryam Kabakov, Gwynn Kessler, Tani Meir, Elliot Pilshaw, David Rogoff, Dawn Robinson Rose, Abigail Ruby, Jonathan Springer, and Laurie Zimmerman.

I would like to thank Eric Cohen and particularly Dawn Rose for their comments on earlier drafts. I am grateful to H. Mark Roelofs, Jan Cohen-Cruz, Augusto Boal, and all those who have taught me about political theater. I also want to show appreciation for the many women, queers, and others with whom I have created and participated in rituals over the years, and particularly acknowledge the work of havurot and the National Havurah Institute as well as Jewish feminist groups such as the Jewish Feminist Resource Center at the National Council of Jewish Women, Ma'yan, and B'not Esh for what they have taught (and are continuing to teach) me about ritual innovation. I also want to thank all of those involved in Ma'yan's Jewish Feminist Research Group, those who attended the special session on this work in progress, in particular, Jennifer Danby and Ruti Kadish for their thoughtful and encouraging reviews.

2. Of course, many of the people who began Jewish feminist ritual innovation were (or are now) also GLTBQ. Ritual innovation continues to be vibrant in myriad Jewish spaces, initiated in large part by Jewish feminists and queers in our overlapping an mutually constitutive spaces. For example, when the organization the Jewish Multiracial Network entered its thirteenth year, members created a bar/

bat mitzvah celebration for the community itself with feminist rabbis and queer leaders bringing together their experiences and knowledges of ritual innovation. www.ritualwell.org has become a good resource for Jewish feminist ritual innovation.

3. The Hebrew word for the English *come*, which is also slang for orgasm, is not also slang for organism in Hebrew. Thus, the diasporic aspect here is worthy of notice. The overlay makes sense to US English speakers.

4. Seidman (2002) explores the notion of closet in the United States in historical context, both public and private. As acknowledged in the NJGLH ritual, Seidman came to understand what he terms "the episodic concealment" (8) of "the psychological and social texture" of the closet (7).

5. Phelan (1994, chapter 3).

6. This could be criticized as an oppressive progressivist modern narrative expectation, a futurity often called into question in queer theory (Edelman 2004). Queers with whom I have discussed this argue that given that oppression can be expected for the futures that we live and can imagine, this moment remains relevant and helpful.

7. Of course, those designing rituals need to take into account peoples' different comfort levels with physical touch and other aspects of intimacy.

8. For Marx's critique of this tact, see his analysis of Critical-Utopian Socialism (1967, 114–118).

9. Ackelsberg has written extensively on feminist anarchism and preparation. (See, for example, 1991 and 2010). She also has worked for many years doing anarchist work (and writing) within Jewish spaces. Dawn Rose's 1998 work on Hanna Levy Haas illustrates this point well. Haas was a communist philosopher who was interned in a concentration camp by the Nazis for being Jewish. With her earlier training in communist theory and strategizing, she was able to organize the Jewish women in the camp. See also Haas (1982).

10. For a discussion of these ideas and practices in historical perspective, see Buber (1949).

11. Brecht is famous for breaking down the "wall" between audience and players in an attempt to be more conscious of and use theater in radical politics. See, for example, Brecht (1964). Boal's (1985) techniques push Brecht's work further in attempting to increasingly democratize theater and better use drama in political practice.

12. For a critical discussion of revolution and postmodernism in this sense, see Buker (1999, 149–152).

13. As an interesting analysis along these lines, see Mitchell's 1988 critique of the role of World's Fairs in the colonizing process.

14. Schechter's 1985 work on clowning, politics, and theater is a helpful illustration of Butler's 1999 ideas concerning the transformative political potential of performativity and parody.

15. Although it is beyond the scope of this article to explore more fully, readers might find interesting that this discussion stimulated a subconversation on using the Jewish holiday Purim for such events. At Purim, Jews traditionally put on

skits and plays about or inspired by the holiday and its story. We asked, how might we use the plays performed at Purim to expose the performances of everyday life that tend to appear natural? The queer potential here is great, given the idea that Purim may be seen as a paradigmatic "coming out" narrative. (See, e.g., Sedgewick 1994, and the JFREJ—Jews For Economic Justice—Purim Shpil http://www.jfrej.org/jfrej-purim-shpil. Accessed 7.20.14.)

16. If readers are interested in getting the flavor of Finley's work and do not have an opportunity to see her live, I suggest, *Shock Treatment* (1990). As a Jewish example, see Aylon (2012) and the work of Jenny Romaine.

Chapter 5

1. See Brettschneider (2015).
2. Jewish Women's Archive. "Fact Sheet on 1654." (Accessed on June 27, 2014.) <http://jwa.org/350years/factsheet1654>.
3. See, for example, http://jwa.org/encyclopedia/article/german-immigrant-period-in-united-states. (Accessed on June 10, 2014.)
4. On racialized treatment of Catholics here, see, for example, Ignatiev (1995).
5. See, for example, Ordover (2003) for her excellent work in this area.
6. Regarding the ways that we often participate in our own oppression, Alexander (2012) notes in her discussion about how the growth of the war on drugs has created a new racial caste system, the ways that many African Americans bought into the paradigm, supported, and played a role in the unprecedented mass incarceration of people of color (males, in her discussion).
7. See, for example, Kaye/Kantrowitz (1992), Brodkin (1998), and Brettschneider (2006).
8. Brodie (1994).
9. See for example, Price (2010), and Silliman and Fried (2004).
10. Special thanks to Jessica Rosenthal for her research assistance in this section.
11. The Comstock Laws, also popularly referred to as the anti-obscenity laws, made it a crime to distribute materials that could be used for contraception or abortion.
12. For example, along with Ben Reitman, Goldman published a pamphlet, "Why and How the Poor Should Not Have Many Children," containing information about condoms, diaphragms, cervical caps, suppositories, and douches (New Internationalist 1998). In 1915 Stokes became the financial secretary of the National Birth Control League, an organization focused on legalizing birth control information and repealing the anti-obscenity laws, which limited the ability of activists to do political work on this issue.
13. Mindell administered the Brownsville clinic in Brooklyn during its first and only week. (It was shut down due to the obscenity laws.) She also assisted

the many Jewish clients by reading them literature on birth control in Yiddish (Lepore 2011).

14. The legal loophole allowed doctors to prescribe medical birth control if it seemed "medically indicated" or if the patient's current physiological state would make pregnancy dangerous. Dr. Hannah Meyer Stone altered the list of medical indications to include the patient's desire for child spacing or psychological factors (Stone 1901).

15. In addition to the National Council of Jewish Women, Hadassah, and the BBW, other Jewish organization endorsers were: the American Jewish Committee, American Jewish Congress, Anti-Defamation League of B'nai B'rith, Jewish Labor Committee, National Federation of Temple Sisterhoods, New Jewish Agenda, Union of American Hebrew Congregations, United Synagogues of America, Women's American ORT, and the Women's League for Conservative Judaism (Global Jewish New Source JTA December 31, 1989 "Behind the Headlines: Abortion Rights Issue Galvanizing Jewish Women's Groups in America").

16. The AJC was founded in 1906 to protect the rights of American Jews, and it works to enhance the well-being of the Jewish people and advance human rights and democratic values.

17. As a more recent public example, in an open letter to Planned Parenthood, Monica Simpson criticized Planned Parenthood for not recognizing the work of reproductive justice organizations when asked about the shift in language away from "pro-choice" (in a *New York Times* article "Advocates Shun 'Pro-Choice' to Expand Message," July 28, 2014).

18. According to the last National Jewish Population Survey (United Jewish Communities 2003, 4), approximately 5 percent of Jewish households have adopted children. Comparatively, the percent for US families in general is 2 to 4 percent (Stolley 1993, 26).

Chapter 6

1. This chapter is developed and adapted from my work (and to see more details on adoption practices) Brettschneider (2006), and was presented in an earlier version as a keynote address at the Adoption: Secret Histories, Public Policies Conference, Cambridge, Massachusetts, 2010. Special thanks to Jessica Compton for research assistance on this chapter.

2. US Public Law 104–193. 104th Cong., 2nd sess., August 22, 1996. Personal Responsibility and Work Opportunity Reconciliation Act of 1996. And see US Public Law 104–188. 104th Cong., 2nd sess., August 20, 1996. Small Business Job Protection Act of 1996. ("Removal of barriers to interethnic adoption" is in section 1808.)

3. Eight percent of U.S. adoptions are interracial. Of those, 6 percent are white adults adopting children of color; 2 percent covers adults of all other races adopting interracially (Stolley 1993, 340).

4. See Williams's 1997discussion regarding adopting her child.

5. There are apparently dual contesting discourses about this historical moment in GLBT US history. One notes DOMA as an antigay initiative that signals the larger retraction of GLBT rights, especially regarding family formation. The other discourse notes changes in adoption and foster care norms and laws regarding GLBT adults as signal of a new age of openness for GLBT people and family formation. As I argue below, this seeming contradiction is primarily a contradiction if only white GLBT people are taken into account. Use of a race-critical analysis which expressly includes experiences of GLBT people of color demonstrates that both moves are destructive of GLBT people's capacities to form families and keep them intact.

6. The primary goal in child welfare had long been reuniting bio-families. Whether this was wise or not requires a long debate. During the 1990s, new legislation was being developed to make it easier to formally cut bio-ties in favor of placing kids in adoptive situations. The experiences of queer youths have run counter to this historical pattern. Getting queer kids in the child welfare system back together with their families of origin was generally not an option. More recently, however, given years of GLBTQ activism, there has been an effort on the part of some in the system to work on the homophobia in the family in order to open up the possibility of reunification. (See Mallon 1998, 98 and passim.)

7. According AFCARS (2014, 5) less than half of "children adopted with public agency involvement in Fiscal Year 2013" were white. The majority were children of color: American/Indian Native, 2%; Black or African American, 21%; Hispanic, 21%; Unknown/Unable to Determine, 1%; more than one race, 7%.

8. While primarily focused on African-American men, see Alexander 2012 to understand the far-reaching implications of the War on Drugs.

9. See Williams (2003) for an historical critique.

10. See Cahill, Battle, and Meyer (2004).

11. There are many news articles and reports, see, for example, Leadership Conference (2011), and Kleiner (2010).

12. See, for example, Shanley (2001).

13. National Association of Black Social Workers (1972).

14. Perhaps further suggesting the ambivalence in the racial reassignment of US Jews, in contrast to problems voiced by majority whites with transracial adoption, Jews were less likely to find TRA a problem for the adopting parents. At the same time, Jews as a community have been better able to understand the logic of the NABSW regarding cultural genocide than many majority whites as well. See, for example, Simon and Altstein (2000, 128–129). Facing issues of cultural genocide themselves in the US context, and the specific situation of the hidden children of the Holocaust (Jewish children taken in by Christian institutions and families and either hidden or raised under an assumed Christian identity in order to save them from Nazi anti-Jewish policies), provide some of the cultural touchstones many US Jews refer to when sympathetically explaining the NABSW rationale. See, for example, Kessel (2000).

15. For central scholarly and popular literature debating transracial adoption, see Roberts (2002), Fogg-Davis (2002), Banks (1998), Bartholet (1999 and 1991), CBS News, "Born in USA, Adopted in Canada" (February 19, 2005), Bowen (1987–88), Howe (1997), Kennedy (1994 and 2003), Perry (1993–34), Shanley (2001), Landes and Posner (1978), Volkman and Katz (2003), and Carroll and Dockery (1995).

16. US Public Law 104–193. 104th Cong., 2nd sess., August 22, 1996. Personal Responsibility and Work Opportunity Reconciliation Act of 1996. US Public Law 104–188. 104th Cong., 2nd sess., August 20, 1996. Small Business Job Protection Act of 1996. ("Removal of barriers to interethnic adoption" is in section 1808.)

17. US "Founding Father" and signer of the Declaration of Independence Benjamin Rush thought similarly. In what was considered by many at that the time a "progressive" stance, Rush sought to confront racism. In his view, the problem for Black slaves was their blackness itself. He was interested in changing the skin color, hair texture, and other "features" of slaves. Making them white, physically to the eye (as if there is a real measure of whiteness to achieve) was Rush's suggested solution to the problem of racist discrimination.

18. Roberts (1997).

19. Roberts (2002).

20. Moynihan (1965). One will recall the discussion in chapter 4 of targeting Euro-heritage Jews for eugenic population reduction. By the new millennium, many Euro Jews were being coded as potentially among the savior whites. It is interesting that the contemporary spin on eugenics via adoption (born marginalized and therefore tainted children can be "saved" by being adoptively "born again" into white middle-class families) stands in direct contrast to the revolutionary adoption agenda of the late-eighteenth-century creation of the early French Republic. Although later rejected, the revolutionary agenda of modernist democracy included forcible adoption as a means of democratizing the republic (a positively valenced notion at the time) by bringing democratizing elements (children of nonaristocratic backgrounds) into the sphere of the former ruling class. Similar to the US case, adoption in revolutionary France was also a matter of poor children being adopted into richer families. Diverging from US patterns, the French example from that historical moment was to change the elite for the better, not to yuppify/gentrify the ordinary and/or formerly outcast. See Gager (1996).

21. Wilkins (2006). http://www.ncsl.org/programs/statetribe/ICWA.htm (Accessed 7/11/06). See Fanshel (1972) and for a contradicting more recent study see Simon and Alstein (2000).

22. Melanson (2000).

Conclusion

1. An earlier version of this argument was published in Bridges in 2010. The author would like to thank Dawn Rose, Clare Kinberg, Barbara Johnson, Judith

Plaskow, and the members of B'not Esh and the Jewish Multiracial Network. For a discussion of the forces behind urban segregation of working-class Jewish and Black neighborhoods, see Levine and Harmon (1992).

2. Good examples of antiracist analyses by Jewish feminists are Ordover (2003), Rothman (2005), Zack (1993), Gordon (1990), and works by Gerda Lerner.

3. Some examples of Jewish feminist antiracist activism may be found in: Butler (1988), Pogrebin (1991), and Talve (2010). See discussion of other examples in Kaye/Kantrowitz (2007).

4. See, for example, work by Yavilah McCoy and Marjorie Agosin. See also Azoulay (1997); *Bridges* (1997 and 2001); Biale, Galchinsky, and Heschel (1998); Brodkin (1998); Kaye/Kantrowitz (1992 and 2007); Levins Morales (1986); Schultz (2001); Tessman and Bar On (2001). See also examples of my edited projects (1996, 2004, and 2003), and with Rose (1999). For other related work by the author see, Brettschneider (2006, 2008, 2007, and 2015).

5. According to the Pew (2013, 13) study, US Jews state the following definitions for what it means to be Jewish: 69 percent leading an ethical life, 56 percent working for justice, 49 percent being intellectually curious. These values are evident in high levels of Jewish activism in social justice work.

6. Tobin, Tobin, and Rubin (2005).

7. The website https://coffeemeetsbagel.com/.../dating-myths-exposed-do-jewish-guys-really-have-a-thing-for-asian-girls/ (accessed August 21, 2014) claims to bust the myth that Jewish (presumed white) guys have "a thing" for Asian (presumed non-Jewish) girls. For a more nuanced exposure to Asian Jews, see http://asianjewishlife.org. Some examples that challenge this paradigm can be found in Jen (1996) and Spigelgass (1959).

8. Graenum (1978, 122). See also Cahnman (1967), Gibel (1965), Gordon (1964), Catherine (2002), and Ross (1974).

9. Helpful resources are Jones (1990), Jones (1994), Walker (2001), Zack (1996). See also Jeffries (2003), and McBride (1996). As another example of related erasures Jews must account for, see Melanson (1999).

10. If you are interested in learning more, a good start includes Agosin (2002), Bruder (2008), Ruby and Johnson (1995), Melammed (2002), Ruggiero (2005), Silliman (2001), Simon (2000), Xin (2003), and Brettschneider (2015).

11. Daniels and Johnson (2001), Delman (2002), Gray (2001), and Khazzoom (2003).

Works Cited

Ackelsberg, Martha. (1991). *Free Women of Spain: Anarchism and the Struggle for the Emancipation of Women.* Bloomington: Indiana University Press.

———. (2010). *Resisting Citizenship: Feminist Essays on Politics, Community, and Democracy.* New York: Routledge.

———. (1986). "Spirituality, Community, and Politics: B'not Esh and the Feminist Reconstruction of Judaism." *Journal of Feminist Studies in Religion* 2.2 (Fall, no. 2): 109–120.

AFCARS. (2014). *Adoption and Foster Care Analysis and Reporting System Report.* Publication no. 21. Washington, DC: U.S. Department of Health and Human Services.

Aylon, Heléne. (2012). *Whatever Is Contained Must Be Released: My Jewish Orthodox Girlhood, My Life as a Feminist Artist.* New York: Feminist Press at the City University of New York.

Adler, Rachel. (1998). *Engendering Judaism: An Inclusive Theology and Ethics.* Philadelphia, PA: Jewish Publication Society.

Adler, Selig, and Thomas E. Connolly. (1960). *From Ararat to Suburbia: the History of the Jewish Community of Buffalo.* Philadelphia: Jewish Publication Society of America.

Agosin, Marjorie. (2002). *Taking Root: Narratives of Jewish Women in Latin America.* Athens: Ohio University Press.

Alarcon, Norma. (1990). "Theoretical Subject(s) of *This Bridge Called My Back* and Anglo-American Feminism," in Gloria Anzaldua, ed., *Making Face, Making Soul; Haciendo Caras; Creative and Critical Perspectives by Feminists of Color.* San Francisco: Aunt Lute.

Alexander, Michelle. (2012). *The New Jim Crow: Mass Incarceration in the Age of Colorblindness.* New York: The New Press.

Alpert, Rebecca T. (1997). *Like Bread on the Seder Plate: Jewish Lesbians and the Transformation of Tradition.* New York: Columbia University Press.

Antler, Joyce. (1990). *America and I: Short Stories by American Jewish Women Writers.* Boston, MA: Beacon Press.

———. (2007). *You Never Call! You Never Write! A History of the Jewish Mother*. Oxford and New York: Oxford University Press.

Anzaldua, Gloria. (1987). *Borderlands/La Frontera: The New Mestiza*. San Francisco: Spinsters/Aunt Lute.

———, ed. (1990). *Making Face, Making Soul/*Haciendo Caras*: Creative and Critical Perspectives by Feminists of Color*. San Francisco: Aunt Lute.

Aviv, Caryn, and David Shneer. (2005). *New Jews the End of the Jewish Diaspora*. New York: New York University Press.

Aviv, Caryn, and David Shneer. (2002). *Queer Jews*. New York: Routledge.

Azoulay, Katya Gibel. (1997). *Black, Jewish, and Interracial: It's Not the Color of Your Skin but the Race of Your Kin and Other Myths of Identity*. Durham, NC and London: Duke University Press.

Balka, Christie, and Andy Rose, eds. (1989). *Twice Blessed: On Being Lesbian, Gay, and Jewish*. Boston: Beacon Press.

Banks, Richard. (1998). "The Color of Desire: Fulfilling Adoptive Parents' Racial Preferences through Discriminatory State Action." *Yale Law Journal* 107 (no. 4): 875–964.

Bartholet, Elizabeth. (1999). *Nobody's Children: Abuse and Neglect, Foster Drift, and the Adoption Alternative*. Boston: Beacon Press.

———. (1991). "Where Do Black Children Belong? The Politics of Race Matching in Adoption." *University of Pennsylvania Law Review* 139: 1163–1256.

Baskin, Judith Reesa. (2002). *Midrashic Women: Formations of the Feminine in Rabbinic Literature*. Hanover, NH: University Press of New England for Brandeis University Press.

Bassel, Leah, and Eleonore Lepinard. (2014). "The Theory and Politics of Intersectionality in Comparative Perspective." *Politics & Gender* 10 (no. 1): 115–117.

Baum, Charlotte, Paula Hyman, and Sonya Michel. (1976). *The Jewish Woman in America*. New York: Dial Press.

Beale, Fran. (1970). "Double Jeopardy: To Be Black and Female," in Robin Morgan, ed., *Sisterhood Is Powerful: Anthology of Writings from the Women's Liberation Movement*. New York: Vintage Books, 340–353.

Beck, Evelyn Torton. (1982). *Nice Jewish Girls: A Jewish Lesbian Anthology*. Boston: Beacon Press.

Beckwith, Karen. (2014). "Gender, Class, and the Structure of Intersectionality: Working-Class Women and the Pittston Coal Strike." *Politics, Groups, and Identities* 2 (no. 1): 17–34.

"Behind the Headlines: Abortion Rights Issue Galvanizing Jewish Women's Groups in America." (2014). *The Global Jewish News Source (JTA)*. http://www.jta.org/1989/10/31/archive/behind-the-headlines-abortion-rights-issue-galvanizing-jewish-womens-groups-in-america; accessed August 21, 2014.

Beinart, Peter. (2012). *The Crisis of Zionism*. New York: Times Books/Henry Holt.

Belzer, Tobin, and Julie Pelc. (2003). *Joining the Sisterhood: Young Jewish Women Write Their Lives*. Albany: State University of New York Press.

Benjamin, Walter. (1999). *The Arcades Project.* Cambridge, MA: Belknap Press.
Berger, Graenum. (1978). *Black Jews in America: A Documentary with Commentary.* New York: Commission on Synagogue Relations/Federation of Jewish Philanthropies of New York.
Berlant, Laura. (1997). *The Queen of America Goes to Washington City: Essays on Sex and Citizenship.* Durham, NC: Duke University Press.
Besnier, N. (2007). "Language and Gender Research at the Intersection of the Global and the Local." *Gender & Language* 1 (no. 1): 67–78.
Biale, David, ed. (2002). *Cultures of the Jews: A New History.* New York: Schocken Books.
———. (1986). *Power & Powerlessness in Jewish History.* New York: Schocken Books.
Biale, David, Michael Galchinsky, and Susannah Heschel, eds. (1998). *Insider/Outsider: American Jews and Multiculturalism.* Berkeley: University of California Press.
Boal, Augusto. (1985). *Theatre of the Oppressed.* New York: Theatre Communications Group.
———. (2001). *Hamlet and the Baker's Son: My Life in Theatre and Politics.* New York and London: Routledge.
Borish, Linda. (2002). "Women, Sport, and American Jewish Identity in the Late Nineteen and Early Twentieth Centuries," in Tara Magdalinski and Timothy Chandler, ed., *With God on Their Side.* New York and London: Routledge, 71–98.
Bowen, James. (1987–1988). "Cultural Convergences and Divergences: The Nexus between Putative Afro-American Family Values and the Best Interests of the Child." *Journal of Family Law* 26: 487–544.
Boyarin, Daniel. (1997). *Unheroic Conduct: The Rise of Heterosexuality and the Invention of the Jewish Man.* Berkeley: University of California Press.
Boyarin, Daniel, and Jonathan Boyarin. (1993). *Diaspora: Generation and the Ground of Jewish Identity,* vol. 9, 4th ed. Chicago: University of Chicago Press. 693–725.
Boyarin, Jonathan, and Daniel Boyarin. (2002). *Powers of Diaspora: Two Essays on the Relevance of Jewish Culture.* Minneapolis: University of Minnesota Press.
Boyarin, Daniel, Daniel Itzkovitz, and Ann Pellegrini. (2003). *Queer Theory and the Jewish Question.* NY: Columbia University Press.
Brecht, Bertolt. (1964). *Brecht on Theatre.* New York: Hill and Wang.
Brettschneider, Marla. (2006). *The Family Flamboyant: Race Politics, Queer Families, Jewish Lives.* Albany: SUNY Press.
———. 2015. *The Jewish Phenomenon in Sub-Saharan Africa: Multiple and Conflicting Discourses.* Lewiston, NY: Mellen Press.
———. 2012. "Kincaid, Diaspora, and Colonial Studies," in Edith Bruder and Tudor Parfitt, eds., *African Zion: Studies in Black Judaism.* Newcastle upon Tyne: Cambridge Scholars Publishing, 287–301.
———. (1996). *The Narrow Bridge: Jewish Views on Multiculturalism.* With a forward by Cornel West. New Brunswick, NJ: Rutgers University Press;

———, guest ed. (2004). *NASHIM: A Journal of Jewish Women's Studies and Gender Issues. Special Issue: Tense Dialogues—Speaking (Across) Multicultural Differences Among U.S. Jewish Feminists* 8.

———, guest ed. with Dawn Rose. (2003). *Journal of Feminist Studies in Religion Special Issue: Meeting at the Well: Multiculturalism and Jewish Feminisms* 19 (Spring, no. 1).

———, guest ed. (1999). *Race, Gender and Class, Special Issue: American Jewish Perspectives* 6 (no. 4).

———. (2001). "To Race, to Class, to Queer: Jewish Contributions to Feminist Theory," in Lisa Tessman, ed., *Jewish Locations: Traversing Racialized Landscapes*. Lanham, MD: Rowan & Littlefield Publishers.

Bridges: A Journal for Jewish Feminists and Our Friends. (1997–1998). Special Issue: *Sephardi and Mizrachi Women Write about Their Lives* 7 (no. 1).

———. (2001). Special Issue: *Writing and Art by Jewish Women of Color* 9 (no. 1).

Brodkin, Karen. (1998). *How Jews Became White Folks and What That Says about Race in America*. New Brunswick, NJ: Rutgers University Press, 1998.

Brodie, Janet Farrell. (1994). *Contraception and Abortion in Nineteenth-Century America*. Ithaca, NY and London: Cornell University Press.

Brook, Vincent. (1999). "The Americanization of Molly: How Mid-Fifties TV Homogenized the Goldbergs (and got Berg-larized in the process)." *Cinema Journal* 38: 45–68.

Brown, Rosellen. (2000). *Half a Heart*. New York: Farrar, Straus, and Giroux.

Brown, Wendy. (1988). *Manhood and Politics: A Feminist Reading in Political Theory*. Totowa, NJ: Rowman & Littlefield.

Bruder, Edith. (2008). *The Black Jews of Africa: History, Religion, Identity*. New York: Oxford University Press.

Buber, Martin. (1949). *Paths in Utopia*. New York: Macmillan Publishing Company.

Buker, Eloise A. (1999). *Talking Feminist Politics: Conversations of Law, Science and the Postmodern*. New York and London: Rowman & Littlefield Publishers.

Bulkin, Elly, Minnie Bruce Prat, Barbara Smith. (1984), *Yours in Struggle: Three Feminist Perspectives on Anti-Semitism and Racism*. Brooklyn: Long Haul Press.

Butler, Judith. (1999). *Gender Trouble: Feminism and the Subversion of Identity* (10th Anniversary Edition). New York and London: Routledge.

———. (2012). *Parting Ways: Jewishness and the Critique of Zionism*. New York: Columbia University Press.

Butler, Shakti, Dir. (1988). *The Way Home*. Hohokus, NJ: World Trust/New Day Films. Film.

Cahill, Sean, Juan Battle, and Doug Meyer. (2004). "Parenting, and Policy: Family Issues Affecting Black Lesbian, Gay, Bisexual, and Transgender (LGBT) People." *Race & Society* 6: 85–98.

Cahnman, Werner. (1967). "The Interracial Jewish Children." *Reconstructionist* 33 (no. 8): 7–12.

Calmes, Jackie. (2014). "Advocates Shun 'Pro-Choice' to Expand Message." *New York Times* July 28; accessed August 25, 2014. http://www.nytimes.

com/2014/07/29/us/politics/advocates-shun pro-choice-to-expand-message.html?_r=2.

Carroll, Rebecca, and Bill Dockery. (1995). "The Debate over Cross-Racial Adoption: An Odd Coalition Takes Aim at a Decades-Old Prejudice against Transracial Placements." *USA Weekend Magazine*, March 17–19.

Cashman, Holly R. (2014). "Queer Latina/o Networks in the City: Languages, Identities and the Ties that Bind," in R. Márquez Reiter and L. Martín Rojo, eds., *A Sociolinguistics of Diaspora: Latino Practices, Identities and Ideologies*, London/New York: Routledge, 66–80.

CBS News. (2005). "Born in USA, Adopted in Canada." February 19, 2005.

Chau, Jennifer. (2004). "More than Chicken Chow Mein." *Nashim* (2004). Special issue on Jewish Feminist Diversity in the US, ed. Marla Brettschneider.

Cho, Sumi, Kimberle Williams Crenshaw, and Leslie McCall. (2013). "Toward a Field of Intersectionality Studies: Theory, Applications, and Praxis." *Signs* 38 (no. 4): 785–810.

Choo, Hae Yeon, and Myra Marx Ferree. (2010). "Practicing Intersectionality in Sociological Research: A Critical Analysis of Inclusions, Interactions, and Institutions in the Study of Inequalities." *Sociological Theory* 28 (no. 2): 129–149.

Chun, Jennifer, George Lipsitz, and Young Shin. (2013). "Intersectionality as a Social Movement Strategy: Asian Immigrant Women Advocates." *Signs* 38 (no. 4): 917–940.

Cliff, Michelle. (1993). *Free Enterprise*. New York: Dutton.

Collins, Patricia Hill. 1990. *Black Feminist Thought*. New York: Routledge.

Crahan, Margaret E., and Franklin Knight. (1979). *Africa and the Caribbean: The Legacies of a Link*. Baltimore: Johns Hopkins University Press.

Crenshaw, Kimberlé. (1989). "Demarginalizing the Intersection of Race and Sex: A Black Feminist Critique of Antidiscrimination Doctrine, Feminist Theory, and Antiracist Politics." *University of Chicago Legal Forum*: 139–167.

———. (1991). "Mapping the Margins: Intersectionality, Identity Politics, and Violence Against Women of Color." *Stanford Law Review* 43 (July, no. 6): 1241–1299.

Cudjoe, Selwyn R. (1989). "Jamaica Kincaid and the Modernist Project: An Interview." *Callaloo* 39 (Spring):396–411.

Danforth, Jessica. (2014). "Understanding Reproductive Justice: A Response to O'Brien." *RH Reality Check*. Last modified May 8, 2013; accessed August 27, 2014. http://rhrealitycheck.org/article/2013/05/08/understanding-reproductive-justice-a-response-to-obrien/.

Davidman, Lynn, and Shelly Tenenbaum. (1994). *Feminist Perspectives on Jewish Studies*. New Haven: Yale University Press.

Davis, Angela. (1981). *Women, Race, and Class*. New York: Random House.

Davis, Kathy. (2008). "Intersectionality as Buzzword: A Sociology of Science Perspective on What Makes a Feminist Theory Successful." *Feminist Theory* 9 (no. 7): 67–80.

Daniels, Ruby, and Barbara Johnson. (1995). *Ruby of Cochin: An Indian Jewish Woman Remembers*. Philadelphia, PA: Jewish Publication Society.

Dekro, Jeffrey. (1996). "Community Economic Development and the American Jewish Community," Marla Brettschneider, ed., *The Narrow Bridge*. New Brunswick, NJ: Rutgers University Press.

Delman, Carmit. (2002). *Burnt Bread and Chutney: Growing Up Between Cultures: A Memoir of an Indian Jewish Girl*. New York: One World/Ballantine Books

Dhamoon, Rita. (2011). "Considerations on Mainstreaming Intersectionality." *Political Research Quarterly* 64 (no. 1): 230–243.

Diamond, Etan. (2000). *And I Will Dwell in Their Midst: Orthodox Jews in Suburbia*. Chapel Hill, NC: University of North Carolina Press.

———. (2002). "The Kosher Lifestyle: Religious Consumerism and Suburban Orthodox Jews." *Journal of Urban History* (May)."Domestic Workers United." http://www.domesticworkersunited.org/index.php/en/.

Dorman, Jacob. (2013). *Chosen People: The Rise of American Black Israelite Religions*. New York: Oxford University Press.

Drescher, Seymour, and Stanley Engerman, eds. (1998). *A Historical Guide to World Slavery*. New York: Oxford University Press.

Duchêne, A., and M. Heller, eds. (2012). *Language in Late Capitalism: Pride and Profit*. London: Routledge.

Edelman, Lee. (2004). *No Future: Queer Theory and the Death Drive*. Durham, NC: Duke University Press.

Elwell, Sue Levi. (1982). "The Founding and Early Programs of the National Council of Jewish Women: Study and Practice as Jewish Women's Religious Expression." PhD diss. University of Indiana.

———. (1987). *The Jewish Women's Studies Guide*. Lanham, MD: University Press of America; Fresh Meadows, NY: Biblio Press.

Elwell, Sue Levi, Shirley Idelson, and Rebecca Alpert. (2001). *Lesbian Rabbis: The First Generation*. New Brunswick, NJ: Rutgers University Press.

Ely, Melvin. (1991). *The Adventures of Amos 'n' Andy: A Social History of an American Phenomenon*. New York: The Free Press.

Falk, Marcia. (1977). *The Song of Songs: Love Poems from the Bible*. New York: Harcourt Brace Jovanovich.

Fanshel, David. (1972). *Far from the Reservation: The Transracial Adoption of American Indian Children*. Metuchen, NJ: Scarecrow Press.

Feld, Merl. (1999). *A Spiritual Life: A Jewish Feminist Journey*. Albany: State University of New York Press.

Ferguson, Kathy E. (2011). *Emma Goldman: Political Thinking in the Streets*. Plymouth, UK: Rowman and Littlefield.

Fernheimer, Janice. (2014). *Stepping Into Zion: Hatzaad Harishon, Black Jews, and the Remaking of Jewish Identity*. Birmingham: University of Alabama Press.

Finley, Karen. (1992). *Shock Treatment*. San Francisco: City Lights.

Fogg-Davis, Hawley. (2002). *The Ethics of Transracial Adoption*. Cornell University Press.

Fonrobert, Charlotte Elisheva. (2007). *The Cambridge Companion to the Talmud and Rabbinic Literature.* Cambridge: Cambridge University Press.
Foucault, Michel. (1975). *Surveiller et punir: Naissance de la prison.* Paris: Gallimard. (*Discipline and Punish: The Birth of the Prison*, Alan Sheridan, trans. (1977). London: Penguin Books.)
Frasier, Nancy. (1989). *Unruly Practices: Power, Discourse, and Gender in Contemporary Social Theory.* Minneapolis: University of Minnesota Press.
Gager, Kristin Elizabeth. (1996). *Blood Ties and Fictive Ties: Adoption and Family Life in Early Modern France.* Princeton, NJ: Princeton University Press.
Gaspar, David Barry. (1993). *Bondmen and Rebels a Study of Master-Slave Relations in Antigua.* Durham: Duke University Press.
Gibel, Inge Lederer. (1965). "The Negro-Jewish Scene: A Personal View." *Judaism* 14 (Winter, no. 1): 12–21.
Giddings, Paula. (1984). *When and Where I Enter: The Impact of Black Women on Race and Sex in America.* New York: Bantam Books.
Gittleman, Sol. (1978). *From Shtetl to Suburbia: the Family in Jewish Literary Imagination.* Boston: Beacon Press.
Goldman, Emma. (1969). *Anarchism and Other Essays.* New York: Dover Publications.
Goldstein, Elyse. (2009). *New Jewish Feminism: Probing the Past, Forging the Future.* Woodstock, VT: Jewish Lights Pub.
Gonzalez, David. (1997). "In Yiddish or English, A Valued Voice." *New York Times*, June 11, B1.
Gordon, Albert Isaac. (1959). *Jews in Suburbia.* Boston: Beacon Press.
Gordon, Albert. (1964). "Negro-Jewish Marriages: Three Interviews." *Judaism* 13 (Spring, no. 2): 64–184.
Gordon, Linda. (1990). *Women, the State, and Welfare.* Madison: University of Wisconsin Press.
Greenwood, Robert. (1991). *A Sketchmap History of the Caribbean.* London: Macmillan Caribbean.
Grzanka, Patrick, ed. (2014). *Intersectionality: A Foundations and Frontiers Reader.* Boulder, CO: Westview Press.
Gray, Ahuvah. (2001). *My Sister, the Jew.* Southfield, Michigan: Targum Press.
Haas, Hanna Levy. (1982). *Belsen Diary.* Brighton, UK: Harvester Press.
Hancock, Ange-Marie. (2007). "Intersectionality as a Normative and Empirical Research Paradigm." *Politics and Gender* 3 (no. 2): 248–254.
Hankivksy, Olena, and Rita Dhamoon. (2013). "Which Genocide Matters the Most? An Intersectionality Analysis of the Canadian Museum of Human Rights." *Canadian Journal of Political Science* 46 (no. 4): 89–120.
Hansberry, Lorraine. (1959). *A Raisin in the Sun: A Drama in Three Acts.* New York: Random House.
Haraway, Donna. (1991). *Simians, Cyborgs, and Women: The Reinvention of Nature.* New York: Routledge.
Heschel, Susannah. (1983). *On Being a Jewish Feminist.* New York: Schocken Books.

Hoberman, J., and Jeffrey Shandler. (2003). *Entertaining America: Jews, Movies, and Broadcasting.* New York: Jewish Museum, under the auspices of the Jewish Theological Seminary of America; Princeton, NJ: Princeton University Press.

Hoggart, L. (2000). "Socialist Feminism, Reproductive Rights and Political Action." *Capital & Class* 23 (no. 70): 95–125.

Hoover, Elizabeth, Katsi Cook, Ron Plain, Kathy Sanchez, Vi Waghiyi, Pamela Miller, Renee Dufault, Caitlin Sislin, and David O. Carpenter. (2012). "Indigenous Peoples of North America: Environmental Exposures and Reproductive Justice." *Environmental Health Perspectives* 120 (December, no. 12): 1645–1649.

Howe, Ruth-Arlene. (1997). "Transracial Adoption (TRA): Old Prejudices and Discrimination Float under a New Halo." *Boston University Public Interest Law Journal* 6 (Winter): 409–472.

Hudnut-Beumler, David. (1994). *Looking for God in the Suburbs: The Religion of the American Dream and Its Critics, 1945–1965.* New Brunswick, NJ: Rutgers University Press.

Hughes, Langston, Arnold Rampersad, and David E. Roessel. (1994). *The Collected Poems of Langston Hughes.* New York: Knopf.

Hyman, Paula. (1995). *Gender and Assimilation in Modern Jewish History: The Roles and Representation of Women.* Seattle, WA: University of Washington Press.

Hyman, Paula, Deborah Dash Moore; Phyllis Holman Weisbard. (1997). *Jewish Women in America: An Historical Encyclopedia.* American Jewish Historical Society. New York: Routledge.

Hull, Gloria, Patricia Bell Scott, and Barbara Smith. (1982). *All the Women Are White, All the Men Are Black: But Some of Us Are Brave.* New York: Feminist Press.

Ignatiev, Noel. (1995). *How the Irish Became White.* Cambridge, MA: Harvard University Press.

Jackson, John. (2013). *Thin Description: Ethnography and the African Hebrew Israelites of Jerusalem.* Cambridge, MA: Harvard University Press.

Jeffries, Dexter. (2003). *Triple Exposure: Black, Jewish and Red in the 1950s.* New York: Kensington Publishers.

Jen, Gish. (1996). *Mona in the Promised Land.* New York: Knopf.

Jews for Racial and Economic Justice. http://www.jfrej.org/.

Jones, Hettie. (1990). *How I Became Hettie Jones.* New York: Penguin.

Jones, Lisa. (1994). *Bulletproof Diva: Tales of Race, Sex and Hair.* New York: Doubleday.

Jordan-Zachery, Julia. (2013). "Intersectionality Studies: Theory, Applications, and Praxis." *Signs* 38 (no. 4): 785–810.

———. (2007). "Am I a Black Woman or a Woman Who Is Black?: A Few Thoughts on the Meaning of Intersectionality." *Politics & Gender* 3 (no. 2): 254–263.

Kaplan, Caren, Norma Alarcón, and Minoo Moallem, eds. (1999). *Between Woman and Nation: Nationalisms, Transnational Feminisms, and the State.* Durham, NC: Duke University Press.

Kaye/Kantrowitz, Melanie. (2007). *The Colors of Jews: Racial Politics and Radical Diasporism.* Bloomington: Indiana University Press.

———. (1992). *The Issue Is Power: Essays on Women, Jews, Violence, and Resistance.* San Francisco: Aunt Lute Books.

Kaye/Kantrowitz, Melanie, and Irena Klepfisz. (1986). *The Tribe of Dina: A Jewish Women's Anthology.* Montpelier, VT: Sinister Wisdom Books.

Kennedy, Randall. (2003). *Interracial Intimacies: Sex, Marriage, Identity, and Adoption.* New York: Pantheon Books.

———. (1994). "Orphans of Separatism: The Painful Politics of Transracial Adoption." *American Prospect* (Spring): 38–45.

Kessel, Barbara. (2000). *Suddenly Jewish: Jews Raised as Gentiles Discover Their Jewish Roots.* Hanover, NH and London: University Press of New England for Brandeis University Press.

Khazzoom, Loolwa, ed. (2003). *The Flying Camel: Essays on Identity by Women of North African and Middle Eastern Jewish Heritage.* NY: Seal Press.

Kincaid, Jamaica. (2005). *Among Flowers: A Walk in the Himalayas.* Washington, DC: National Geographic.

———. (1985). *Annie John.* New York: Farrar, Straus, Giroux.

———. (1983). *At the Bottom of the River.* New York: Farrar, Straus, Giroux.

———. (1996). *Autobiography of My Mother.* New York: Farrar, Straus, Giroux.

———. (1983). "Columbus in Chains." *New Yorker,* October 10.

———. (1992). "Flowers of Evil: In the Garden." *New Yorker,* October 5.

———. (1990). *Lucy.* New York: Farrar, Straus, Giroux.

———. (2002). *Mr. Potter.* New York: Farrar, Straus, Giroux, 2002.

———. (1997). *My Brother.* New York: Farrar, Straus, Giroux, 1997.

———. (1991). "On Seeing England for the First Time." *Transitions* 51: 32–40. Indiana University Press on behalf of the W. E. B. Du Bois Institute.

———. (1989). "Ovando." *Conjunctions* 14 (1989): 75–83.

———. (2013). *See Now Then.* New York: Farrar, Straus, Giroux.

———. (1988). *A Small Place.* New York: Farrar, Straus, and Giroux.

———. (2001). *Talk Stories.* New York: Farrar, Straus, Giroux.

Klagsbrun, Francine. (1997). "Sarah and Hannah: The Laughter and the Prayer," in Gail Twersky Reimer and Judith A. Kates, eds., *Beginning Anew: A Woman's Companion to the High Holy Days.* New York: Simon & Schuster, 91–105.

Kleiner, Yevgenia S. (2010). "Racial Profiling in the Name of National Security: Protecting Minority Travelers' Civil Liberties in the Age of Terrorism." *Boston College Third World Law Journal* 30 (November, no. 1): 103–144, http://lawdigitalcommons.bc.edu/twlj/vol30/iss1/5; accessed July 1, 2014.

Klepfisz, Irena. (1990). *Dreams of an Insomniac: Jewish Feminist Essays, Speeches, and Diatribes.* Portland, OR: Eighth Mountain Press, 1990.

Koltun, Elizabeth. (1976). *The Jewish Woman: New Perspectives.* New York: Schocken Books.

Landes, Elisabeth, and Richard Posner. (1978). "The Economics of the Baby Shortage." *Journal of Legal Studies* 7: 323–348.

Larson, Nella. (1986). *Quicksand and Passing*. New Brunswick, NJ: Rutgers University.
Leadership Conference. (2011). *Restoring a National Consensus: The Need to End Racial Profiling in America*. Washington, DC: Leadership Conference on Civil and Human Rights.
Lepore, Jill. (2011). "Birthright." *New Yorker*, November 14, http://www.newyorker.com/magazine/2011/11/14/birthright-2.
Lerner, Gerda. (1997). *Why History Matters: Life and Thought*. New York: Oxford University Press.
Lev, Sarra. (2004). "Genital Trouble: On the Innovations of Tannaitic Thought Regarding Damaged Genitals and Eunuchs." PhD diss. New York: New York University, Graduate School of Arts and Science.
———. (2007). "How the *'Aylonit* Got Her Sex." *AJS Review* 31 (no. 2): 297–316.
———. (2010). "They Treat Him as a Man and See Him as a Woman: The *Seris Hammah* in Tannaitic Literature," *Jewish Studies Quarterly* 17 (September, no. 3): 213–243.
Levine, Hillel, and Harmon, Lawrence. (1992). *The Death of an American Jewish Community: A Tragedy of Good Intentions*. New York: Free Press.
Levins Morales, Aurora, and Rosario Morales. (1986). *Getting Home Alive*. Ithaca, NY: Firebrand Books.
Levitt, Laura. (1997). *Jews and Feminism: The Ambivalent Search for Home*. New York: Routledge.
Lewis, Robert, ed. (2004). *Manufacturing Suburbs; Building Work and Home on the Metropolitan Fringe*. Philadelphia: Temple University Press.
LifeLong Adoptions. (2014). "LGBT Adoption Statistics." *LGBT Adoption*, http://www.lifelongadoptions.com/lgbt-adoption/lgbt-adoption-statistics; accessed August 20, 2014.
Lorde, Audre. (1984). *Sister Outsider: Essays and Speeches*. Trumansburg, NY: Crossing Press.
Luft, Rachel E., and Jane Ward. (2009). "Toward an Intersectionality Just Out of Reach: Confronting Challenges to Intersectional Practice." *Advances in Gender Research* 13: 9–37.
Luna, Zakiya T. (2010). "Marching Toward Reproductive Justice: Coalitional (Re)Framing of the March for Women's Lives." *Sociological Inquiry* 80 (no. 4): 554–578.
Luna, Zakiya, and Kristin Luker. (2013). "Reproductive Justice." *Annual Review of Law & Social Science* 9 (no. 11): 327–352.
Lux, William. (1975). *Historical Dictionary of the British Caribbean*. Metuchen NJ: Scarecrow Press.
Mallon, Gerald P. (1998). *We Don't Exactly Get the Welcome Wagon: The Experiences of Gay and Lesbian Adolescents in Child Welfare Systems*. New York: Columbia University Press.
Marc, David. 1984. *Demographic Vistas*. Philadelphia: University of Pennsylvania Press.

Marchetti, Kathleen. (2014). "Crossing the Intersection: The Representation of Disadvantaged Identities in Advocacy." *Politics, Groups, and Identities* 2 (no. 1): 104–119.

Marx, Karl and Friedrich Engels. (1967). *The Communist Manifesto*. New York: Penguin Books.

Massey, Douglas. (1993). *American Apartheid: Segregation and the Making of the Underclass*. Cambridge, MA: Harvard University Press.

McBride, James. (1996). *The Color of Water: A Black Man's Tribute to His White Mother*. New York: Riverhead Books.

McCall, Leslie. (2005). "The Complexity of Intersectionality." *Journal of Women in Culture and Society* 30 (Spring, no. 3): 1771–1800.

McKinley, Catherine. (2002). *The Book of Sarahs: A Family in Parts*. Washington, DC and New York: Counterpoint.

Melammed, Renée Levine. (2002). *Heretics or Daughters of Israel? The Crypto-Jewish Women of Castille*. New York: Oxford University Press.

Melanson, Yvette. (2000). *Looking for Lost Bird: A Jewish Woman Discovers Her Navajo Roots*. New York: Harper Collins.

Meyerowitz, Joanne. (2002). *How Sex Changed: A History of Transsexuality in the United States*. Cambridge: Harvard University Press.

Miri, Kush. (2009). *Seasons in Sheol: A Black Woman's Nightmare Journey Through Synagogue Culture*. Cranbury, NJ: BCA Books.

Mirzoeff, Nicholas, ed. (2000). *Diaspora and Visual Culture: Representing Africans and Jews*. London and New York: Routledge.

Mitchell, Timothy. (1988). *Colonising Egypt*. Cambridge and New York. Cambridge University Press.

Mohanty, Chandra. (1988). "Under Western Eyes: Feminist Scholarship and Colonial Discourses." *Feminist Review* (1988): 61–88.

Moore, Deborah Dash. (2008). *American Jewish Identity Politics*. Ann Arbor, MI: University of Michigan Press.

Moraga, Cherri, and Gloria Anzaldua, eds. (1982). *This Bridge Called My Back: Writings by Radical Women of Color*. 2nd ed. New York: Kitchen Table: Women of Color Press.

Morrison, Toni. (1992). *Playing in the Dark: Whiteness and the Literary Imagination*; Cambridge, MA: Harvard University Press.

Moynihan, Daniel Patrick. (1965). *The Negro Family: The Case for National Action*. March. Office of Policy Planning and Research, United States Department of Labor.

Narayan Uma. (1998). "Rethinking Cultures: A Feminist Critique of Cultural Essentialism and Cultural Relativism." Keynote address at the Annual Society of Women in Philosophy Eastern Division Spring Conference, Durham, University of New Hampshire, April.

Nash, Jennifer. (2008). "Re-thinking Intersectionality." *Feminist Review* 89: 1–15.

———. (2011). "Practicing Love: Black Feminism, Love-Politics, and Post-Intersectionality." *Meridians* 11 (no. 2): 1–24.

National Association of Black Social Workers. (1972). "Position Statement on Trans-Racial Adoption." The Adoption History Project, http://darkwing.uoregon.edu/~adoption/archive/NabswTRA.htm.

National Council of Jewish Women. (2013). "Jewish Women to Tackle Reproductive Justice, Gun Violence, Immigration Reform at National Conference." Press Release. (March 17–19, 2013), http://www.ncjw.org/content_9733.cfm; accessed August 27, 2014.

———. (2014). "NCJW Denounces Supreme Court Decision in *Burwell v Hobby Lobby.*" *Press Release.* (June 30, 2014); accessed August 28, 2014. http://www.ncjw.org/content_10902.cfm?navID=218.

New Internationalist. (1998). "A History of Reproduction, Contraception and Control." 303 (no. 7).

"NYC Statistics." NYC: The Official Guide, http://www.nycgo.com/?event=view.article&id=78912. Accessed July 2014.

Nyong'o, Tavia. (2005). "Punk'd Theory." *Social Text* 23 (Winter, no. 3/4): 19–34, 84–85.

Ochs, Vanessa L. (1990). *Words on Fire: One Woman's Journey into the Sacred.* San Diego: Harcourt Brace Jovanovich.

———. (2007). *Inventing Jewish Ritual.* Philadelphia: Jewish Publication Society.

Opper, Nicole. (2010). *Off and Running.* Film.

Ordover, Nancy. (2003). *American Eugenics: Race, Queer Anatomy, and the Science of Nationalism.* Minneapolis: University of Minnesota Press.

Ostriker, Alicia. (1996). "A House of Holies: The Song of Songs as Counter Text." Paper presented to Ma'yan's Jewish Feminist Research Group, New York.

———. (1982). *A Woman Under the Surface: Poems and Prose Poems.* Princeton, NJ: Princeton University Press.

Paley, Grace. (1974). *Enormous Changes at the Last Minute: Stories.* New York: Farrar, Straus, Giroux.

Parfitt, Tudor. (2013). *Black Jews in Africa and the Americas.* Cambridge, MA: Harvard University Press.

Patil, Vrushali. (2013). "From Patriarchy to Intersectionality: A Transnational Feminist Assessment of How Far We've Really Come." *Signs* 38 (Summer, no. 4), Intersectionality: Theorizing Power, Empowering Theory: 847–867.

Perry, Twila. (1993–1994). "The Transracial Adoption Controversy: An Analysis of Discourse and Subordination." *New York University Review of Law and Social Change* 21: 33–108.

Peskowitz, Miriam. (1997). *Spinning Fantasies: Rabbis, Gender, and History.* Berkeley: University of California Press.

Peskowitz, Miriam, and Laura Levitt. (1997). *Judaism Since Gender.* New York: Routledge.

Pew Research Center. (2013). *A Portrait of Jewish Americans.* Publication. Washington, DC: Pew Research Center.

Phelan, Shane. (1994). *Getting Specific: Postmodern Lesbian Politics.* Minneapolis: University of Minnesota Press.

———. (1989). *Identity Politics: Lesbian Feminism and the Limits of Community*. Philadelphia: Temple University Press.
Piercy, Marge. (1976). *Woman on the Edge of Time*. New York: Fawcett Crest.
Pinsky, Dina. (2010). *Jewish Feminists: Complex Identities and Activist Lives*. Urbana: University of Illinois Press.
Plaskow, Judith. (1991). *Standing Again at Sinai: Judaism from a Feminist Perspective*. New York: HarperCollins.
Plaskow, Judith, and Carol Christ. (1979). *Women's Spirit Rising: A Feminist Reader in Religion* San Francisco: Harper San Francisco.
Pogrebin, Letty Cottin. (1991). "Ain't We Both Women? Blacks, Jews, and Gender," in *Deborah, Golda, and Me: Being Female and Jewish in America*. New York: Crown Publishers, pp. 275–311.
Pons, Frank. (2007). *History of the Caribbean: Plantations, Trade, and War in the Atlantic World*. Princeton, NJ: Markus Wiener Publishers.
Prell, Riv-Ellen. (1999). *Fighting to Become Americans: Jews, Gender, and the Anxiety of Assimilation*. Boston, MA: Beacon Press.
———. (1989). *Prayer and Community: The Havurah in American Judaism*. Detroit: Wayne State University Press.
Price, Kimala. (2010). What Is Reproductive Justice?: How Women of Color Activists Are Redefining the Pro-Choice Paradigm. *Meridians: Feminism, Race, Transnationalism* 10 (no. 2): 42–65.
Puar, Jasbir. (2007). *Terrorist Assemblages: Homonationalism in Queer Times*. Durham, NC: Duke University Press.
Rand, Robert. (2001). *My Suburban Shtetl: A Novel About Life in a Twentieth-Century Jewish American Village*. Syracuse: Syracuse University Press.
Reitman, Jason, dir. (2009). *Up in the Air*. Hollywood: Paramount Pictures. Film.
Rich, Adrienne. (1976). *Of Woman Born: Motherhood as Experience and Institution*. New York: Norton.
———. (1980). "Compulsory Heterosexuality and Lesbian Existence." *Signs: Journal of Women in Culture and Society* 5 (no. 4): 631.
Rose, Or, Jo Ellen Green Kaiser, and Margie Klein, eds. (2008). *Righteous Indignation: A Jewish Call for Justice*. Woodstock, VT: Jewish Lights Publishing.
Roberts, Dorothy. (2002). *Shattered Bonds: The Color of Child Welfare*. New York: Basic Books.
———. (1997). *Killing the Black Body: Race, Reproduction, and the Meaning of Liberty*. New York: Pantheon Books.
Rodriguez, Junius P., ed. (1997). *The Historical Encyclopedia of World Slavery*, vol. 1. Santa Barbara, CA: Oxford University Press.
Rogow, Faith. (1993). *Gone to Another Meeting: The National Council of Jewish Women, 1893–1993*. Tuscaloosa: University of Alabama. Press.
Ronell, Avital. (2004). *Crack Wars: Literature Addiction Mania (Texts and Contexts)*. Urbana and Chicago: University of Illinois Press.
Rose, Dawn. (1998). "Inmate Ethics at Bergen Belsen: The Measure of Humanity in Hanna Levy-Haas' Holocaust Philosophy." Paper Presented at the 10th

Conference of North American and Cuban Philosophers and Social Scientists, Havana, Cuba.

———. (1999). "Class as Problematic in Jewish Feminist Theology." *Race, Gender, and Class: American Jewish Perspectives* 6 (no. 4).

Ross, Fran. (2000). *Oreo*. Boston, MA: Northeastern University Press.

Rothman, Barbara Katz. (2005). *Weaving a Family: Untangling Race and Adoption*. Boston: Beacon Press.

Ruggiero, Kristin, ed. (2005). *The Jewish Diaspora in Latin America and the Caribbean: Fragments of Memory*. Portland, OR: Sussex Academic Press.

Ruttenberg, Danya. (2001). *Yentl's Revenge: The Next Wave of Jewish Feminism*. Seattle, WA: Seal Press.

Saunder, Nicholas J. (2005). *The Peoples of the Caribbean an Encyclopedia Archeology and Traditional Culture*. Santa Barbara, CA: ABC-CLIO.

Schechter, Joel. (1985). *Dubrov's Pig: Clowns, Politics and Theatre*. New York: Theatre Communications Group.

Schultz, Debra L. (2001). *Going South: Jewish Women in the Civil Rights Movement*. New York and London: New York University Press.

Schwartz, Lacey, and James Adolphus. (2014). *Little White Lie*. Montclair, NH: Truth Aid. Film.

Scott, Joan Wallach. (1999). *Feminism and History*. Oxford and New York: Oxford University Press.

Sedgwick, Eve Kosofsky. (1994). *Epistemology of the Closet*. London: Penguin.

Segal, Josylyn C. (1997). "Shades of Community and Conflict: Biracial Adults of African-American and Jewish-American Heritages." PhD diss. Berkeley: The Wright Institute.

Seidman, Steven. 2002. *Beyond the Closet: The Transformation of Gay and Lesbian Life*. New York Routledge.

"Seven Jewish Groups Join Forces to Mobilize for Abortion Rights." (2014). *The Global Jewish News Source (JTA)*. Last modified September 14, 1989. http://www.jta.org/1989/09/14/archive/seven-jewish-groups-join-forces-to-mobilize-for-abortion-rights; accessed August 21, 2014.

Shanley, Mary Lyndon. (2001). *Making Babies, Making Families: What Matters Most in an Age of Reproductive Technologies, Surrogacy, Adoption, and Same-Sex and Unwed Parents*. Boston: Beacon Press.

Shanley, Mary Lyndon, and Adrienne Asch. (2009). "Involuntary Childlessness, Reproductive Technology, and Social Justice: The Medical Mask on Social Illness." *Signs: Journal of Women in Culture and Society* 34 (no. 4): 851–874.

Shepard, Sadia. (2008). *The Girl from Foreign: A Search for Shipwrecked Ancestors, Forgotten Histories, and a Sense of Home*. New York: Penguin Press.

Silberman, Marsha. (2009). The Perfect Storm: Late Nineteenth-Century Chicago Sex Radicals: Moses Harman, Ida Craddock, Alice Stockham and the Comstock Obscenity Laws. *Journal of the Illinois State Historical Society* 102 (no. 3): 324–367.

Silliman, Jael Miriam. (2001). *Jewish Portraits, Indian Frames: Women's Narratives from a Diaspora of Hope*. Hanover, NH: Brandeis University Press.

Silliman, Jael, Marlene Gerber Fried, Loretta Ross, and Elena R. Gutierrez. (2004). *Undivided Rights: Women of Color Organize for Reproductive Justice*. Cambridge, MA: South End Press.

Simon, Rachel. (2000). "Between the Family and the Outside World: Jewish Girls in the Modern Middle East and North Africa." *Jewish Social Studies* 7 (no. 1): 81–108.

Simon, Rita J., and Howard Altstein. (2000). *Adoption across Borders: Serving the Children in Transracial and Intercountry Adoptions*. Lanham, MD: Rowman & Littlefield Publishers.

Simpson, Monica. (2014). "Reproductive Justice and 'Choice': An Open Letter to Planned Parenthood." *RH Reality Check*. Last modified August 5, 2014. http://rhrealitycheck.org/article/2014/08/05/reproductive-justice-choice-open-letter-planned-parenthood/; accessed August 25, 2014.

Singer, Saul. (2006). "Day Schools Don't Isolate, They Foster Jewish Identity." Institute for Jewish & Community Research. July 28, 2006. http://www.jewishresearch.org/v2/2006/articles/philanthropy/7_28_06.htm; accessed February 10, 2015.

Sklare, Marshall, and Joseph Greenblum. (1967). *Jewish Identity on the Suburban Frontier: A Study of Group Survival in the Open Society*. New York: Basic Books.

Slater, Mary. (1968). *The Caribbean Islands*. New York: Viking Press.

Smith, Andrea. (2005). "Beyond Pro-Choice Versus Pro-Life: Women of Color and Reproductive Justice." *NWSA Journal* 17 (Spring, no. 1): 119–140.

Smith, Barbara. (1979). "Notes for Yet Another Paper on Black Feminism, or Will the Real Enemy Please Stand Up," *Conditions* 5: 123–132.

———, ed. (1983). *Home Girls: A Black Feminist Anthology*. New York: Kitchen Table: Women of Color Press.

Spade, Dean. (2011). *Normal Life: Administrative Violence, Critical Trans Politics, and the Limits of Law*. Brooklyn, NY: South End Press.

Spelman, Elizabeth V. (1988). *Inessential Woman: Problems of Exclusion in Feminist Thought*. Boston, MA: Beacon Press.

Spigelgass, Leonard. (1959). *A Majority of One: A Comedy in Three Acts*. New York: Samuel French.

Spivak, Gayatri Chakravorty. 1988. *Can the Subaltern Speak?* Basingstoke: Macmillan.

Starhawk. 1987. *Truth or Dare: Encounters with Power, Authority, and Mystery*. San Francisco: Harper & Row.

Stokes, Rose Pastor. (1916). *The Woman Who Wouldn't*. New York: G. P. Putnam's Sons.

Stolley, Kathy. (1993). "Statistics on Adoption in the United States," *The Future of Children* 3: 26.

Stone, Hannah Mayer. (1901). "Birth Control and Population." *America Now* (01/01): 456–468.

Talve, Susan. (2010). "Synagogue: Breaking the Color Barrier." *Reform Judaism Magazine Online* (Spring), http://reformjudaismmag.org/Articles/index.cfm?id=1563.

Tessman, Lisa, and Bat-Ami Bar On, eds. (2001). *Jewish Locations: Traversing Racialized Landscapes.* Lanham, Maryland: Rowman & Littlefield Publishers.

Tobin, Diane, Gary Tobin, and Scott Rubin. (2005). *In Every Tongue: The Racial and Ethnic Diversity of the Jewish People.* San Francisco, CA: Institute for Jewish & Community Research.

Thomsen, Carly. (2013). "From Refusing Stigmatization Toward Celebration: New Directions for Reproductive Justice Activism." *Feminist Studies* 39 (Spring, no. 1): 149–158.

Umansky, Ellen, and Dianne Ashton. (1992). *Four Centuries of Jewish Women's Spirituality: A Sourcebook.* Boston, MA: Beacon Press.

United Jewish Communities. *The National Jewish Population Survey 2000–01: Strength, Challenge and Diversity in the American Jewish Population.* Publication. New York, NY: United Jewish Communities, 2003.

US Public Law 104–193. (1996). 104th Cong., 2nd sess., August 22. Personal Responsibility and Work Opportunity Reconciliation Act of 1996.

US Public Law 104–188. (1996). 104th Cong., 2nd sess., August 20. Small Business Job Protection Act of 1996. ("Removal of barriers to interethnic adoption" is Section 1808.)

Volkman, Toby Alice, and Cindi Katz, eds. (2003). Special Issue on Transnational Adoption. *Social Text* 21 (no. 1).

Wadsworth, Nancy. (2011). "Intersectionality in California's Same-Sex Marriage Battles: A Complex Proposition." *Political Research Quarterly* 64 (no. 1): 200–216.

Walby, Sylvia, Jo Armstrong, and Sofia Strid. (2012). "Intersectionality: Multiple Inequalities in Social Theory." *Sociology* 46 (no. 2): 224–240.

Walker, Rebecca. (2001). *Black, White, and Jewish: Autobiography of a Shifting Self.* New York: Riverhead Books.

Wardell, Dorothy. (1980). "Margaret Sanger: Birth Control's Successful Revolutionary." *American Journal of Public Health* 70 (no. 7): 736.

Weber, Donald. (1998). "The Jewish-American World of Gertrude Berg: *The Goldbergs* on Radio and Television, 1930–1950," in Joyce Antler, ed., *Talking Back: Images of Jewish Women in American Popular Culture.* Hanover, NH: University Press of New England, 85–102.

———. (1999). "Taking Jewish-American Popular Culture Seriously: The Yinglish Words of Gertrude Berg, Milton Berle and Mickey Katz," *Jewish Social Studies* 5 (nos. 98/99): 124–154.

Weissler, Chava. (2010). *Art as Spiritual Practice in the Jewish Renewal Movement.* Ann Arbor, MI: University of Michigan.

———. (1989). *Making Judaism Meaningful: Ambivalence and Tradition in a Havurah Community.* New York: AMS Press.

———. (1998). *Voices of the Matriarchs: Listening to the Prayers of Early Modern Jewish Women*. Boston: Beacon Press.
Wertheimer, Jack. (2007). "Recent Trends in Supplementary Jewish Education Report." New York, NY: AVI CHAI Foundation.
West, Robin. (2009). "From Choice to Reproductive Justice: De-Constitutionalizing Abortion Rights." *The Yale Law Journal* 118 (no. 7): 1394–1432.
Wilkins, Andrea. (2006). "The Indian Child Welfare Act and the States." The National Conference of State Legislatures (April), http://www.ncsl.org/programs/statetribe/ICWA.htm; accessed September 11, 2006.
Williams, Linda Faye. (2003). *The Constraint of Race: Legacies of White Skin Privilege in America*. University Park: Pennsylvania State University Press.
Williams, Patricia. (1991). *The Alchemy of Race and Rights*. Cambridge, MA: Harvard University Press.
———. (1997). "Spare Parts, Family Values, Old Children, Cheap," in Adrien Wing, ed., *Critical Race Feminism: A Reader*. New York: New York University Press, 151–158.
Wilson, Samuel M. (1997). *The Indigenous People of the Caribbean*. Gainesville, FL: University Press of Florida.
Xin, Xu. (2003). *The Jews of Kaifeng, China*. Jersey City, NJ: KTAV Publishers.
Yeskel, Felice. (1996). "Beyond the Taboo: Talking about Class," in Marla Brettschneider, ed., *The Narrow Bridge Jewish Views on Multiculturalism*. New Brunswick, NJ: Rutgers University Press.
Young, Iris Marion. (1990). *Justice and the Politics of Difference*. NJ: Princeton University Press.
Zack, Naomi. (1996). "On Being and Not: Being Black and Jewish," in Maria P. P. Root, ed., *The Multiracial Experience: Racial Borders as the New Frontier*. Newbury Park, California: Sage Publications, 140–151.
———. (1993). *Race and Mixed Race*. Philadelphia: Temple University Press.
Zisper, Arthur, and Pearl Zisper. (1989). *Fire and Grace: The Life of Rose Pastor Stokes*. Athens: University of Georgia Press.
Zurawik, David. (2003). *The Jews of Prime Time*. Hanover, NH: Brandeis University Press/University Press of New England.

Index

Abayudaya (Uganda), 140
ableism, 5, 6
abortion, 73, 103, 105, 107–108, 113, 163n11, 164n15
Abraham, 47, 49
additive approach, 20, 24, 28, 151n25
adoption, 73, 110–111, 113–115, 116–118, 120–121, 122, 123, 124, 126, 135–136, 164n1, 164n2, 164n3, 165n5, 166n16, 166n20; agencies, 73; rights, 110; transracial, 14–15, 122–124, 125, 126 (*see also* Interethnic Adoption Provisions)
Adoption and Safe Families Act (ASFA), 113, 117, 120–122
Affordable Care Act, 108
Africa, 45, 49, 50, 59, 155n23, 155n24, 156n37; Central, 2; North, 3; Sub-Saharan, 1, 142; Western, 2, 100
Africana studies, 42
African Americans, 2, 4, 5, 18, 22, 63, 64, 70, 72, 106, 115, 118, 124, 125, 127, 128, 132, 140, 145, 156n31, 163n6, 165n7. *See also* Black men; Black women
African diaspora. *See* diaspora, African
African heritage, 57, 59, 100, 135, 137, 153n7. *See also* Jews: African-heritage; slaves: African-heritage
Africans, 51, 154

Afro-Caribbean, 12, 40, 41, 45, 48, 50, 51, 53, 59, 157n46
agency, 47, 58, 60, 104, 118, 123, 129; as privilege, 1
Albright, Madeline, 136
Alpert, Rebecca, x, 11, 19, 31–32, 33, 34, 35, 36, 152n35, 160n11
alterity, 92
American Jewish Committee (AJC), 108, 164n16
Amos 'n' Andy, 62, 64, 65, 160n4
anarchist ideas, 75, 76, 77, 88, 89, 92, 94, 95, 96
anarchist movement, 103
anarchists, 86, 87, 88, 91
anticolonial politics, 54
Antigua, 42, 44, 47, 50, 51, 52, 54, 56, 57, 58, 59, 60, 154n19, 155n23, 155n26, 156n33, 156n38
anti-immigration laws, 115, 121, 126
antimilitarism, 36
anti-miscegenation, 110
anti-Muslim, 9
anti-Muslimists, 146
anti-obscenity laws, 106, 163
antiracism, 5, 7, 15, 38, 59, 73, 129, 130, 131, 133, 138, 140, 141, 142, 143, 144, 145, 167n2, 167n3
anti-Semitism, 5, 6, 8, 9, 11, 34, 35, 36, 38, 54, 90, 103, 116, 125, 128, 134, 141, 144

anti-Zionism, 43
Arabs, 120
Aristotle, 12, 20, 21, 22, 23, 24, 27, 29, 149, 150
Ashkenazi Jews, 30, 70, 99, 111, 112, 132, 134, 140, 143, 160n7. *See also* Jews: of European heritage
Ashkenazi norms, 11, 79, 80, 132, 139
Asians, 70, 71, 72, 133, 167, 173. *See also* South Asians
assimilation, 9, 31, 36, 37, 43, 62, 66, 69, 70, 74, 102, 104, 124, 144, 159n1
Athenians, 20, 21, 150
Aviv, Caryn, 11, 43, 55, 153

bastards, 26–29
beatings, 2, 3
Beck, Evelyn Torton, 10
(be)coming out. *See* coming out
behavioralism, 94
Berg, Gertrude, 4, 13, 61–67, 69–73
Berlin, Isaiah, 57
Biale, David, 11, 43, 45, 55, 153n7, 167n4
bi/multi/pan-sexual, 82
birth control, 3, 104–105, 106–107, 163n12, 164n13, 164n14; clinics, 107, 163n13; movement, 104
Birth Control Clinical Research Bureau (BCCRB), 107
birth mothers, 115, 116, 124
bisexuals, 32, 33, 34, 35, 81, 98
Black-ish, 65, 71, 124
"Black-Jewish Question," 38
#blacklivesmatter, 5
Black men, 5, 6, 18, 22, 135, 150n19, 158n60, 165n8
Blackness, 122, 124, 166n17
Blacks, as Jews, 4, 38, 53. *See also* Black men; Black women
Black women, 5, 20, 38, 114, 117, 118, 119, 120, 121, 125, 126, 150n17, 150n19, 158n60
B'not Esh, ix, 4, 87, 161n1, 167n1

Boal, Augusto, 75–76, 90–93, 161n1, 162n11
Boko Haram, 1
Boyarin: Daniel, 11, 43, 55, 151n29, 153n4; Jonathan, 43, 55, 153n4
Bronx, 4, 13, 61, 63, 65–66, 68, 136
Brooklyn, 35, 71, 72, 107, 163n13
Brown, Michael, 2, 6, 127
Bulkin, Ellie, 9, 147n12
Bush, George W., 57
Butler, Judith, 43, 55, 76, 92–96, 147n8, 149n6, 149n12, 153n7, 154n15, 160n5, 162n14, 167n3

Canaanites, 48
capitalism, 39, 55, 57, 101
Carib, 48, 49, 57, 154n20
Caribbeans, 12, 40, 41–43, 44, 45, 47, 48, 49, 50–53, 54, 56, 57, 59, 136, 137, 155n23, 156n31, 156n32, 156n33, 156n41, 157n46
Casablanca. *See* Morocco
caste, 26–30, 151n31, 151n32, 163n6
Central Africa. *See* Africa: Central
Charlie Hebdo, 144
Chibok. *See* Nigeria
Chicago Women's Aid, 107
Christian as nonmarked category, 33, 59, 67, 72
Christian Americans, 9, 70, 101, 114, 118, 123, 135
Christianity, 70, 105, 108, 124, 136, 146, 148n13, 165n14
Christian right-wing, 5, 9, 109, 145
cisgender, 78–81
citizenship, 2, 20, 21, 66, 106, 115, 158
civil rights movement, 11, 35, 38, 73, 123, 135
classism, 5, 6
co-construction, 8, 14, 58, 60, 66, 89, 90, 91, 114
co-constructionist intersectional approach, 27, 61, 92
Cohens, 26–30

cold war, 62
colonialism, 12, 14, 42, 46, 47, 49, 51, 52, 53, 54, 57, 80, 92, 139, 141, 142
Combahee River women's collective, 7, 148
coming out, 13, 37, 75–85, 88–89, 95–96, 97, 98, 137, 163
communitarian socialists, 88
communities: African American, 70, 122, 135, 146; diaspora 57, 58, 59, 60; mutually constructed, 83, 85, 90, 98; queer, 77, 78, 82, 83, 96, 97, 98, 152n3
Comstock Laws, 106, 163
contraception, 103, 106, 107, 108, 113, 163
constructionism, 27, 61, 86, 88, 92
Council on Urbal Affairs, the, 4
counterperformance, 94
countertexts, 12, 23–25, 29, 38–39
couples: different-gender, 34, 72; same-gender, 117, 119, 120
criminal justice, 102, 111, 118
critical race theory, 10, 11, 12, 15, 18, 22, 24, 43, 114, 116, 130
critical theory, 12, 34, 76, 97, 130
cultural capital, 53
culture, 4, 17, 18, 25, 34, 36, 38, 39, 43, 48, 49, 51, 52, 53, 56, 57, 59, 60, 75, 77, 94, 145, 156n41; dominant, 38, 39; Jewish, 26, 37, 151n29, 151n34, 160n25; Native, 124; popular, 13, 39, 62, 69, 96, 102, 130, 161n28; queer, 33, 77, 79, 81, 96

Defense of Marriage Act (DOMA), 119, 120, 123, 125, 133, 165n5
democracy, 87, 88, 145, 166n20
Department of Homeland Security, 124
diaspora, 12, 13, 41, 42, 43, 44, 46, 47, 48, 49, 50, 51, 52, 53, 54, 55, 56, 57, 58, 59, 60, 154n15, 155n16, 158n55, 162n2; African, 12, 42, 44, 45, 48, 50, 59, 153, 57, 59, 156n32; Afro-Caribbean 12, 42, 45, 48, 50; barrenness, linked to, 49–50; Jewish 12, 43, 45, 46, 48, 49, 55, 60, 156n31; theorizing and studies, 12, 40, 41, 42, 43, 44, 47, 50, 56, 130, 153n7, 154n15
disabled women, 22
discrimination, 4, 10, 28, 103, 110, 116, 144; against Jews, 144; in adoption, 116, 117, 125; racist, 123, 166n17
disenfranchisement, 68
divorced women, 29
Domestic Workers United, 58, 159n66
double jeopardy, 7
drag, 13, 33, 69
drug sentencing, 118, 121
dual axis, 21

egalitarianism, 87, 88, 89
empowerment, 68, 79, 81
England, 41, 52, 53, 54, 56, 57, 154n18, 156n32, 157n42, 157n45, 157n47
equity, 2
erev Shabbat, 127–129
essentialism, 14, 18, 22, 24, 25, 32, 33, 34, 35, 41, 48, 75, 76, 80, 81, 95, 98, 123, 151n26, 151n30
estrangement, 56, 60
eugenics, 3, 14, 101–103, 104, 105–106, 107, 109, 166n20
Europe, 49, 54, 62, 99, 103, 136, 156n32
European heritage, of Jews. *See* Jews: of European heritage
Europeans, 48, 51, 52, 79, 136, 141, 142, 151n29, 155n23, 155n24
excommunication, 79
exile, 2, 42, 43, 44, 46, 47, 48, 49, 50, 52, 53, 55, 56, 57, 59, 60, 135, 154n16

Exodus, 47, 109

"fair access" issues, 110
families, x, 4, 13, 14, 26, 29, 42, 45, 47, 53, 58, 61–71, 73, 82, 83, 100, 102–110, 112, 113–126
family planning, 105, 107, 110
femaleness, 21. *See also* maleness
feminism: lesbian, 30–35; of color, 7, 28, 142; queer, 75–78, 94, 96
feminist scholarship/theory, 7, 8, 10–15, 17–20, 23–25, 30–35, 41, 43, 44, 46, 48, 49, 57, 60, 62, 67, 75–78, 110, 115, 116, 150n13, 152n35
Ferguson, 2–5, 127
fertility, 106, 108, 109
Findley, Karen, 95
foster care, 111, 113–114, 116, 117, 119, 121–122, 125, 165n5
freedom, 10, 48, 57, 68, 97, 103, 104, 105, 109, 116, 144; sexual, 104, 105, 110, 112
Fresh off the Boat, 71

GLBTQ, 11, 13, 14, 75, 77, 98, 114, 113, 115, 119, 125, 145, 165n5, 165n6
Garden of Eden, 46, 47
Garner, Eric, 6
gay men, 11, 32, 33, 34, 76, 78, 80, 81, 83, 116, 117, 118, 119, 121, 146, 159n4, 165n5
Gaza, 1, 2
Gemara. *See* Talmud
gender. *See* couples: opposite gender; couples: same gender; femaleness; justice: sexual and gender; maleness
gender nonconformity, 80
genocide, 48, 62, 122, 123, 125, 165n14; anti-Jewish, 62, 165n14; Native American, 48, 124
germ theory, 102
Germany, 100

Ghana, 140
Goldbergs, The, 72–74, 102, 106, 159n1, 160n4, 160n13, 160n14, 160n18, 161n28
golden bergs/towns, 71
Goldman, Emma, 87, 88, 90, 104, 106, 107, 163n12
guerilla theater, 91. *See also* theater

Hadassah, ix, 108, 153n2, 164n15
Hancock, Ange-Marie, 7, 147n9n13
Hansberry, Lorraine, 64, 65, 160n12; *A Raisin in the Sun* 64, 65
Haverville, 63
health care, 120
Hebrew Bible, 44–45
Hebrews, 46–48
hegemony, 9; Christian, 5, 81, 104, 105, 141, 144, 146, 149n6 (*see also* privilege, Christian)
Heschel, Susannah, 10, 11, 167n4
heteronormativity, 32, 88, 144
hetero-patriarchal indoctrination, 78
heterosexism, 9, 23, 37, 80, 81, 93, 125, 132, 133, 143
heterosexuality, 18, 52, 80
heterosexuals, 34
hierarchies, 24, 27, 28, 91, 115, 141, 144; complex, 24, 30
Hitler, 3
Hobby Lobby Supreme Court decision, 108, 145
Hollywood, 36
Holocaust 2, 36, 148n13, 154n16, 165n14
homophobia, 5, 6, 23, 35, 52, 90, 125, 165n6
honorary whites, 4, 67, 71
Hughes, Langston, 91

identitarianism, 8, 18, 151n26
identity, 7, 8, 11, 17, 18, 21, 24, 27, 28, 32, 33, 34, 36, 37, 48, 61, 63, 66, 68, 69, 70, 75, 81, 82, 83, 84,

85, 86, 87, 93, 94, 98, 113, 114, 123, 124, 149n4, 149n7, 160n23; theory, 8, 18, 19, 20, 21, 24, 150n13, 152n35, 165n14
imagery, linear, 85
immigration, 11, 84, 99, 100, 101, 120, 121, 126, 145; Eastern European 101–103
immigrants, 41, 52, 53, 63, 67, 71, 100, 101–103, 106, 107, 117, 120, 159n62
Immigration and Naturalization Service (INS), 124
imperialism, 9, 42, 51, 54, 80, 142
imperialists, 48
Indian Child Welfare Act, 124
individualism, 39, 57
individualist. *See* individualism
inequality, 41
institutionalization, 105
Interethnic Adoption Provisions 117, 121, 164n2, 166n16
intermarriage, 133, 136
International Association of Gay and Lesbian Jews, 83
interracial peace, 72
IQ test, 101
Iron Dome, 1
Islam, Nation of. *See* Nation of Islam
Islamic fundamentalism, 1, 148
Islamic State, 2
Israel, 1, 2, 26, 27, 43, 45–50, 53, 55, 59, 88, 107, 145, 150n20, 151n31, 153n7, 154n15, 155n24
Israelites 26–29, 46, 70, 100, 135, 151n31

Japan, 72
Jen, Gish, 70
Jewish activists, 146
Jewish elite men, 77
Jewish New Year, 96
Jewish Organizations, 3, 5, 106–108, 110

Jewish scholars, 8, 146, 151n27
Jewish Life Television, 62
Jewish Multiracial Network, ix, 5, 161n2, 167n1
Jewish Queer Think Tank, ix, 75, 76, 98
Jewish-Asian relationships, 71
Jewishness, 24, 30, 37, 42, 63, 70, 76, 93, 114, 136, 137, 140, 149n4, 151n26
Jews: African, ix, 3, 11, 43, 140, 155n24; African-American, 4, 5, 80, 128, 140; African-heritage, 43, 48, 100, 110, 135; Asian, 167n7; of color, 3, 35, 131, 132, 134, 137–138, 140, 143, 148n14; of European heritage, 3, 4, 14, 30, 43, 58, 61, 64, 66, 67, 69, 70, 71, 72, 73, 99, 100, 101, 102, 103, 104, 105, 106, 111, 114, 115, 116, 117, 121, 123, 124, 125, 126, 132, 134, 135, 136, 137, 138, 139, 140, 141, 143, 161n28, 166n20; Middle Eastern, 3, 11; Mizrachi, 34, 35, 140; non-Ashkenazi, 34, 111, 132, 139; non-European, 70, 139, 141; nonwhite, 67, 79, 111, 132; poor, 37, 67, 101, 105; Portuguese, 100; queer (*see* queer Jews); radical, 36, 37; Sephardi, 100, 140; white, 30, 67 79, 134, 135, 138, 139; working class, 37, 167n1
Jews for Racial and Economic Justice ix, 4, 38, 58
joker system, 91
Jorgensen, Christine, 63
Judaic studies, 55
justice, 5, 11, 25, 37, 38, 39, 40, 78, 84, 106, 109, 123, 132, 139, 141, 144, 167n5; criminal, 102, 111, 118; economic, ix, x, 4, 38, 58, 108, 163n15; racial, 4, 38, 58, 131, 138; reproductive, 109–110, 105, 106, 108, 109, 123–124, 164n17;

justice *(continued)*
  sexual and gender, 3, 13, 14, 75, 76, 77, 78, 99, 100, 105, 109, 110, 112; social, 9, 15, 35, 39, 40, 43, 58, 59, 80, 108, 109, 111, 138, 144, 167n5

Kaye/Kantrowitz, Melanie X, 10, 11, 19, 31, 35–38, 43, 55, 147n1, 152n35, 152n37–48, 152n51–54, 153n6–7, 159n67, 160n16, 161n34, 163n7, 167n3–4
kibbutz movement, 88
Kincaid, Jamaica 12, 40–42, 44–60, 92, 152n1, 153n2n8–12, 154n13–14, 154n16–20, 155n21–23, 155n25–26, 155n29–30, 156n31–32, 156n38–40, 157n42–50, 158n53, 158n60
King, Rodney, 6
Klagsbrun, Francine, 50, 155n27
Klepfisz, Irena, 10–11

Lazarus, Emma, 100
learning cooperatives, 88
Lehman College, 136, 137
Lemba priests, 140
lesbian identities, 33
lesbians, x, 10, 18, 31, 32, 33, 34, 35, 75, 78, 81, 82, 83, 98, 102, 104, 116, 117, 118, 119, 121, 152n36; Black, 119–120, 125; European heritage, 30, 117; Jewish, 10, 11, 18, 24, 30, 31, 76, 117, 149n4, 161n1
Levite, 26–28, 29, 151n33
life-cycle events, 77
Lifschiz, Anna, 107
liminality, 78, 89
Lot: wife of, 49
Lucille Ball Show, 13

maleness, 21, 22. *See also* femaleness
male privilege. *See* privilege, male

markers of otherness, 70
Martin, Trayvon, 6
Marx, Karl, 17, 162n8
marxism, 86–87
Marxists-Leninists, 86–89
McCoy, Yavila, 4, 147, 147n1, 167n4
masturbation, 102
medical ethicism, 25, 39, 148n1
mezuzah, 89–90, 93
micropractices, 90
middle class, 65, 67–69, 71, 73, 79, 103, 106, 111, 124, 166n20
Middle Easterners, 120
mikvah, 80, 97
military industrial complex, 120
Mindell, Fania, 107, 163n13
miscegenation, 72. *See also* anti-miscegenation
Mishnah. *See* Talmud
Mobilize for Women's Lives Rally, 108
modernism, 24, 89, 91, 166n20
Mona, 71
Morocco, 2
Mosul, 2
multiculturalism, 8, 11, 19
multicultural studies, 8
multisexual, 82
mutual constitution 8, 12, 18, 19, 22, 23, 24, 31, 36, 38, 40, 49, 59, 76, 92, 161
mutual construction, 8, 12, 13, 19, 39, 40, 90, 114, 146
Muslims, 120, 146

nathins, 27, 28, 151n31
Nation of Islam, 70
National Association of Black Social Workers (NABSW), 122, 165n14
National Council of Jewish Women, 106, 108, 161n1, 164n15
National Jewish Population Survey, 111, 164n18
natural, concept of, 21, 94, 95, 98, 102, 155n28, 159n65, 163n15

Nehirim, ix, 97
neocolonialism, 41, 42, 52, 53, 56, 57
New England, 53–56, 59, 60, 136, 144, 152n1, 153n2, 157n46, 157n47, 158n55; Black, 53, 153n2; Black-Jewish, 53; Jewish, 53
New Hampshire, ix, 117, 136, 153n2
New Jersey Gay and Lesbian Havurah, 83
Nietzsche, 103
Nigeria, 1
Noah, 49; sons' wives, 49
non-Ashkenazi Jews, 34, 111, 132
non-Christians, 19, 22, 45
non-identitarian paradigm, 8
nonwhite people, 4, 19, 34, 45, 52, 67, 103, 111, 122, 136, 137, 140
normativity, 32, 80, 88, 94, 95, 105

Occupied Territories, 1. *See also* Gaza
Oleary, Mrs., 127–129
oppression, 7, 9, 10, 18, 19, 21, 47, 79, 85, 90, 92, 93, 97, 98, 108, 114, 115, 142, 151n25, 156n31, 162n6, 163n6
originary, 94
outmarriage, 133, 137
outness, 88

Palestinians, 1, 145
paradigms, 7, 38, 39, 74, 91, 115, 131, 133, 137, 141, 142, 150n13, 163n6; assimilationist, 144; progressivist, 91; totalizing, 91
parental rights. *See* rights: parental
parody, 93, 162n14
patriarchy, 22, 33, 34, 52, 57, 58, 78, 80, 103, 131, 139, 141, 142, 143
people of color, 59, 111, 119, 132–138, 143, 163n6, 165n5. *See also* women of color
performance, 69, 75, 83, 90, 93–96, 163n15

performativity, 76, 92, 162n14
Personal Responsibility Act. *See* Welfare Reform
Phelan, Shane, 81–83, 88, 92, 152n36, 162n5
Planned Parenthood, 107, 164n17
Plaskow, Judith, 10, 148n14, 149n3, 153n2, 167n1
Plato, 20
political sovereignty, 55
popular culture, 4, 13, 62, 102, 130
postcolonial studies, 42, 47
postdiaspora, 43, 57
postrevolutionary moments and time, 86, 87, 91
power relations, 25, 29, 30, 38, 56
preparation, 75, 87, 88, 91, 94, 104; anarchist, 86
prison-industrial complex, 118
privilege, 1, 35, 37, 53, 54, 60, 76, 86, 87, 144, 154n19, 168n55; Christian, 5, 33, 38, 102, 144, 145, 146 (*see also* hegemony, Christian); male, 22, 129; of agency, 1; white, 38, 114, 137
Progressive Jewish Alliance, the, 4
proselytes, 26, 151n26
Puerto Ricans, 63
Purim, 71

queer activists, 8
queer communities. *See* communities: queer
queer Jews, 6, 8, 30, 39, 76–79, 80, 83, 84, 86, 88, 89, 90, 92, 93, 94, 96, 97, 98, 117, 149n3
queer studies. *See* queer theory
queer theory, 6, 8, 10, 11, 13, 17, 19, 23, 24, 30, 32, 75, 76, 81, 91, 92, 93, 98, 116, 162n2

reassignment, 67, 103–104, 110, 165
race/class line, 21, 74, 159
race studies, 17, 30, 32, 130

racism, 5, 6, 9, 22, 35, 38, 52, 70, 80, 90, 110, 118, 122, 123, 125, 128–131, 134, 136, 138, 140–145, 150, 156, 166
Red Scare, The, 62–64
relationships, 59, 77, 85, 87; communal, 60; egalitarian, 87, 116, 154; Jewish-Asian, 71
religion, 10, 63, 69, 86, 91, 145, 150, 151, 152, 160
Religious Action Center of Reform Judaism, 108
Religious Coalition for Reproductive Choice, 109
rights: adoption, 110; civil, 11, 35, 38, 73, 123, 135; parental, 3, 14, 73, 111, 115, 121, 122; reproductive, 3, 14, 100, 105–110, 113, 123
right-wing, 5, 9, 109
ritual innovation, 92, 95, 96, 98, 109, 161n1, 161n2, 162n2
rituals, 3, 14, 39, 75–86, 88–90, 92–98, 161n1
Roberts, Dorothy, 110, 125, 135, 166n15n18
Roe vs. Wade, 107, 108
Rogoff, David, 83, 161
Roth, Philip, 66

sameness, 8, 18, 24, 31. See also non-identitarian paradigm
Sanger, Margaret, 104, 107
Sarah, 47–50, 155
segregation, 134, 135, 137, 141–143, 167
self: as social construction, 18, 75, 93; disempowered, 47; empowered, 85, 93–94
separative, 31, 36, 84, 89, 94, 95
servile status. See slaves, status of
sexism, 5–7, 23, 32, 35, 80, 90, 125, 132, 133, 143, 144, 150n14
sex reassignment surgery, 63
sexual minorities, 32, 76

Shakespeare, 95
Shalom Center, 3
Shneer, David, 11, 43, 55, 153n7
simcha, 85
slaves, 20–22, 24, 26, 28, 29, 127, 149n11, 150n17, 156n37, 166n17; African, 156n37; African-heritage, 52; Black, 150n17, 166n17; emancipated, 27; Israelite-heritage, 100; slave trade, 48, 51, 135, 154n16, 155n23, 156n33, 157n46; status of, 150n13
slavery, 51, 52, 59, 65, 70, 127
slavery, sexual, 1
Smith, Barbara, 9
social hierarchy, 21
social justice, 106, 108, 110, 111, 138, 144, 167n5
social relations, 87, 88, 92, 94
Sodom and Gomorra, 49
Sojourner Truth, 7
solidarity, 2, 37
Songhai, 140
South Asians, 120
Spelman, Elizabeth, 35, 38–40, 147n8, 149n8, 149n9, 149n11, 150n12, 150n13, 150n14, 150n15, 150n17, 150n18, 150n19, 151n25, 152n35
Spigelglass, Leonard, 71
spirituality, 76, 86, 89
spontaneity, 89, 96
stereotypes: gender, 160n4, 150n18; of the "Jewish mother," 66
sterilization, forced, 105, 106, 110, 113
Stokes, Rose Pastor, 106
subaltern cultures, 39
Sub-Saharan Africa. See Africa, Sub-Saharan
suburbs: middle-class, 64, 65, 69, 71; working-class, 64
surveillance, sexual, 105, 106, 119, 125
syndicated labor movements, 88

Talmud, 12, 19, 23–31, 36–39, 135, 150n20, 151n29, 151n32
Talve, Susan, 3, 4, 147n1, 167n3
terrorism, 120
theater, 75, 76, 88, 90–93, 95, 161n1, 162n11, 162n14
tikkun olam, 40, 138
Torah, 23, 135, 138
Trans Day of Remembrance, 96
transgender, 15, 22, 32–34, 79
transitions, urban-suburban, 64, 85, 156n41
trans people, 22, 32, 34, 35, 81, 82, 97, 98, 116
transphobia, 6, 52, 80, 88, 90, 93
transracial adoption. *See* adoption: transracial
T'ruah: The Rabbinic Call for Human Rights, 3
two-tiered model, 19, 22, 150n15

ultraconservatism, Christian. *See* Christian right-wing
US Coming Out Day/Week, 96

Vermont, 45, 49, 53–55, 59, 117, 157n47, 158n55, 159n63
victims, 2, 36, 46
vilification, Jewish/gender, 66
violence, 2–3, 35, 36, 46, 52, 54, 58–60, 67, 68, 86, 129, 152n39; against girls, 129; against Israelis, 2 against Jews, 2; against women, 36; colonial, 46; patriarchal, 58; racial, 36; retaliatory, 2

Washington, 71
welcoming rituals, 79, 81, 82, 89
Welfare reform, 115, 119, 120, 121, 123
West, Cornel, 8
Western Africa. *See* Africa: Western
Western Canon, 23
whiteness, 72, 80, 132, 133, 166n17
Wilde, Oscar, 87
women: African American, 22, 106, 118, 156n31; Black (*see* Black women); Native American, 106; of color, 3, 14, 18, 111, 112, 114, 115, 118, 119, 120, 121, 122, 123, 125, 133, 136, 143; queer, 33; white, 19, 22, 115, 118, 128 150n19
Women of Reform Judaism, 109
women's studies, ix
worker-run factories, 88

xenophobia, 65

Yiddish, 106, 164n13

Zion, 43, 44, 46, 48, 50, 55, 60, 154n15